DEMANDING GOOD

GOVERNANCE

D0887153

DEMANDING GOOD

GOVERNANCE

Lessons from Social Accountability Initiatives in Africa

MARY McNEIL

AND

CARMEN MALENA

Editors

THE WORLD BANK
Washington, D.C.

ISBN: 978-0-8213-8380-3
eISBN: 978-0-8213-8383-4
DOI: 10.1596/978-0-8213-8380-3

Cover photo: Arne Hoel/World Bank.
Cover design: Drew Fasick.

Library of Congress Cataloging-in-Publication Data
Demanding good governance : lessons from social accountability initiatives in Africa / edited by Mary
    McNeil and Carmen Malena.
       p. cm.
    Includes bibliographical references and index.
    ISBN 978-0-8213-8380-3 — ISBN 978-0-8213-8383-4 (electronic)
    1. Social accounting—Africa—Case studies. I. McNeil, Mary, 1956- II. Malena, Carmen. III.
World Bank.

HN774.D46 2010
320.6096—dc22

2010008390

To

George Washington Matovu

CONTENTS

BOXES

FIGURES

TABLES

FOREWORD

This is a challenging time for Africa. The combined effects of the global economic crisis, the need for equitable allocation of natural resource assets, and the ever-changing balance of influence and power between the developed and developing worlds are requiring African countries to re-evaluate their governance structures. These challenges are accompanied by new opportunities. For example, the proliferation of information and communication technologies (ICTs)—such as cell phones and SMS text messaging, among others—is opening up government processes to a larger public and empowering ordinary citizens to demand accountability from their leaders. Although in many countries these trends are still nascent, they have the potential to radically change democratic processes.

"Social accountability," as defined in this book, is an approach to enhancing government accountability and transparency. It refers to the wide range of citizen actions to hold the state to account, as well as actions on the part of government, media, and other actors that promote or facilitate these efforts. Social accountability strategies and tools help empower ordinary citizens to exercise their inherent rights and to hold governments accountable for the use of public funds and how they exercise authority. Global experience has shown that such initiatives can be catalytic and that they increasingly play a critical role in securing and sustaining governance reforms that strengthen transparency and accountability.

The case studies presented in this book represent a cross-section of African countries, drawing on initiatives launched and implemented both by civil society groups and by local and national governments in countries with different political contexts and cultures. They demonstrate that although social accountability approaches are strongly influenced by many underlying legal, social, cultural, and economic factors, they can still be implemented in difficult political environments (for example, in Zimbabwe). They point to the overriding problem of access to information (Ghana, Malawi, and Zimbabwe), and the low readability of information when it is available (Benin). They demonstrate what can happen when governments and civil society work together to institute accountability measures (Nigeria), and the implementation challenges they face in environments ranging from decentralized (Tanzania) to more centralized (Senegal). In the introductory and concluding chapters, the editors explain what social accountability means in the African context and distill some common success factors and lessons that can help other practitioners and innovators in the field.

I am especially pleased that this volume emphasizes the "how to" of reform, as described by those who have implemented such approaches on the ground. The World Bank Institute plans to draw on and integrate this kind of knowledge into its global learning programs, relying increasingly on South-South exchanges of experience.

The credit for this volume belongs to the authors of the case studies, who have shared many astute and personal insights into the challenges they faced. Despite such challenges, each has succeeded in helping citizens make their voices heard and shape the way they are governed.

Sanjay Pradhan
Vice President
World Bank Institute

ACKNOWLEDGMENTS

In October 2004, 20 African practitioners—from civil society and government—met in Kampala, Uganda, to discuss a range of initiatives they had launched under the broad rubric of social accountability. They had been drawn from a larger group identified through a stocktaking of social accountability initiatives in Anglophone Africa launched in 2004 by the Municipal Development Partnership for Southern and Eastern Africa (MPD-ESA) and the World Bank Institute (WBI). Since this initial meeting the work on social accountability in Africa has continued to gain momentum. Through regional conferences on the theme in Accra, Ghana, in May 2005 and Addis Ababa, Ethiopia, in May 2008, and the establishment of a dedicated facility to support practitioners on the continent—the Affiliated Network for Social Accountability (ANSA)—in Africa in 2006, an increasing number of citizens, civil society organizations, NGOs, local and national government officials, and academics have championed the social accountability cause on the continent.

It is therefore with great humility that we attempt to thank the numerous supporters who have aided in the preparation of this book. We begin with George Matovu (to whom this volume is dedicated) and Takawira Mumvuma of MDP-ESA who were supporters of this work from the very beginning. Reiner Forster (now with GTZ), Janmanjay Singh, and Jeff Thindwa of the World Bank's Social Development Department were instrumental in developing the early conceptual frameworks. Drew Harton shepherded the volume through its beginning stages. Our colleagues on WBI's Community Empowerment and Social Inclusion Learning Program—Jerri Dell, Maria Gonzalez de Asis, Veronica Nyhan Jones, Marcos

Mendiburu, Marguerite Monnet, Karen Sirker, Pietronella Van Den Oever, and Victor Vergara—made this work possible by their early and sustained commitment to community-driven and participatory development, upon which this work is based. Vinod Thomas, former vice president of WBI, gave us the freedom to launch a new agenda. His successor, Frannie Léautier, supported its extension. Beatrix Allah-Mensah, Ian Bannon, Mary Bitekerezo, Sarah Keener, Jacomina de Regt, and Carolyn Winter from the World Bank's Africa region have led this work regionally and long championed the cause of citizen-led accountability. Finally, we'd like to thank James Wolfensohn, whose acknowledgment of civil society's vital role in development opened the door to this work and created a new paradigm of development without which this book could not have been undertaken.

The authors of the individual chapters—Charles Abbey, Vitus A. Azeem, Cyrille Chabi Eteka, Anne Floquet, Dauda S. Garuba, Bara Guèye, John G. Ikubaje, Renatus Kihongo, Dalitso Kinglsley Kubalasa, Cuthbert Baba Kuupiel, John Lubuva, Bob Libert Muchabaiwa, and Limbani Bartholomew Elia Nsapato—demonstrated considerable patience in an editing process that at times seemed to never end. John Clark, Helene Grandvoinnet, George Matovu, and Sina Odugbemi provided valuable review comments. Ed Campos and Randi Ryterman supported its completion and final publication. Warren Van Wicklin moved the project forward with his impeccable editing, and Lauren Kunis ensured on numerous fronts that the volume would be published.

Finally we'd like to thank the many practitioners of social accountability on the African continent who, despite great challenges, continue to forge ahead to improve citizen voice and government accountability. We feel privileged to have participated in and coordinated this effort and to have worked alongside such talented and inspiring colleagues.

Mary McNeil
Carmen Malena

ABOUT THE EDITORS

Mary McNeil is senior operations officer and team lead in the Governance Practice of the World Bank Institute (WBI). While at WBI, she has led global programs on socially sustainable development and community empowerment and social inclusion, and is the founding editor of its flagship publication *Development Outreach*. She is the author of numerous articles and publications on civic participation and empowerment of the poor. During her career at the World Bank, she has held positions in the water and sanitation and in the urban sectors where she managed projects and provided technical assistance, and in the International Finance Corporation, where she coordinated relations with the NGO community. She currently manages World Bank grant-funded facilities in Africa and Asia, the Affiliated Networks for Social Accountability (ANSAs) that work to build civil society's capacity to hold government accountable. Her work has spanned all regions, with a continued focus on community participation, social inclusion, and equitable governance. She holds a master's degree in public administration from the John F. Kennedy School of Government, where she was the Joel Leff Fellow in Political Economy (1993–94), and is a visiting professor in the economics department at Wake Forest University.

    Carmen Malena works as an independent consultant and part-time director of the Participatory Governance Programme of CIVICUS: World Alliance for Citizen Participation. She is a political sociologist with special interest in civil society, participatory governance, social accountability, and gender. Malena has more than 20 years of experience as a development practitioner, researcher, writer, facilitator, and trainer and has authored a wide range of academic and operational publications. Previously, she held positions as a civil society and participation specialist at the World Bank and the African Development Bank and has worked for a range of multilateral and bilateral donors and NGOs. She holds a master's degree in international development from the University of Sussex, U.K.

ABOUT THE CONTRIBUTORS

Charles Abbey is executive director of the African Development Programme, Ghana, and global vice president of the International Council on Social Welfare (ICSW). Previously, he was ICSW regional president for Central and West Africa. Abbey also is an international visiting fellow at the Taiwan Foundation for Democracy and a member of the Child Rights Information Network (U.K.) and the Ghana Association of Private Voluntary Organisations in Development. Over the past couple of years, Abbey has served as a local facilitator for the World Bank Institute's distance learning program on local growth and economic development at the Ghana Institute of Management and Public Administration. He is also a member of the Experts Group of the Department of Gender and Human Development (Social Affairs) of the Economic Commission of West African States.

Vitus A. Azeem, an anticorruption campaigner, is the executive secretary of the Ghana Integrity Initiative, the local chapter of Transparency International. Previously, he was program coordinator of the Centre for Budget Advocacy within the Integrated Social Development Centre, a Ghanian rights-advocacy organization.

Cyrille Chabi Eteka is a social anthropologist who has served since 2003 as a research assistant and consultant at the International Forum for Development and Knowledge Exchange for the Promotion of Rural Entrepreneurship, a multidisciplinary collaborative institution of the University of Abomey-Calavi in Benin. He is also an associate researcher at the Laboratory of Studies and Research on Social Dynamics and Local Development, an affiliate of the University of Abomey-Calavi.

Anne Floquet is an agronomist and a rural economist who has worked for many years for a Beninese NGO, the Benin Centre for Environment and Economic and Social Development (CEBEDES). She is currently CEBEDES's department head for agriculture and the environment. As a scientist, Floquet also works in the university and is a main contributor and critical observer of the development of citizen control initiatives in the primary education sector (participatory local impact monitoring methodology, or SILP) and at the communal level.

Dauda S. Garuba is Nigeria program coordinator at the Revenue Watch Institute (RWI). (He coauthored the chapter on Nigeria in this volume before joining RWI.) Previously, Garuba worked as senior program officer in governance, security, and development at the Centre for Democracy and Development (CDD) West Africa. In 2005–07 and July–October 2008, he represented CDD on the steering committee of Publish What You Pay (PWYP) Nigeria. He was also national civil society representative on the monitoring and evaluation team that collaborated with the Office of the Senior Special Assistant to the President on the Millennium Development Goals to assess projects financed through the Debt Relief Gain under the 2006 budget. Garuba's experience includes extensive work in the Niger Delta. He is coauthor of *Democracy, Oil, and Politics in the Niger Delta: Linking Citizens' Perception with Policy Reform.*

Bara Guèye is a rural economist who has worked for more than 25 years to promote local development and participatory approaches in West Africa. Before he joined the International Institute for Environment and Development (IIED) in 1993, he was an academic trainer and researcher. He set up and coordinated the IIED Drylands Programme's Sahel office from 1993 to September 2005, when the program became an independent organization: *Innovations, Environnement et Développement en Afrique* (IED Afrique). Over the past seven years, Guèye's work has focused on supporting the decentralization process in West Africa, with an emphasis on building inclusive and transparent institutions and on providing citizens with the skills and tools to exert effective control on local government decisions through participatory budgeting and participatory monitoring and evaluation.

John G. Ikubaje is the technical officer for voice and accountability with the U.K. Department for International Development program on Partnership for Transformation in the Health Sector in Nigeria (PATHS2). Previously, he was the program coordinator for anticorruption and good governance with the U.S. Agency for International Development (USAID) project on Advocacy, Awareness Creation, and Civic Empowerment (ADVANCE), managed by the Pact International office in Nigeria. He has also worked as senior program officer in charge of governance, security, and development at the Centre for Democracy and Development in both London and Nigeria. Ikubaje has consulted for many national and international organizations concerning anticorruption, good governance, and development.

Renatus Kihongo is the special programs coordinator for the Tanzania Commission for AIDS (TACAIDS). As a senior economist with more than 15 years' experience in managing development projects and promoting local development and participatory approaches, Kihongo has coordinated participatory projects at the local and central government levels in partnership with international organizations such as the Netherlands Development Organization and the World Bank. Previously, he worked for the Local Government Capital Development Grant project, a component of the Local Government Support Project; the Tanzania Social Action Fund; and as national project coordinator of the Community AIDS Response Fund, a component of the Tanzania Multisectoral AIDS Project at TACAIDS. Kihongo has also participated in various participatory research, policy, and advocacy initiatives such as a Participatory Poverty Assessment coordinated by the Economic and Social Research Foundation; formative process research on the local government reform program in Tanzania, coordinated by Research on Poverty Alleviation (REPOA); and the research project on Improving Local Revenue Generation through Participatory Budgeting, coordinated by the Municipal Development Partnership for Eastern and Southern Africa (MDP-ESA).

Dalitso Kingsley Kubalasa has extensive experience in the fields of participatory governance, development policy analysis, and advocacy. In his current role as director of programs for the Malawi Economic Justice Network (MEJN), he is responsible for establishing and sustaining the civil society program on pro-poor participatory economic governance. He joined MEJN as a Poverty Reduction Strategy Paper (PRSP) and budget monitoring program manager in 2003 and, in 2005–06, also served as MEJN's acting director of programs and as budget monitoring program manager. Before joining MEJN, Kubalasa worked as a branch manager for an international microfinance institution, PRIDE Malawi, and as an intern with the Planning Division of Malawi's Ministry of Agriculture and Irrigation. He also has experience as a fiction writer, journalist, and development policy analyst.

Cuthbert Baba Kuupiel has 12 years of experience in starting up, working with, and managing development projects in Ghana, gaining considerable expertise in the management of community capacity-development activities, including institutional capacity strengthening and organizational development of civil society organizations. Kuupiel has also pioneered, in concert with other development actors, the development of mechanisms and systems for civil society engagement with local government and traditional institutions for sustainable and equitable development. He has actively promoted learning and experience sharing among development practitioners as well as joint action among them.

John Lubuva is a senior consultant with AMKA Consult Consortium Ltd., based in Tanzania. He has extensive experience in the fields of urban development, local government management, good governance reforms, and participatory budgeting following a long career in local government service. He served as deputy commission secretary of the Dar es Salaam City Commission (1996–2000), chief executive officer of the Ilala Municipal Council in Dar es Salaam (2000–08), and chief executive officer of the Shinyanga District Council (2008–09) before stepping down from civil service. Previously, Lubuva served as a senior principal town planner in the Ministry of Lands, Housing and Human Settlements Development (1979–96), gaining extensive experience in urban planning, urban development policy and legislation, land policy, and environmental management. In addition, Lubuva has ample experience in training, as a part-time university lecturer and external examiner, and as coordinator and facilitator of distant learning programs for the World Bank Institute and the Municipal Development Partnership for Eastern and Southern Africa (MDP-ESA) (2002–08).

Bob Libert Muchabaiwa is the research, policy, and advocacy manager of the South African Development Community Council of NGOs, based in Botswana. Before that, he was the programs director of the National Association of Non-Governmental Organisations in Zimbabwe. Especially interested in social development policy and regional integration issues, Muchabaiwa has authored several articles and training manuals on participatory budgeting and other social accountability topics, including *Child Friendly Budgeting in Zimbabwe* and a social accountability handbook for civil society in Zimbabwe.

Limbani Bartholomew Elia Nsapato has been Southern Africa program officer for the Africa Network Campaign on Education for All in Lusaka, Zambia, since 2008. Previously, he worked for four years with civil society organizations in Malawi as national coordinator of the Civil Society Coalition for Quality Basic Education (CSCQBE), a coalition of education advocacy NGOs. During his tenure, CSCQBE collaborated with national networks such as the Council for Non-Governmental Organisations in Malawi and the Malawi Economic Justice Network (MEJN) to monitor the country's Poverty Reduction Strategy Paper (PRSP), the Malawi Growth and Development Strategy, and the national education budget in light of the nation's Education for All goals and Millennium Development Goals (MDGs). Nsapato's areas of professional experience and interest include coalition building, networking, budget tracking, policy research, and analysis as well as evidence-based advocacy concerning all education goals and MDGs.

ABBREVIATIONS

ADP	African Development Programme
AFRODAD	African Network on Debt and Development
BMPIU	Budget Monitoring and Price Intelligence Unit (Nigeria)
CAGD	Controller and Accountant General's Department (Ghana)
CBA	Centre for Budget Advocacy (Ghana)
CBO	community-based organization
CCPA	Citizen Control of Public Action (Benin)
CDD	community-driven development
CEBEDES	Benin Centre for Environment and Economic and Social Development
CEDAW	Convention on the Elimination of Discrimination against Women
CFNBI	Child-Friendly National Budget Initiative (Zimbabwe)
CISANET	Civil Society Agriculture Network (Malawi)
CLP	community-level planning and budgeting support [team] (Tanzania)
CRC	citizen report card
CSCQBE	Civil Society Coalition for Quality Basic Education (Malawi)
CSO	civil society organization
DA	district assembly (Ghana)
DACF	District Assemblies Common Fund (Ghana)
DFID	Department for International Development (U.K.)
EITI	Extractive Industries Transparency Initiative

EPM	Environmental Planning and Management
GDP	gross domestic product
GNP	gross national product
GRBP	Gender Responsive Budgeting Project (Zimbabwe)
HIPC	heavily indebted poor countries
IED Afrique	Innovations Environment Development Africa
IBA	independent budget analysis
ILO	International Labour Organization
IMC	Ilala Municipal Council (Tanzania)
IMF	International Monetary Fund
LGA	Local Government Authority (Tanzania)
LGRP	Local Government Reform Program (Tanzania)
MDG	Millennium Development Goal
MEJN	Malawi Economic Justice Network
MEPD	Ministry of Economic Planning and Development (Malawi)
MFEP	Ministry of Finance and Economic Planning (Ghana)
MHEN	Malawi Health Equity Network
MLGRD	Ministry of Local Government and Rural Development (Ghana)
MMDAs	metropolitan, municipal, and district assemblies (Ghana)
MPRS	Malawi Poverty Reduction Strategy
MTEF	Medium Term Expenditure Framework (Tanzania)
NANGO	National Association of Non-Governmental Organisations (Zimbabwe)
NEITI	Nigeria Extractive Industries Transparency Initiative
NGO	nongovernmental organization
NNPC	Nigerian National Petroleum Corporation
NSWG	National Stakeholders Working Group [of NEITI] (Nigeria)
OECD	Organisation for Economic Co-operation and Development
OSIWA	Open Society Initiative in West Africa (Nigeria)
OVC	orphans and other vulnerable children
PETS	Public Expenditure Tracking Survey (Malawi)
PPA	participatory poverty assessment
PPEs	Protected Pro-Poor Expenditures (Malawi)
PRS	Poverty Reduction Strategy
PRSP	Poverty Reduction Strategy Paper

PWYP	Publish What You Pay (Nigeria)
RECODEF	Fissel Community Group for Self-Development (Senegal)
SADC	Southern African Development Community
SDSS	Service Delivery Satisfaction Survey [of MEJN] (Malawi)
SUDP	Strategic Urban Development Plan (Dar es Salaam, Tanzania)
UN	United Nations
UNDP	United Nations Development Programme
UNICEF	United Nations Children's Fund
USAID	United States Agency for International Development
Z-CYBN	Zimbabwe Child and Youth Budget Network
ZWRCN	Zimbabwe Women's Resource Centre and Network

Note: All dollar amounts are U.S. dollars unless otherwise indicated.

SOCIAL ACCOUNTABILITY INITIATIVES FROM SEVEN
SELECTED COUNTRIES

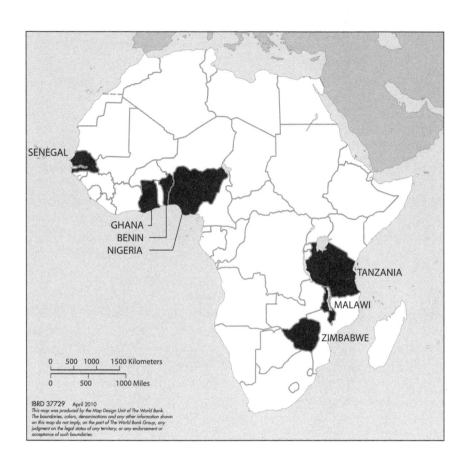

CHAPTER 1

SOCIAL ACCOUNTABILITY IN AFRICA: AN INTRODUCTION

Carmen Malena and Mary McNeil

Accountability is the cornerstone of good governance. Unless public officials can be held to account, critical benefits associated with good governance—such as social justice, poverty reduction, and development—remain elusive.

"Social accountability" refers to the wide range of citizen and civil society organization (CSO) actions to hold the state to account, as well as actions on the part of government, media, and other societal actors that promote or facilitate these efforts. Across the globe, citizens are increasingly active in challenging their governments, citing lack of transparency, responsiveness, and accountability as important problems, especially in relation to disadvantaged social groups (Commonwealth Foundation 1999, Narayan and others 2000). In many countries, CSOs no longer rely on top-down measures to improve governance but instead are demanding good governance by participating in public decision making and resource allocation, monitoring government performance, and ensuring accountability in the use of public resources.

The impacts of nonresponsive and unaccountable governance are perhaps most harshly felt by people in Africa, where corruption and governance failures are broadly acknowledged as major obstacles to achieving critical poverty reduction and human development goals. Lack of public accountability not only results in corruption and the waste of precious development resources but also seriously compromises the quality and effectiveness of public policy making, planning, and the provision of services to meet basic needs. Lack of accountability denies citizens their inherent right

to influence decisions that directly affect their lives and to hold state officials accountable for the public resources with which they are entrusted.

Over the past decade, a wide range of social accountability practices—
such as participatory budgeting, independent budget analysis, participatory monitoring of public expenditures, and citizen evaluation of public
services—have been developed and tested in countries such as Brazil,
India, the Philippines, and South Africa. In less developed Sub-Saharan
African countries, civil society and government actors are also actively
creating and experimenting with social accountability approaches (and
tools), but these experiences, their outcomes, and lessons have received
less attention and been less documented, studied, and shared. This volume aims to help fill this gap by describing and analyzing a selection of
social accountability initiatives from seven Sub-Saharan countries:
Benin, Ghana, Malawi, Nigeria, Senegal, Tanzania, and Zimbabwe.

PURPOSE AND TARGET AUDIENCES

This volume is written primarily by and for social accountability practitioners. Case study chapters are authored by civil society and government
practitioners who describe their firsthand experiences in designing,
promoting, and applying social accountability strategies in the African
context. The authors share the growing conviction that enhanced social
accountability is fundamental to achieving good governance and development in Africa. These practical experiences demonstrate that social
accountability approaches have the potential to bring important benefits to African citizens and governments, but that such approaches also face
significant challenges and require a demanding mix of technical expertise,
outreach, and sustained commitment to overcome obstacles. The book
seeks answers to the following questions:

• What kind of social accountability initiatives are being pursued in Sub-
  Saharan Africa?
• What are these accountability initiatives achieving?
• What obstacles do these initiatives face?
• What factors are critical to the initiatives' success?
• What can be done to promote social accountability in Africa?

We hope that social accountability practitioners in Africa and elsewhere
will glean operationally relevant lessons from the case studies highlighted

here. The descriptions and analyses of these seven initiatives can also serve as a source of information (and inspiration) for government and civil society representatives who lack firsthand experience with social accountability approaches but are interested in exploring such possibilities. Finally, the analysis of obstacles, factors of success, lessons learned, and recommendations may interest the research community and those donors and development partners who seek to promote and support enhanced social accountability and demand for good governance in Africa.

METHODOLOGY

Most of the case studies in this volume were identified in the context of two multicountry social accountability stocktaking exercises commissioned by the World Bank Institute; they were carried out in Anglophone countries by the Municipal Development Partnership for Eastern and Southern Africa (McNeil and Mumvuma 2006) and in Francophone countries by Innovations Environnement Développement Afrique (IED Afrique).[1] We chose the initiatives presented here from a much larger sample of close to 60 social accountability experiences, selecting the seven cases based on the results and lessons they offer as well as to represent a variety of approaches, strategies, and objectives. To enhance opportunities for comparative learning, the initiatives also represent a range of political, social, cultural, and organizational contexts. See table 1.A.1 in the annex to this chapter for a summary matrix of some key country indicators with regard to each case study.

OVERVIEW

This book focuses on the accountability of public power holders—political leaders, public officials, and civil servants—to ordinary citizens. The remainder of this introductory chapter sets the stage by clarifying what social accountability means, what it looks like in practice, and why it is crucially important in the African context. Each of the following seven chapters describes and analyzes one social accountability experience.

Chapters 2 and 3 describe efforts to introduce participatory planning and budgeting processes at the local level. Bara Guèye describes the experience of the rural commune of Fissel in Senegal. John Lubuva and

Renatus Kihongo recount the experience of the Ilala Municipal Council in Tanzania.

In Chapter 4, Charles Abbey, Vitus A. Azeem, and Cuthbert Baba Kuupiel describe CSOs' efforts in Ghana to monitor the transfer of resources from the central government to district councils through participatory expenditure tracking and to influence the national budget through independent budget analysis.

In Chapter 5, Dalitso Kingsley Kubalasa and Limbani Bartholomew Elia Nsapato describe the strategies of the Malawi Economic Justice Network to promote social accountability and economic justice through budget analysis and demystification, public education and mobilization, participatory monitoring, advocacy, and media activities.

In Chapter 6, Bob Libert Muchabaiwa describes another example of applied budget work, this time targeted at making the Zimbabwe national budget more responsive to the needs of women and children.

In Chapter 7, Dauda S. Garuba and John G. Ikubaje discuss the highly challenging and pathbreaking efforts of CSOs, working with government and private sector actors, to enhance government revenue transparency through two parallel initiatives: the government-led Nigeria Extractive Industries Transparency Initiative (NEITI) and the civil society-led Publish What You Pay (PWYP) campaign.

In Chapter 8, Cyrille Chabi Eteka and Anne Floquet convey the experience of Social Watch Benin, in which a network of more than 150 CSOs seeks to monitor government implementation of its Poverty Reduction Strategy (PRS) and Millennium Development Goals (MDGs).

Chapter 9 summarizes the key findings and conclusions of the seven case studies, beginning with an analysis of the most important factors that enable societies to create an environment for social accountability. The chapter goes on to discuss key challenges, factors of success, lessons learned, and conclusions about enhancing social accountability in Africa.

DEFINITION OF ACCOUNTABILITY

In the social context, accountability is often defined as the obligation of public power holders to account for or take responsibility for their actions. Accountability exists when power holders must explain and justify their actions or face sanctions.

The accountability of state actors is a consequence of the implicit social compact between citizens and their delegated representatives and agents in a democracy. The social compact, in turn, derives from notions of human and citizen rights, as enshrined in the General Assembly of the United Nations' Universal Declaration of Human Rights[2] and in many national constitutions. A fundamental principle of democracy is that citizens have both the *right* and the *responsibility* to demand accountability and to ensure that government acts in the best interests of the people. Public actors can and should be held accountable for both their conduct and performance. In other words, citizens have the right to ensure that public actors (a) obey the law and not abuse their powers, and (b) serve the public interest in an efficient, effective, and fair manner.

In an institutional environment for good governance, certain conditions underpin the ability of governments to *be* accountable (supply-side conditions) and the ability of citizens and civil society to *hold* governments accountable (demand-side conditions). Supply-side and demand-side mechanisms of accountability are complementary and mutually reinforcing. All states have some form of internal mechanisms to promote or ensure accountability of public servants, including

- Political mechanisms, such as constitutional constraints, separation of powers, the legislature, and legislative investigative commissions
- Fiscal mechanisms, such as auditing, financial management, and procurement regulations
- Administrative mechanisms, such as reporting systems, norms of public sector probity, public service codes of conduct, rules and procedures regarding transparency, and public oversight
- Legal mechanisms, such as corruption control agencies, ombudsmen, and an independent judiciary (Goetz and Gaventa 2001)

While such internal or supply-side mechanisms of accountability are necessary for good governance, experience has shown that they are not sufficient. States are rarely effective at holding themselves accountable. To achieve accountability, citizens must also demand it. Unless CSOs and other external actors can demand government transparency, responsiveness, and accountability, current governance failures are unlikely to be resolved.

In democracies, elections are the principal means by which citizens can hold the state to account. Elections, however, have frequently proven to be a weak and blunt instrument with which to hold government accountable.

Even if citizens were fully and accurately informed of the views and actions of every political candidate (which is far from the case), elections still allow citizens to select from only a limited number of individuals or political parties. They do not offer citizens the opportunity to express their preferences on specific issues, to contribute in a meaningful way to public decision making, or to hold public actors accountable for specific decisions or behaviors (World Bank 2004).

Social accountability is about affirming and making operational the direct accountability relationships between citizens and the state. In practical terms, accountability refers to (a) the broad range of actions and mechanisms (beyond voting) that citizens can use to hold the state to account, such as access to and ability to monitor public budgets, participation in budget formation, and citizen report cards on service delivery; and (b) actions on the part of government, civil society, media, and other societal actors that promote or facilitate these efforts.

SOCIAL ACCOUNTABILITY STRATEGIES AND METHODS

In practice, social accountability encompasses an array of approaches, strategies, and methods that may

- Be initiated by a wide range of actors (citizens, CSOs, communities, government agencies, parliamentarians, media, and others)
- Occur at different levels (from the community level to the national and international levels)
- Use diverse strategies (for example, research, monitoring, civic education, media coverage, advocacy, and coalition building)
- Employ different forms of formal and informal sanctions (for example, judicial enforcement of freedom of information laws and public exposés in the media)
- Vary by the extent to which they are institutionalized and collaborative

Traditionally, citizen or civil society-led efforts to hold government accountable have included public demonstrations, protests, advocacy, and lobbying. In recent years, the expanded use of participatory data collection and analytical tools, combined with enhanced space and opportunity for citizen and civil society engagement with the state, has led to a new generation of social accountability practices that emphasize a solid evidence base and direct dialogue and negotiation with government counterparts.

These social accountability practices include, for example, participatory public policy making, participatory budgeting, public expenditure tracking, and citizen monitoring and evaluation of public services.

The opportunities for social accountability exist in all aspects of governance. Among the wide range of mechanisms to build social accountability, those that directly involve ordinary citizens in the allocation, disbursement, monitoring, and evaluation of public resources have proved effective because these are the resource flows that translate public policy into action.

Table 1.1 summarizes how the case studies in this book illustrate promotion of social accountability at both the national and local levels as well as at various stages throughout the public policy and budget cycles: policy making and planning; revenue reporting, auditing, and analysis; budget formulation, advocacy, and analysis; expenditure reporting and tracking; and service delivery evaluation. Interesting to note is the lack of on-the-ground experience in measuring the impact of social accountability approaches on revenue generation—an area that needs further study.

Social Accountability and Public Revenues

In most countries around the world, citizens know little about how much money their government has at its disposal, where that money comes from, and how it is managed and accounted for. Public revenue transparency is particularly weak in Sub-Saharan Africa where, due to corruption, there is significant misuse of public resources. Robert Rotberg of Harvard's John F. Kennedy School of Government estimates that in Nigeria, for example, 30 of the 36 state governors are corrupt, which in turn feeds corruption among local officials (Rotberg 2007).

That a relatively large proportion of government revenues in Sub-Saharan Africa come from international aid and the export of primary resources (rather than tax revenues) further diminishes a sense of accountability to citizens for public revenues. In 2007, for example, total inflows of combined Overseas Development Assistance (ODA) and foreign direct investment into Africa reached $91 billion (Boko and McNeil 2010).

Enhancing social accountability with regard to public revenues is therefore both essential and highly challenging in the African context. The NEITI and PWYP campaign in Nigeria are important and pathbreaking examples of multistakeholder efforts to improve transparency

Table 1.1 Social Accountability Practices in the Seven Case Studies

	National level ← → Local level	
Policies and plans	• Policy advocacy (Benin; Civil Society Manifesto, Malawi; NEITI bill, Nigeria) • Participatory formulation of the poverty reduction strategy (Benin) • Independent monitoring of the PRS and MDGs implementation (Benin, Malawi)	• Participatory urban planning (Tanzania) • Participatory rural commune planning (Senegal) • Independent monitoring of commune development plans (Benin)
Revenues	• Public revenue monitoring and reporting (Nigeria) • Advocacy for transparent revenue management (Nigeria) • Independent audit of oil sector revenues (Nigeria) • Public revenue and taxation analysis (Ghana)	
Budgets	• Independent budget analysis (Benin, Ghana, Malawi, Zimbabwe) • Budget literacy, budget demystification, and capacity building (Ghana, Malawi, Zimbabwe) • Assessing budget impact on women and children (Zimbabwe) • Budget advocacy (Ghana, Malawi, Zimbabwe) • Participatory national budget formulation (Benin, Malawi, Ghana, Zimbabwe)	• Participatory municipal budget formulation (Tanzania) • Participatory rural commune budget formulation (Senegal)
Expenditures	• Independent monitoring of public transfers of the District Assembly Common Fund (Ghana) • Participatory public expenditure tracking surveys in the education sector (Malawi)	• Public reporting of expenditures and budget implementation by local government (Ghana, Senegal, Tanzania)
Service delivery	• Citizen evaluation of public services (service delivery satisfaction surveys, Malawi)	• Participatory evaluation of local service delivery (user satisfaction surveys, Malawi, Tanzania) • Community scorecards (Malawi)

Source: Authors.

and accountability in Africa's most populous country and in the highly lucrative and problematic extractive industries sector. Other examples include revenue analysis efforts in Ghana by the Centre for Budget Advocacy, which aims to help ordinary citizens understand the tax system in the country and its implications.

Social Accountability and Public Budgets

Citizen involvement in preparing and analyzing public budgets is another important category of social accountability practices. Participatory budget formulation is most common at the local level (as in the case studies from Senegal and Tanzania) but can also be found at higher levels to varying degrees—for example, in the Ghana Ministry of Finance's public consultations or the Zimbabwe government's welcoming of oral and written submissions before budget formulations. More common examples of budget-related social accountability practices at the national level include independent civil society efforts to demystify the technical content of the budget and undertake public education campaigns to

- Improve budget literacy (in Benin, Ghana, Malawi, and Zimbabwe)
- Analyze the impact and implications of budget allocations overall (in Ghana) or for specific social groups such as women and children (in Zimbabwe)
- Advocate for public influence on national budget decisions (in Ghana, Malawi, Zimbabwe) and budgeting processes (in Ghana)

As these case studies demonstrate, independent applied budget work, in which CSOs combine specialized analysis with popular education and mobilization techniques, is an important and growing phenomenon in Sub-Saharan Africa.

Social Accountability and Public Expenditures

The formulation of public budgets is one thing, but whether and how public resources are actually used (according to budget provisions) is another. Another important aim of social accountability is to enable citizens to hold government accountable for how public monies are managed, transferred, and used.

A growing number of local governments (as the Senegal and Tanzania case studies show) publicly announce, post, or disseminate information about public expenditures. Public expenditure tracking exercises—initiated either by government (as in the education expenditure tracking surveys in Malawi, discussed in box 1.1) or by civil society (as in the monitoring of public transfers to the District Assembly Common Fund in Ghana)—are examples of expenditure-related social accountability practices that can be applied at the national level to monitor the flow of financial (or physical) resources and identify leakages or bottlenecks in the system.

These approaches often involve the comparison of information from disbursement records of central ministries, accounts of line agencies or decentralized government structures, and independent enquiries (using tools such as social audits, for example). Public sector entities or CSOs subsequently disseminate the information through books, the news media, and public meetings. If these approaches uncover mismanagement or misuse of funds, then calls for corrective measures and sanctions may also be made in the public arena to create popular pressure and momentum for action.

Box 1.1 Civil Society Organization Conducts Education Expenditure Tracking Surveys in Malawi

The Civil Society Coalition for Quality Basic Education (CSCQBE), created in 2000, consists of 67 civil society groups in Malawi, including nongovernmental organizations, community organizations, teachers' unions, religious organizations, and district networks. In response to suspicions of government corruption and mismanagement in the education sector, CSCQBE aims to prevent such corruption by closely monitoring government budgets and spending. It also seeks to enhance public understanding of education and budget policies and the need for accountability.

Through its network, CSCQBE has established 13 district networks to decentralize the monitoring of education budgets, and it provides these networks with technical assistance. Using Public Expenditure Tracking Surveys (PETS), the organization tracks the flow of resources through various levels of government to the end users to identify leakages.

CSCQBE has used PETS three times between 2002 and 2007, gathering information from teachers, students, and public sector agencies and employees in the education sector around the country. It holds public meetings to unveil findings to ministry officials, parliamentarians, development partners, and the media during the annual parliamentary budget deliberation. It then holds district meetings during which district assembly officials, district education officials, nongovernmental organizations, and school officials can discuss the results and, if necessary, formulate action plans.

Source: Ramkumar 2008.

Social Accountability and Public Service Delivery

Another social accountability category seeks accountability with regard to the relevance, accessibility, and quality of public goods and services. Typically, these practices involve citizen participation in the monitoring and evaluation of service delivery, often according to indicators that citizens have selected.

At the national level, methods such as public hearings or public opinion polls (for example, Service Delivery Satisfaction Surveys in Malawi) solicit citizen feedback that can be disseminated and presented to government officials to promote accountability and lobby for change (for example, see box 1.2). At the local level, both service providers and CSOs use a variety of participatory tools to help citizens monitor, evaluate, and seek accountability for effective public service delivery. Community scorecards in Malawi, for example, allow both service providers and users to independently evaluate public services and then come together at interface meetings to share their findings, discuss problems,

---

Box 1.2 Citizen Report Card "Roadshows" in Kenya

In Kenya, the Public Affairs Foundation and the Water and Sanitation Program–Africa used creative methods to strengthen consumers' voice in the water and sanitation sector, aiming to better understand issues that affect the poor and, ultimately, to improve service delivery.

To build awareness of the Citizen Report Card (CRC) as a social accountability tool, the team employed an innovative approach of "Report Card Roadshows," a five-day event involving both individual consultations with stakeholders and multistakeholder workshops. The Roadshow events created better awareness and understanding of the CRC concept and methodology while also creating the space for public dialogue and deliberation on the merits of the tool and its contextual fit.

A broad alliance of diverse partners involved in providing water supply and sanitation services had participated in public dialogues before the launch of the CRC. A slogan was even created in Kiswahili that means "Water and sanitation? Come all, let's discuss and agree," which was used on all promotional materials. The implementing agencies worked closely with the media to cover the process and to disseminate findings. CRC findings were discussed on television, radio, and in print media. As a result, senior policy makers made public commitments to address the problems identified.

Source: Thampi 2007.

and seek solutions. In Tanzania, the Ilala Municipal Council uses citizen surveys, elected service management boards, and local-level monitoring committees to enhance the quality and accountability of public services.

Early experience has shown that each of these methods has the potential to produce significant operational results (for example, improved performance and introduction of corrective measures) as well as process outcomes (for example, institutional, behavioral, and relational changes).

WHY SOCIAL ACCOUNTABILITY IS IMPORTANT IN AFRICA

Progress in governance, development, and citizen empowerment is crucial to societies and citizens around the world. Africa, however, is arguably the region where governance failures, underdevelopment, and disempowerment are most pronounced, where the need for enhanced social accountability is most pressing, and where the potential benefits of social accountability are greatest. Exacerbating these needs is the move toward more decentralized governance, which has yielded few clear signs that public service delivery and local economic development have been enhanced. Consequently, social accountability may be a crucial missing component of many decentralization programs.

Experience shows that social accountability practices, such as those described in this book can make important contributions toward improved governance, enhanced development, and citizen empowerment (figure 1.1).

Figure 1.1 Key Benefits of Social Accountability

Source: Authors.

Improved Governance

Governance, broadly defined, is the means by which the state acquires and exercises authority to provide for citizens. The outputs of governance processes and systems, at their most basic, are at the core of what affects citizens on a daily basis—roads being built and repaired, health services being delivered properly, and public school teachers getting the supplies they need. Although governance systems vary greatly, they all tend to have three parts: how governments make things happen, how institutions hold government accountable through checks and balances, and how citizens are actively engaged in the governance process. The objectives of social accountability summarized below, if achieved, can improve these crucial elements of good governance and lead to improved development outcomes.

Strengthened democracy. Although most African countries have made a formal transition to democracy (through regular multiparty elections), these incipient democratic structures are often weak or dysfunctional. Many African countries, sometimes referred to as "hybrid regimes," combine formal democratic systems with authoritarian features and are characterized by highly concentrated political power, flawed election processes, and inconsistent application of the rule of law.

Even those emerging democracies that have freed themselves from authoritarian rule often suffer from weak democratic institutions, lack of transparency, traditions of top-down political control and decision making, and shallow citizen participation. As the case studies show, social accountability practices can make an important contribution to overcoming these democratic deficits. By enhancing the capacity and opportunities of ordinary citizens (not just elite groups) to have information and knowledge about public affairs, voice their needs, monitor government actions, engage public actors, and demand accountability, the social accountability approaches presented in this book have been made operational and deepened democracy.

Enhanced accountability. Unfortunately, many African regimes are currently characterized by extremely weak accountability. The democratic deficits described above, combined with capacity and resource constraints, often limit the effectiveness of conventional internal mechanisms of accountability. For example, political and legal mechanisms of accountability are frequently compromised by executive dominance over the legislative and judicial branches of government and independent control agencies (such as anticorruption commissions or ombudsmen) and often lack genuine powers of sanction. Fiscal and administrative accountability mechanisms often suffer from weak management and auditing systems, low compliance with established rules and procedures, and human and financial capacity constraints.

Under such circumstances, social accountability approaches can improve accountability, both by complementing conventional practices (for example, through citizen-led audit or expenditure tracking exercises, as in Malawi and Ghana) and by reinforcing existing mechanisms (for example, when CSOs collaborate with parliamentarians to enhance their capacities of representation, analysis, and oversight, as in Malawi and Zimbabwe).

Reduced corruption. Corruption at all levels of government plagues many African nations. Despite governments' stated commitment to fight corruption and implement transparency and anticorruption initiatives, important problems persist: abuse of powers, patronage, mismanagement, and embezzlement of public resources. Almost all of the case studies presented in this book cite government corruption or mismanagement as driving forces behind their initiatives.

Social accountability approaches are potentially powerful tools against public sector corruption. They can serve both to detect and to prevent corruption—for example, by enhancing public transparency and oversight (as in the NEITI and PWYP campaign in Nigeria) and by exposing leakages (as through the education expenditure tracking surveys in Malawi).

A common challenge faced by social accountability initiatives is the failure to prosecute wrongdoers once evidence of corruption has been revealed. Here, the public nature of social accountability initiatives is extremely important, in that these initiatives can both create informal sanctions (in the form of public shaming) and increase the chances of applying formal sanctions (through public pressure and sustained public monitoring).

Greater government legitimacy and credibility. Many governments around the world currently suffer a lack of legitimacy. Citizens cite a lack of responsiveness on the part of government, corruption, and weak accountability as the main sources of their disillusionment. Conversely, citizens' trust in government grows when they feel they have a say in government decisions and an eye on government activities, and when government listens and responds to their concerns. Social accountability mechanisms, therefore, play an important potential role in enhancing government credibility and legitimacy. As the Senegal and Tanzania case studies show, enhanced accountability and legitimacy can translate into greater popularity and increased public support for both government actors and programs, including tax increases.

Improved citizen-state relations. Some government officials perceive citizen or civil society demands for accountability as threatening. Indeed, most social accountability approaches must overcome some initial resistance or reluctance and will frequently involve some level of critical or contentious engagement. It is striking, therefore, that social accountability approaches frequently result in stronger and more positive and productive relationships between citizens and the state.

Almost all the case studies in this volume cite improved relations and greater mutual trust and appreciation between citizens, or CSOs, and government counterparts as a result of social accountability intervention. In many cases, the fact that social accountability approaches open up channels of communication and put citizens and CSOs in direct contact with state actors (sometimes for the first time) is enough to help overcome initial mutual distrust, lack of information, and misunderstanding. In Tanzania, for example, citizens immediately became less critical and more understanding of local government officials when they were accurately informed about the limited resources available to the municipality and how those resources were used.

New and emerging social accountability practices significantly enhance citizens' ability to move beyond mere protest or opposition and toward engagement with bureaucrats and politicians in a more informed, organized, constructive, and systematic manner, thus building more productive relations and increasing the chances of effecting positive change. In several case study countries—including Benin, Nigeria, and Zimbabwe—civil society representatives report having earned greater recognition and respect from state actors as a result of their social accountability activities. In fact, in Zimbabwe, despite significant tensions between government and CSOs, the government (parliament and relevant ministries) has come to welcome and even rely on CSOs' analyses of policy and budgetary impacts on women and children.

Political stability and peace. Finally, enhanced social accountability can ultimately contribute to political stability and peace. The risk of political instability clearly increases when citizens distrust government, perceive government as corrupt or unresponsive, or cannot get the basic services they need. Actions such as public protests and popular uprisings result when channels for more constructive dialogue and negotiation are lacking. Social accountability mechanisms create opportunities for informed, constructive dialogue and negotiation between citizens and government and the identification of mutually agreed-upon solutions, thus contributing to better and more stable government over time. Government stability is a critically important, long-term benefit of enhanced social accountability, especially in those African states emerging from or threatened by civil conflict or unrest.

Enhanced Development

In addition to important governance benefits, social accountability mechanisms have led to concrete improvements in government policies, programs, services, and development. By enhancing citizens' information and voice, introducing incentives for downward accountability, and creating mechanisms for participatory monitoring and citizen-state dialogue and negotiation, social accountability mechanisms can contribute to better policy, program design, more development resources, more equitable and efficient public spending, and greater and more sustainable development outcomes.

Better-designed policies, budgets, and plans. In many countries in Africa and around the world, government policies, budgets, and plans have traditionally been designed away from public view. Bureaucrats and teams of experts have led these processes and provided little opportunity for input from ordinary citizens or community members. Therefore, government policies, budgets, and plans can fail to reflect societal priorities and local context or overlook the needs of various societal groups, especially traditionally marginalized groups such as women, youth, and people with disabilities.

Some of the case studies in this book (Senegal and Tanzania, for example) demonstrate how citizen participation can contribute to better-designed, more effective policies, budgets, and plans that are more responsive to citizen preferences and better adapted to their needs.

Participatory processes of policy making, budget formulation, and planning also enhance citizen knowledge of and interest in these key public decisions, increasing the opportunities for subsequent engagement and monitoring and improving the chances of compliance and uptake.

Increased resources. Enhanced social accountability can also lead to increased government resources for development, both from international donors (who increasingly request or require enhanced accountability mechanisms) and from tax-paying citizens. In both Senegal and Tanzania, for example, local government officials saw the payment of municipal taxes significantly increase once citizens understood how these resources were being used and were confident that they could hold local authorities accountable. In Tanzania, the municipality of Ilala also saw private sector contributions increase after it introduced participatory and social accountability-oriented processes.

More equitable public spending and services. Because of problems of elitism, patronage, and social and political exclusion, citizens who are in greatest need (relatively poorer and less powerful groups) have often benefited the least from public spending and services. The *2004 World Development Report: Making Services Work for Poor People*, argues that much of the solution to these inequities lies in strengthening relationships of accountability between policy makers, service providers, and citizens (World Bank 2003). This is exactly what social accountability approaches seek to do.

A key benefit of many social accountability initiatives, including several of the examples cited in this book, is to increase equity in public spending and services. Virtually all the case studies in this book emphasize equity issues, with the enhanced well-being of disadvantaged and disempowered groups as the initiatives' core objective. Applied budget work in Zimbabwe, for example, has led to increased budgets for programs and services that directly benefit women and children. In Ilala, Tanzania, participatory planning and budgeting has improved equity of services through more targeted spending on services for the poor and enhanced information and access for the poor.

Greater efficiency, less waste. An important obstacle to development in Africa has been the inefficient or wasteful use of limited development resources. The important role that social accountability practices can play in fighting corruption and checking leakages of public funds has already been discussed. Another important advantage of social accountability approaches is their potential to promote more efficient and effective public spending and service delivery.

In Ghana, for example, participatory expenditure tracking helped to identify bottlenecks in the system and analyze the reasons for serious and costly delays in the transfer of funds to local government authorities. In Ilala, Tanzania, local government officials say that community-led procurement has ensured greater monetary value in working with local contractors. Locally elected management committees and community monitoring teams have also led to more efficient public spending and less waste. In countries such as Malawi, citizen and community evaluations of public services (through user satisfaction surveys and community scorecards, for example) have provided feedback on problems and shortcomings and proposed collective solutions for enhanced service delivery.

Better development results. Social accountability approaches have shown strong potential to contribute to greater and more sustainable development. Among the examples highlighted in this book (which are, for the most part, more recent and modest in scope than initiatives in countries like Brazil), only a few initiatives can claim to have achieved concrete improvements in citizens' well-being and quality of life. The Ilala Municipal Council in Tanzania, however, reports a significant increase in the number of municipal-level development projects and employment opportunities as a direct result of its participatory planning and budgeting strategies. Other case studies report more intermediate-level results for now—including improved development processes and enhanced institutional capacities—and predict that sustained effort will bring more medium- to long-term development impacts.

Citizen Empowerment

People everywhere want to be treated fairly and have a say in the decisions that affect their lives. Many citizens across Africa, especially those from disadvantaged groups, have felt incapable of engaging public actors, unable to influence public decisions or demand fair treatment, and powerless to improve their own lives. Social accountability approaches are based upon empowering ordinary citizens—in particular, disadvantaged citizens with the least voice and influence—to know and exercise their rights, obtain information and knowledge, make their voices heard, negotiate change, and hold public power holders to account. These aspects of empowerment and the promotion of citizen rights are a final and crucially important potential benefit of social accountability approaches.

Greater awareness of citizen rights. A crucial component of empowerment is raising awareness of citizen and human rights among citizens (rights claimers) and public power holders (duty bearers). In most African countries, the law protects basic human and citizen rights such as freedom of information, expression, association, and assembly.

Many citizens, however, remain unaware of their rights and, all too frequently, these rights are violated despite legal guarantees. Social accountability is based on notions of citizen rights, and the starting point of many social accountability initiatives is to raise awareness of these rights and advocate for their protection both in law and in practice. Almost all of the examples in this book adopt a rights-based approach to advocacy and development, and many of them cite greater rights awareness as an important outcome of their social accountability initiative. Citizens who know their rights and their corresponding responsibilities are more likely and better placed to engage with public actors and to demand accountability and good governance. Democracy requires active and empowered citizenship, and rights awareness is an important first step.

More information. Information is power. Citizens have frequently lacked the information they need to demand good governance and social accountability. The ability to generate and gain access to relevant information—and thereby to build a credible evidence base for holding public officials to account—is critical to social accountability. For example, the NEITI and PWYP campaigns in Nigeria focus on making essential information about transfers of funds from oil companies to the government available to the public. Initiatives in Ghana and Malawi help ordinary citizens become better informed about the content of the national budget by simplifying and publicly disseminating essential budget information.

In fact, every social accountability initiative described in this book includes efforts to promote transparency and enhance public access to essential information about government resources, policies, commitments, laws and regulations, budgets, programs, actions, and results. Enhancing the quantity and quality of information in the public arena, and building the capacity of citizens to digest and use that information, constitute a core element of citizen empowerment and social accountability. While there has been some progress in legislating access to information on the continent, much work still needs to be done.[3]

Stronger citizen voice. Citizens have the right to speak up and be heard. Strengthening the citizen voice is another key element of empowerment and a central feature of most social accountability initiatives. The case studies presented in this book use a variety of strategies both to help citizens speak up and to help ensure that government actors listen and respond to these voices.

Almost all of the case studies include capacity-building activities that aim to give ordinary citizens—especially those with the weakest political voice such as women, children, and other traditionally marginalized groups—the confidence and capacity to voice their views, questions, concerns, and needs. Other important strategies include creating spaces for public debate and dialogue (as in the organization of public debates in Malawi); consolidating citizen voices (for example, through the formation of broad-based coalitions in Benin and opinion leader strategies in Nigeria); and amplifying citizen voices (for instance, through community radio in Senegal and CSO-media partnerships in Malawi).

A principal challenge, and important potential benefit, of social accountability initiatives is to help ensure that the voices of the poor and other marginal groups are not drowned out or dominated by more powerful interests.

Enhanced agency and opportunity. The degree to which a person or group is empowered is influenced by agency (the capacity to make purposive choice) and opportunity structure (the institutional context in which choice is made) (Alsop and Heinsohn 2005). By providing critical information, building citizen capacity, and strengthening citizen voice, social accountability initiatives clearly contribute to increased agency.

An important characteristic of social accountability approaches is that they also aim to improve opportunity structures—for example, by

- Creating or expanding opportunities and mechanisms for citizen-state engagement, such as public budget consultations in Ghana, public debates in Malawi, and the development of an evaluation tool for service delivery in Colombia (see box 1.3)
- Clarifying and mutually agreeing to the terms of that engagement, such as through meaningful CSO involvement in PRS formulation processes in Benin
- Negotiating new institutional forms that allow citizens a more meaningful and influential role in governance processes, such as elected management committees and community monitoring teams in Tanzania

---

Box 1.3 Bogotá Cómo Vamos: Citizen Evaluation of Public Services in Colombia

Bogotá Cómo Vamos was created in 1997 to monitor political campaign promises and their impact on the quality of life in the city. A citizen-based social accountability initiative, Bogotá Cómo Vamos works closely with government, the private sector, and the media.

The evaluation tool that this initiative developed is based on a set of key indicators of outcomes, technical standards, and public perception. Information submitted by the district offices every six months informs the technical portion, whereas an annual opinion survey of 1,500 citizens of Bogotá informs the public perception portion. Results are presented in public forums, with the mass media playing a central role in the dissemination and deliberation of evaluation findings.

The project's most significant contribution to ensuring accountability is the development of performance indicators that provide benchmarks for citizens to use as a basis for demanding accountability from city officials. It effectively improved the quality of reporting and shifted the focus from inputs and activities to impacts and outcomes.

Bogotá Cómo Vamos has demonstrated its effectiveness as a forum for public debate where strategic issues affecting the city can be examined and deliberated by broad segments of society. By raising the citizen voice and strengthening the accountability relationships between citizens and government officials, it hopes to further stimulate public debate, influence policy dialogue, and improve development outcomes for the people of Bogotá.

Source: Sánchez 2003.

Social accountability approaches, therefore, empower citizens through both enhanced agency and opportunity. Of particular importance is the potential of social accountability initiatives to empower those social groups that are systematically underrepresented in formal political institutions (such as women, youth, and poor people). Numerous social accountability tools—including women- and children-friendly budgeting processes in Zimbabwe and participatory monitoring and evaluation in Benin—are specifically designed to address issues of inequality and to ensure that less powerful societal groups also have the agency and opportunity to express and act upon their choices and to demand accountability.

CONCLUSION

This introductory chapter has sought to clarify the concept of social accountability and explain why enhanced social accountability is crucially important for Africa. It has also introduced some of the key characteristics and achievements of the social accountability initiatives highlighted in this book.

In the following chapters, readers are invited to gain a more in-depth understanding of how courageous and committed practitioners from both civil society and government are working to enhance social accountability in their own community, sector, or country. The case studies, based on hands-on experience, describe and analyze the challenges that African social accountability practitioners face and the strategies they use to overcome challenges and constraints. The case studies also describe how social accountability initiatives are helping to achieve critical governance, development, and empowerment goals from the national to the local level and are making a difference in the daily lives of communities and individuals.

Readers are welcome to review all of the case studies—each of which offers unique findings and lessons—or to focus on select case studies based on specific country or sector interest. Table 1.A.1 summarizes the key characteristics of each case study to guide readers in their choices.

ANNEX

Table 1.A.1 Case Study Characteristics

Country	Organizations involved	Social accountability tools	Challenges	Outcomes
Benin	Social Watch Benin	• Participatory formulation of PRS (Poverty Reduction Strategy) • Independent monitoring of PRS and MDG (Millennium Development Goal) implementation • Independent monitoring of communal development plans	• Raising resources • Mobilizing grassroots organizations • Ensuring credibility and accountability within civil society • Increasing inclusiveness	• Enhanced CSO capacity • Increased support for community action • Improved relations with the media • Had informal impact on budget allocations • Improved civil society credibility • Impact on formulation and monitoring of development policies
Ghana	African Development Programme Integrated Social Development Centre Friends of the Nation Muslim Relief Association of Ghana	• Public revenue and taxation analysis • Independent budget analysis • Analysis of national budgeting process • Budget literacy and capacity building	• Mobilizing grassroots organizations • Raising resources • Ensuring credibility and accountability within civil society • Institutionalization	• Increased citizen interest in use of public funds and independent budget analysis • Increased government willingness to consult with and involve civil society in budget policies

(Table continues on the following page)

Table 1.A.1 (continued)

Country	Organizations involved	Social accountability tools	Challenges	Outcomes
	Centre for the Development of the People Centre for Budget Advocacy	• Budget advocacy • Independent monitoring of public transfers • Public reporting of local government expenditures	• Building capacities and skills for social accountability	• Enhanced status of civil society and increased government willingness to engage with civil society
Malawi	Malawi Economic Justice Network	• Policy advocacy		• Scaling up of CSO budget monitoring
		• Independent budget analysis	• Raising resources	• Increased public interest in, access to, and awareness of public budgets
		• Budget literacy and capacity building	• Mobilizing grassroots organizations	• Enhanced local capacity
		• Budget advocacy	• Ensuring credibility and accountability within civil society	
		• Participatory expenditure tracking surveys	• Building trust	
		• Citizen evaluation of public services	• Establishing effective interface mechanisms	
		• Community scorecards	• Increasing inclusiveness	

24

Country	Organization	Practice	Challenges	Results
Nigeria	NEITI (Nigeria Extractive Industries Transparency Initiative) PWYP (Publish What You Pay) Nigeria	• Public revenue reporting	• Building capacities and skills for social accountability • Mobilizing grassroots organizations • Establishing effective interface mechanisms • Increasing political will and leadership	• Signing of enabling legislation for EITI • Raised awareness of need for, and improved transparency and accountability in, extractive industries sector • Institutionalized NEITI
Senegal	IED Afrique RECODEF (Fissel Community Group for Self-Development)	• Participatory rural communal planning • Participatory tax collection • Participatory communal budgeting • Public reporting of local government expenditures	• Raising resources • Building capacities and skills for social accountability • Reducing low education and widespread illiteracy • Decreasing the high turnover of facilitators • Institutionalization: lack of political will, lack of citizen knowledge of rights and responsibilities • Difficulty of reconciling budgeting process and participatory process	• Improved understanding among traditionally excluded groups about local planning processes • Increased community capacity • Improved relationship between rural council and grassroots organizations • Raised the priority given women's needs in budget allocation • Scaling up of practice beginning across Senegal (organized forum for 30 rural communmities)

(Table continues on the following page)

Table 1.A.1 (continued)

Country	Organizations involved	Social accountability tools	Challenges	Outcomes
Tanzania	Ilala Municipal Council	• Participatory urban planning	• Urban setting challenges degree of participation	• Increased budget effectiveness
	Institute of Regional Development Planning	• Participatory tax collection	• Raising resources	• Increased community involvement in projects
		• Participatory municipal budgeting	• Building capacities and skills for social accountability	• Enhanced sustainability of local development projects
		• Participatory monitoring and evaluation of local service delivery	• Political conflict	• Increased community capacity
			• Increasing inclusiveness	• Improved government-community relations
				• Improved accountability
Zimbabwe	National Association of Non-Governmental Organisations	• Independent budget analysis	• Building capacities and skills for social accountability	• Increased transparency and accountability regarding budgeting processes and information
	Zimbabwe Women's Resource Centre and Network	• Budget literacy and capacity building	• Ensuring credibility and accountability within civil society	• Decentralized and democratized budget debates
		• Assessment of budget impact on women and children	• Overcoming problems of patronage and partisanship	• Increased budget allocations for women and children's issues
		• Budget advocacy	• Building trust	• Enhanced local capacity: parliament, civil society, and citizens
			• Increasing inclusiveness	• Made positive policy changes
			• Establishing effective interface mechanisms	

Source: Authors.

NOTES

1. The case study from Tanzania was prepared for another WBI-commissioned research project on participatory budgeting, and the Nigeria case study was identified directly by the research team and prepared specifically for this book.
2. The Universal Declaration of Human Rights is accessible at http://www.un.org/en/documents/udhr.
3. Five Southern African Development Community (SADC) countries—the Democratic Republic of Congo, Madagascar, Malawi, Mozambique, and South Africa—have the right to information expressly guaranteed within their constitutional frameworks. Nine other SADC countries have protected this right only within the context of the broader right of freedom of expression, which normally includes the right to "seek, receive, and impart information." Those nine countries are Angola, Botswana, Lesotho, Mauritius, Namibia, Swaziland, Tanzania, Zambia, and Zimbabwe. In addition, Zambia has an Access to Information Bill at an advanced stage (Mukelani 2009).

REFERENCES

Alsop, Ruth, and Nina Heinsohn. 2005. "Measuring Empowerment in Practice: Structuring Analysis and Framing Indicators." Policy Research Working Paper 3510. World Bank, Washington, DC.

Boko, Sylvain and McNeil, Mary. 2010. "Monitoring Resource Flows in Decentralizing States." In *Sourcebook on Social Accountability in Africa*. Pretoria: Affiliated Network for Social Accountability (ANSA)-Africa.

Commonwealth Foundation. 1999. *Citizens and Governance: Civil Society in the New Millennium.* London: Commonwealth Foundation.

Goetz, Anne Marie, and John Gaventa. 2001. "Bringing Citizen Voice and Client Focus into Service Delivery." Institute of Development Studies (IDS) Working Paper 138. IDS, Brighton, U.K.

McNeil, Mary, and Takawira Mumvuma. 2006. *Demanding Good Governance: A Stocktaking of Social Accountability Initiatives by Civil Society in Anglophone Africa.* Washington, DC: World Bank Institute.

Mukelani, Dimba. 2009. "Mapping the Right to Information Legislation in Africa." *Full Circle*, newsletter of ANSA-Africa, December 2009. http://www.ansa-africa.net/uploads/documents/newsletters/Full_Circle_Dec2009.pdf.

Narayan, Deepa, Raj Patel, Kai Schafft, Anne Rademacher, and Sarah Koch-Schulte. 2000. *Voices of the Poor: Crying Out for Change.* Washington, DC: World Bank.

Ramkumar, Vivek. 2008. *Our Money, Our Responsibility: A Citizens' Guide to Monitoring Government Expenditures.* Washington, DC: International Budget Project.

Rotberg, Robert I. 2007. *Nigeria: Elections and Continuing Challenges.* Council Special Report 27. Council on Foreign Relations, New York.

Sánchez, Maria Fernanda. 2003. "Evaluation of Changes in the Quality of Life in Bogotá, Colombia, from a Civil Society Perspective: Bogotá Cómo Vamos." In *Voice, Eyes, and Ears: Social Accountability in Latin America—Case Studies on Mechanisms of Participatory Monitoring and Evaluation*, ed. Civil Society Team, Latin America and the Caribbean Region, 77–82. Working Paper 30413, Civil Society Series. World Bank, Washington, DC.

Thampi, Gopakumar. 2007. "From 'Brakes' to 'Accelerators': How Informed Public Opinion Facilitates Behavior Changes in Public Officials." Paper prepared for the Public Affairs Foundation, Bangalore. http://www.sasanet.org/documents/Curriculum/ Strategic%20Communication/G%20Thampi.pdf

World Bank. 2003. *World Development Report 2004: Making Services Work for Poor People.* Washington, DC: World Bank.

———. 2004. "State-Society Synergy for Accountability: Lessons for the World Bank." World Bank Working Paper 30. World Bank, Washington, DC.

CHAPTER 2

PARTICIPATORY BUDGETING
IN FISSEL, SENEGAL

Bara Guèye

This chapter presents a case study on participatory budgeting as a tool to promote inclusive and transparent mechanisms of local governance. The initiative took place in the *communauté rurale* (rural commune) of Fissel, one of the first rural communes in Senegal to be decentralized in 1972. Fissel also benefits from many years of active community life, which has encouraged the creation of dynamic local organizations.

A long process led Fissel to participatory budgeting. It started when people became aware of their weak participation in local decision making, despite national government support for decentralization and natural resource management, and in spite of capacity-building programs on local administration initiated by local officials. Once aware of the situation, local government and nongovernmental actors decided to start a participatory process that would help them identify the factors that promote or inhibit citizen participation.

It is within this context that a nongovernmental organization (NGO)— Innovations, Environnement et Développement en Afrique (Innovations Environment Development Africa, or IED Afrique)[1] helped Regroupement Communautaire pour le Développement de Fissel (Fissel Community Group for Self-Development, or RECODEF) to develop a pilot research program on monitoring and reinforcement of citizen participation in local development.

Fissel's participatory budgeting initiative is the result of not only the community's research but also the implementation of the community's recommendations. While the product of indigenous collective analysis promoted by local civil society through RECODEF, the participatory budget process was also strongly supported by the rural council,[2] the local government management body.

The process required a lot of time and patience, and was challenged by the relatively low education level of some councilors, the high illiteracy rate among the local population, and the high turnover of facilitators. The biggest challenge to supporting the participatory budgeting process was finding sufficient funding.

Despite these challenges, however, the participatory budgeting process has spread. In 2004, Fissel organized a forum on budget transparency for 30 rural communities. Then in 2006, Fissel presented a workshop in which members of the Decentralization Commission of the National Assembly took part. Over the two-year period of 2008–09, almost 70 municipalities sent councilors to visit Fissel and learn about its experience. Two mayors from Burkina Faso visited Fissel in March 2009, and Fissel and four other communes were selected to host field visits during the international conference organized by the World Bank in partnership with other African institutions, including IED Afrique. Since Fissel's experience, two Senegalese municipalities (Matam and Guediawaye) and one other rural commune (Ndiaganiao) have adopted the participatory budgeting process. Despite this progress, traditional resistance to some aspects of the process persists, especially to the empowerment of women.

This chapter describes the conditions under which the experience emerged. The chapter also analyzes the methods of implementing the participatory budgeting process, the most important challenges to be faced before it is institutionalized, the results and impacts, and the lessons learned.

POLITICAL AND ECONOMIC CONTEXT

Senegal's economy is still dependent on its agricultural sector, which employs more than half the population. Due to the combined effects of globalization, recurrent droughts, structural adjustment policies, and inadequate national policies, the agricultural sector is going through a structural crisis. The country is faced with extreme poverty; 65 percent of the population falls below the poverty line. One-third of the nation's poor live in the cities, while two-thirds reside in rural areas. The Kolda region, and to a lesser extent Rambacounda, which are the most impoverished, are also the richest in natural resources, demonstrating that poverty in Senegal is not always due to the lack of resources but to the lack of adequate policies to share the nation's benefits more equitably.

Like most French-speaking countries, Senegal's executive, legislative, and judicial systems have been inspired largely by the French system. Senegal has significant experience with a multiparty political system, and since its independence, it has benefited from political stability—holding regular elections that allowed for a change in power in 2000. It is one of the few African countries that, since independence, have been governed by elected civil administrations. Three political regimes have ruled Senegal since its independence. The most recent one encourages liberalism, and the first two were socialist governments. Religion plays an important role in the mobilization and choice of candidates for election, even though its influence has diminished.

Senegal's position as the capital territory of West Africa during the colonial period made it a crucible of workers' movements. As a result, the dynamism of the union movement and of civil society in general has been a key factor in reinforcing freedom of association and expression. This freedom is reflected by the particularly strong presence of NGOs, associations, press organizations, newspapers, private television channels, and private and community radio stations. Experience shows, however, that continuous efforts are needed to protect freedom of expression, even in democracies, because the usual tensions between civil society and government often induce government reactions that may attempt to constrain this freedom. Senegal is no exception, and there have been recent conflicts between the state and the media.

Social practice is not always in line with the values underpinning this open political context and its legislative and regulatory standards. The political and economic power of women is still quite limited. Efforts are being made to guarantee some of their rights, but the balance of power in traditional society does not always allow effective enforcement. For example, women have the constitutional right to own land, but this is not allowed in practice because of the predominance of customary law over modern land access legislation. Similarly, the power of women in decision making is limited. In 2008, of the 320 rural councils, only one was headed by a woman. There was only one woman president among the 11 regional councils, and 25 women out of 120 deputies. Women represent 19 percent of municipal councilors and 11 percent of rural councilors (Ngaidé 2006).

These gender gaps prompted civil society organizations (CSOs) and political parties to campaign for the adoption of a law on gender parity for candidates in the June 2007 legislative elections. The National Assembly adopted the law, but it has not been enforced due to an action for annulment brought by the opposition party and some CSOs. The matter remains controversial because large sectors of civil society are against the adoption of the law, arguing that the issue of representation is not only a question of quantity, and that more emphasis should be given to the capacity of women to influence decisions.

Senegal has extensive experience in decentralization. The first urban communes date back to the 19th century. Rural decentralization began in 1972 with the creation of the first rural communes. A gradual pilot approach was adopted, and it took 10 years to complete the network of rural communes throughout the nation. Today, 320 rural communes are distributed across 11 administrative regions. Urban administrative organs include 67 *communes de villes* (urban communes or municipalities) and 43 *communes d'arrondissement* (subdivisions of urban communes).

Since 1972, several reforms have aimed at strengthening the power of local governments. With the 1990 reform, the president of the rural council became the main authorizing officer for the budget, replacing the subprefect (representative of the administration), who still has control over decisions before they are taken up by the rural council (management body of the rural commune). During the same period, municipal status changed considerably when the mayor became the executive body, with reinforced powers, and also replaced the municipal administrator, who had been a government official. The definite break took place in 1996, when the regions became *collectivités territoriales* (territorial authorities), and responsibility in nine areas[3] was devolved to local governments. The financial means to implement these responsibilities effectively, however, have not been transferred.

The implementation of decentralization in rural areas faces several problems, including the following:

- Scant resources available to local authorities, limiting their intervention capacity
- Lack of adequately trained elected officials who, for the most part, have only a vague idea of their mission
- A highly politicized process for choosing elected representatives and for decision making in rural councils

- Sporadic or nonexistent mechanisms to monitor local public action
- Most citizens' lack of awareness of, or disinterest in, their right to control the actions of their elected representatives

Even if progress has been made in good governance (Transparency International's 2006 Corruption Perceptions Index ranked Senegal 70th among 163 countries), problems persist. Senegal has created a national commission for the fight against corruption and misappropriation of public funds. A new code on public procurement is also being prepared, with the primary objective of making public procurement more transparent and equitable. Some CSOs and development partners are concerned about delays in the adoption and application of this code—delays that may be due to the government's reluctance to adopt the code. CSOs also regret that parliamentary action is limited to budget analysis by specialized committees before its adoption and that any monitoring action is rarely taken after budget approval.

CSOs also have undertaken actions to promote good governance. For example, Forum Civil, the CSO that represents Transparency International in Senegal, recently launched a series of research programs to collect information on corruption in key sectors such as health services and natural resource management. The independent press also plays an active role by publishing any corruption cases brought to its attention. Nonetheless, the reinforcement of a culture of transparency and social responsibility is undermined by the fact that few CSOs in rural areas are capable of understanding the decentralization process and of developing citizen capacity to hold their local councilors accountable.

THE PARTICIPATORY BUDGETING PROCESS

The process that led to adoption of participatory budgeting in Fissel started in 2002. It was initiated by local civil society through RECODEF, with the support of the rural council and village and religious chiefs as representatives of traditional authorities. RECODEF and the council asked for IED Afrique's support to carry out a local planning process. The entry point was a forum to assess the impact of decentralization on Fissel, better understand the factors that limit local actors' participation in decentralization, and improve decentralization performance in the rural commune. Participatory budgeting was not one of the initial objectives but became one of the results of the deliberative process. Figure 2.1 portrays the participatory budgeting process in Fissel, the steps and stages of which are described in detail below.

Step 1: Organizing a Community Forum

Four work groups were set up to reflect on the following themes:

- Local planning approach and methods
- Decentralization, participation, and local institutions (local authorities, farmers' organizations, and traditional institutions)

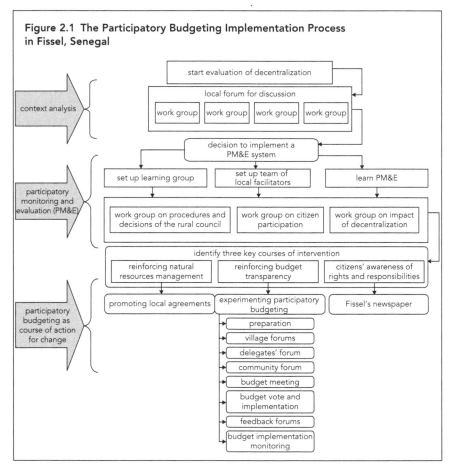

Figure 2.1 The Participatory Budgeting Implementation Process in Fissel, Senegal

Source: Guèye 2005.

Note: PM&E = participatory monitoring and evaluation.

- Forms and impact of participation in local development
- The role of communication and information in citizen participation

Each group analyzed the strengths and weaknesses in each thematic area and suggested actions aimed at improving local development performance and decentralization of the rural commune.

Step 2: Deciding to Implement a Participatory Monitoring and Evaluation System

The work carried out in the work groups revealed constraints related to the lack of coordination of various actors, limited popular participation in the decision-making process, the lack of adequate mechanisms and procedures to account for rural council decisions, citizens' lack of knowledge about their rights and responsibilities—particularly on monitoring the performance of elected officials—and the lack of adequate information and communication tools. To tackle these problems, the forum decided to implement a participatory monitoring and evaluation (PM&E) system for the decentralization process.

Step 3: Establishing a Learning Group

In consideration of the repetitive nature of the process and the need to enhance the knowledge of various actors, it was decided to establish a learning group as an inclusive and participatory mechanism through which key players could share their knowledge. To function effectively, the learning group had to meet certain conditions:

- All actors involved must clearly see their participation in the evaluation process as useful to them.
- The participants must be open-minded and willing to accept that the group will analyze their perceptions and ideas.
- The participants must respect prerogatives of various actors and agree on the need to use visualization tools in learning groups to facilitate general participation.

Step 4: Choosing and Training a Team of Local Facilitators

The team had 14 members, 6 of whom were women. Facilitators were chosen according to the following criteria: facilitation skills; fluency in

Wolof, Serere (two main local languages), or French; availability and commitment to serve the community; personal motivation; not being a member of the rural council; and approval by all members of the learning group. Geographic criteria were introduced to represent various zones of the rural commune. The facilitators received PM&E training.

Step 5: Organizing a Community Forum on PM&E of Decentralization

A community forum brought together facilitators, heads of rural council technical committees, village chiefs, chairpersons of village development committees, and representatives of women's associations. During debates, three themes were identified that would underpin the PM&E system:

1. Participation of actors in the decentralization process
2. Decision-making mechanisms and procedures within the rural council
3. The impact of decentralization on living standards

Table 2.1 summarizes the PM&E criteria for each theme generated by the community forum.

Step 6: Applying PM&E to the Chosen Priorities

During the evaluation process, each thematic group ranked criteria on a 1-to-10 scale. Figure 2.2 shows the evaluation tools used for citizen participation and for decision-making mechanisms and procedures within the rural council. For a better assessment of the scores, see table 2.A.1 in the annex for a collective analysis that identified the constraints, opportunities, and strengths related to various criteria.

Step 7: Identifying Actions for Change

Results of the evaluation were presented and validated during a community meeting. To address the most important problems found during the evaluation, three actions were identified:

1. Increase the transparency of rural council budget management through participatory budgeting
2. Strengthen natural resource management by implementing local agreements
3. Improve citizen knowledge and awareness of their rights and responsibilities by formulating a strategy for information and communication

Table 2.1 PM&E Criteria Identified by the Learning Group

Criteria for citizen participation in the decentralization process	Criteria for decision-making mechanisms and procedures within the rural council	Criteria for impact of decentralization on living standards
• Organization of population • Dissemination of decisions • Nature of participation • Importance of financial participation • Influence on decisions • Roles of participants	• Citizen attendance at rural council meetings • Number of decisions by rural council • Number of meetings organized by rural council • Councilors' knowledge of their roles and responsibilities • Councilor attendance at meetings • Frequency of reports prepared by councilors • Diversity of information tools • Accessibility of information • Availability of participatory planning tools	• Changes observed • Investments by rural council • Matching investments and needs • Local participation in choice of investments • Improved access of vulnerable groups to natural resources • Improved access of vulnerable groups to basic social services

Source: Author.

Note: PM&E is participatory monitoring and evaluation.

Step 8: Implementing Actions for Change: Participatory Budgeting

The following stages summarize the participatory budget process implemented in Fissel.

Preparation. The participatory budgeting participants needed to understand the concept and modalities of implementation and to clearly define their roles and responsibilities. Emphasis was made on the advantages this approach can bring to local authorities and people by enabling them to better identify the population's needs, improve the rural council's performance, and restore trust between elected officials and local people through more transparent management of public affairs. During this stage, the various actors attended courses on budget preparation that prepared them for the participatory budgeting process.

Figure 2.2 Criteria for Citizen and Council Participation in Participatory Budgeting

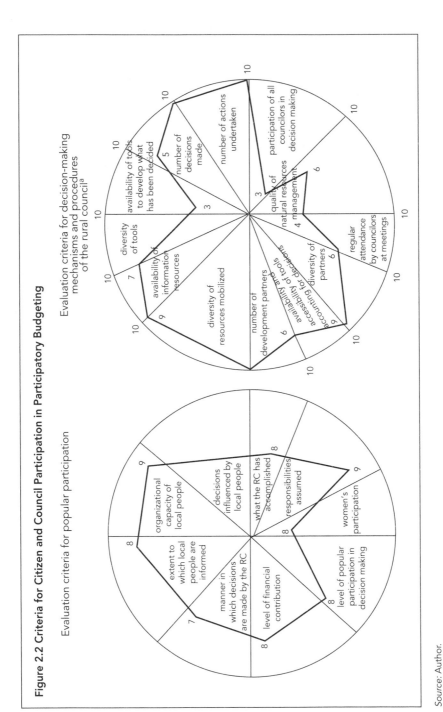

Evaluation criteria for popular participation

Evaluation criteria for decision-making mechanisms and procedures of the rural council[a]

Source: Author.

Notes: This figure shows the evaluation tools used for citizen participation and for decision-making mechanisms within the rural council.

Numerals represent work groups' score of each criterion on a 1-to-10 scale.

RC = rural council.

a. See annex table 2.A.1 for further assessment of rural council criteria.

Village forums. The rural council presented the fiscal-year budget in village forums, where citizens identified constraints and priorities and inventoried existing infrastructure. The rural council's presentation of budgetary implementation was a key moment in the process and a major innovation. Interesting debates took place between local authorities and citizens who had the opportunity to ask questions about budget implementation.

Local facilitators helped to organize forums in each of the 28 villages in Fissel according to the needs of each group.[4] In each village, separate focus groups were held for men and women to identify the most urgent problems and priority actions. Each group (men and women) identified a maximum of five key problems and suggested five priority actions. After the focus groups, men and women met together to prepare a synthesis of their proposals. After the synthesis, the five most important problems and the five highest priority actions were identified through a process of collective analysis and negotiation, taking into account the separate views of men and women. Men did not dominate these meetings because the results of the synthesis carried out in various villages showed that, in most cases, the priorities identified by women came out on top (for example, in 22 villages, the highest priority was access to water). Once the local diagnosis was completed, each village chose two delegates, one man and one woman, to represent them in the delegates' forum.

Delegates' forum. Fifty-six delegates, two (one man and one woman) for each village, met to synthesize the proposals from all 28 villages in Fissel. To facilitate prioritization, the delegates identified the 10 most important problems for Fissel as a whole and the 10 highest-priority actions using a five-point scale. Proposals made during the delegates' forum served as guidelines for the preparation and organization of the next stage, during which the budget was formulated. Table 2.2 shows the results for Fissel.

Community forum. Next, delegates and elected officials came together in a forum where delegates presented the community synthesis (the priority action matrix) and rural council members presented their budget estimates for the upcoming year. Based on these estimates, investment proposals were made. This information was complemented by the results of the infrastructure inventory to guide decisions on the location of infrastructure. The delegates also selected a monitoring committee for budget implementation. This committee is composed of seven members, including three women, chosen from among the delegates.

Table 2.2 Fissel Priority Action Matrix (2004 Budget)

Actions	Number of times ranked as a top-four priority				Total	Rank
	1	2	3	4		
Water supply	17	4	2	2	25	1
Millet mill for women	2	3	3	3	11	2
Vocational training for women	1	2	2	3	8	3
Funding	1	4	1	2	8	3
Construct classrooms		2	3	1	6	5
Build classroom for younger children	1	1		4	6	5
Enclose schools	1	3		1	5	7
Construct village shops	2		3		5	7
Enclose health centers		2	1	1	4	9
Provide rooms for literacy classes		1	2	1	4	9
Provide areas for children and young people			1	3	4	9

Source: Guèye 2005.

Budget meeting. Proposals made during the community forum were studied, and decisions were made on the actions to be undertaken, based on estimated resources. This is a joint deliberative process with village delegates. Budget decisions conform to the proposed priority list and validate the proposals made. It is noteworthy that the forum also takes into account the types of investments made in previous years, beneficiary villages and groups, and compliance with budgetary nomenclature.

Budget vote and implementation. The budget is submitted to the subprefect, and implementation may start only after subprefect approval. Even if members of the monitoring committee are present during the budget vote, the law does not allow their participation, conferring this power exclusively on locally elected officials.

Feedback forum. In the past two years, the introduction of three feedback forums has further strengthened the accountability process:

- The first forum, called the restitution forum, is held just after the subprefect approves the budget. Its objective is to present the new budget to the communities to allow them to assess how well it aligns with the set priorities.

- The second forum, in July, is called the mid-term feedback forum. Its objective is to assess budget implementation halfway through the fiscal year. It also provides the opportunity for the council to raise any concerns regarding resource mobilization. Usually this forum serves as a sensitization platform for tax payment.
- The third forum is held at the end of the fiscal year in November or December. During this forum, the final budget results are presented and a collective evaluation carried out. It also launches the planning process for next year's budget.

Budget implementation monitoring. Another major innovation of this initiative is the formation of a citizen committee to organize forums that present budget results at the end of the fiscal year, ensure that budget review meetings are held, use adequate tools to disseminate information to local people, collect feedback from the people, and submit its requests to the rural council.

KEY CHALLENGES AND CONSTRAINTS

The participatory budgeting process requires a lot of time and patience because of the capacity-building needs of the various participants. Moreover, the rural commune's scarce resources cannot cover related expenses—a situation exacerbated because the responsibilities devolved to local authorities have not been matched with corresponding transfers of financial resources, making local governments even more dependent on the central government and external partners. This dependence undermines sustainability. The problem could be addressed by providing funds for the participatory budgeting process in the rural commune budget. The long-term solution would be for public authorities to earmark support funds to urban or rural communes that have adopted participatory budgeting, which would encourage more local authorities to adopt the process.

Local Challenges

Another constraint is the relatively low educational level of some councilors, which limits their capacity to disseminate information in their villages. The rural councilor's education is especially critical in Fissel, where his or her responsibility of informing the population is particularly important. Some councilors are illiterate and have difficulty preparing tools or recording information on meetings and forums for feedback to their villages. The high rate of illiteracy among the local population is also a challenge for effective participation, especially in the absence of adequate information tools.

High turnover of facilitators is another concern. Facilitators with extensive family responsibilities could not participate regularly, and some even asked to be replaced. That facilitators work on a voluntary basis worsens the situation because, during certain periods of the year, some give priority to other activities to meet their families' needs. Eventually, the commune budget could pay facilitators for some of the time they spend on the participatory budgeting process. Such a decision would be justified because it contributes to commune performance.

The budget planning process is subject to a fixed and rigid schedule that is sometimes incompatible with the flexible and repetitive nature of the participatory process. Nevertheless, over time, the participants began to accept this and planned their activities to meet the legal deadlines for budget presentation.

Nationwide Challenges

At the national level, the main obstacle to institutionalizing the participatory budgeting process is the highly political nature of the mechanisms and procedures to designate councilors, which depend more on political parties' decisions than on the local people's choice. In communities where civil society's role is not strong enough to counterbalance this pressure, councilors feel more accountable to their political party than to their constituents. Citizens' lack of knowledge about their rights and responsibilities adds to the problem and can slow down the introduction of participatory mechanisms.

The results of the March 2009 local elections raised a new challenge as Fissel, like many municipalities in Senegal, saw the opposition party return to power. The challenge may depend less on the local communities' willingness and commitment to strengthen their citizen engagement than on the new ruling coalition's readiness to genuinely accept and build on the previous councils' achievements. However, the first signals from the new council are positive. In any case, it is the role of local CSOs to act as watchdogs for the consolidation of the process regardless of the politics of the council.

RESULTS AND IMPACT

Although the initiative is still in its early stages, a recent external evaluation found that social groups traditionally less involved in local decision making (in particular, women and young people) declared that participatory budgeting had allowed them to better understand the local planning process and now gives them a say on the allocation of local resources. The participatory process and its village forums have generated great enthusiasm among participants, who naturally expect that most of the proposed actions will be taken into account in the rural commune budget. Because available resources cannot fund all proposals, however, choices must be made. Even so, villages represented in the community forum in charge of setting priorities and making decisions trust the results that emerge from this inclusive process.

Eventually, it will be necessary to diversify financial resources. During the meetings, proposals have already been formulated concerning the reinforcement of decentralized cooperation; support to sectors with high potential to generate revenue (such as tourism based on the area's rich cultural heritage); and better control and monitoring of traditional fee collection (licenses, rural taxes, and so forth).

Another important result of the participatory process is that it strengthens community capacity. Since the beginning, more than 10 thematic workshops have prepared various actors for effective participation in the process. Contrary to common practice, these workshops are not addressed primarily to local officials. Instead, they target local people even though officials also take part in the training. Workshops were held on decentralized natural resource management, budget structure, budgetary nomenclature, PM&E, facilitation techniques, gender and decentralization, and writing local newspaper articles. These workshops enabled some facilitators to become resource persons for other organizations working in Fissel.

Popular participation in the decentralization process has improved significantly. Even if it seems difficult to associate all the progress made in tax recovery with the participatory process, many citizens have declared that, since the participatory initiative, they are more willing to pay their rural taxes because they have more control over the use of their contributions and because they have a monitoring mechanism. A member of the budget monitoring committee attests to this progress perfectly (Dioh 2007): "Before the participatory budget initiative, many in my village were not interested in matters concerning the budget because they didn't know much about it. I remember my thoughts were elsewhere when I heard people talking about the budget. Today, it is different. Thanks to participatory budgeting, I have learned to plan and to adopt a systematic approach to solve problems."

It is important to point out another significant impact of this experience: a stronger, more confident relationship between the rural council and grassroots organizations in programs related to devolved responsibilities such as natural resource management, health, education, and culture. Even though the village and community forums were organized within the framework of participatory budgeting, they also gave stakeholders the opportunity to discuss other programs in Fissel. The participatory process improved the reputation of local officials. Previously, citizens saw local officials as a privileged group engaged in the opaque management of local resources.

In addition, participatory budgeting yielded this primary innovation: more relevant infrastructure choices and more objective decisions—particularly, higher ranking of women's needs on the priorities list. All local stakeholders, beginning with women themselves, agree that participatory budgeting made it possible to place the needs expressed by women among the highest priorities for the commune investment plan. Fissel is preparing a local development plan that will integrate actions decided through participatory budgeting. The plan will allow Fissel to ask other sources (NGOs and government) for actions that will complement those of the rural council. Funds from these other sources could be used for priority actions that the commune cannot finance itself.

Perhaps it is too early to speak of impact; sustainable change from institutionalizing the participatory budgeting approach takes time. However, recent actions or initiatives at both the local and national levels show that Fissel's experience is beginning to influence other Senegalese communities and even international development efforts.

After establishing its own participatory budgeting initiative, Fissel shared its experience with visitors from NGOs, government, and the National Assembly. Fissel itself launched the first action to scale up the experience when it organized a 2004 forum on budget transparency, which representatives from more than 30 rural communities throughout Senegal attended. In 2006, Fissel and IED Afrique were invited to an international participatory budgeting colloquium in France, in which the mayor of Fissel and a female councilor participated.

Also in 2006, the Fissel experience was presented at a workshop on participatory budgeting that was organized at the request of the National Assembly and facilitated by IED Afrique with the financial support of the Ministry of Economy and Finance. Members of the financial committee of the National Assembly participated in the workshop, which resulted in several proposals, including the following:

- Translating the national budget into national languages
- Organizing field visits for members of parliament who will explain the national budget to local people
- Creating a parliamentary committee on participatory budgeting within the National Assembly
- Creating awareness on participatory budgeting in associations of local officials
- Implementing a national advocacy program on participatory budgeting with members of parliament, local officials, civil society, and the administration
- Printing and disseminating material on participatory budgeting experiences

From 2008 through 2009, almost 70 municipalities sent councilors to visit Fissel and learn about its experience. Even two mayors from Burkina Faso visited Fissel in March 2009. Fissel and four other communes were selected to host the field visits organized during an international conference in Dakar organized by the World Bank in partnership with other African institutions including IED Afrique.

As previously mentioned, two Senegalese municipalities (Matam and Guédiawaye) and a rural commune (Ndiaganiao)[5] already have adopted the participatory budgeting process. Based on the Fissel and Ndiaganiao experiences, IED Afrique issued a manual on participatory budgeting and a short film portraying these experiences. These materials are in high demand from communes and CSOs in the region.

In addition, the National School of Applied Economy and the National School of Administration have introduced courses on participatory budgeting. Three of their students, supervised by IED Afrique, are preparing theses about the Fissel experience.

Finally, some of the collaborative activities between the Decentralization Directorate and IED Afrique focus on the dissemination of participatory budgeting experiences in Senegal.

LESSONS LEARNED

Several factors contributed to the success of the participatory budgeting process. First, Fissel has many years of experience in community development. Its local organizations, among the most dynamic in Senegal, have been engaged in awareness and capacity building for decades. Many local officials are experienced in local development and are therefore more inclined to be open to a participatory approach to decentralization. Therefore, Fissel is fertile ground for strong civil society.

Second, Fissel was one of the first rural communes chosen to pilot rural decentralization. Several tools for local development and decentralization were tested in Fissel, promoting a positive attitude toward innovation.

Third, the partnership of RECODEF, the rural commune, and IED Afrique over a relatively long period reinforced the capacities, methods, and techniques essential for stakeholders' effective participation in, and full ownership of, the participatory process.

Fourth, the rural council's open-mindedness and a long tradition of collaboration between the council and grassroots community organizations were critical in securing the council's strong support for the budgeting process. The council quickly realized the advantages that could result from a partnership with community organizations for budget transparency. For example, by improving the council's performance and effectiveness, the participatory process would increase citizen participation and commitment to the council's actions. The council president's open approach is explained by his personal knowledge and experience in rural activities, his active participation in community life, the experience he acquired during several terms as council president, and the dynamism of grassroots organizations that have sound knowledge on local development.

Finally, a local radio station was an essential tool for extensive information dissemination.

Persistent Challenges

These findings highlight the importance of building the capacity of the various actors, a dynamic local civil society, and good communication and information dissemination. However, the still-predominant position of traditional institutions and a persistent power struggle prevent vulnerable groups from having stronger representation in strategic positions.

Achieving such inclusive representation is most certainly one of the long-term challenges that the process in Fissel must address. Social pressures still relegate women to a secondary role, emphasizing their domestic responsibilities instead of the role they could play in Fissel's political life. Most political parties want to reassure their electorate, and their candidate lists for the rural council reflect their reluctance to upset tradition.

Conditions for Emulation

To replicate Fissel's successful participatory budgeting initiative, certain conditions must be met.

First, local or central governments must be committed not only to actively participate in the process but also to present participatory budgeting as a political option and not as a simple test or exercise. The cost in terms of the time invested and expectations created is so significant that the process must be conceived as a long-term effort and supported with adequate means to ensure its sustainability.

Second, strong and well-structured local organizations are necessary to carry out the deliberative process. Certain aptitudes, such as being able to read and write in national languages, played a decisive role in the Fissel experience. Facilitators were able to record the main stages of the process and publish an information bulletin.

Third, a simple methodological tool should be created based on the Fissel experience. This tool is particularly important during the dissemination stage because not all local authorities will have the substantial guidance and training that was available in Fissel.

THE OUTLOOK FOR PARTICIPATORY BUDGETING IN SENEGAL AND BEYOND

Clearly, the participatory process must be included in national institutional and legislative mechanisms to ensure large-scale adoption. To date, it is difficult to say when there will be any legislation on participatory mechanisms such as participatory budgeting. In the meantime, it could be useful to develop a coalition of local authorities currently working on participatory budgeting and to obtain financial support from the state that would ensure the initiative's sustainability.

The Fissel experience is admittedly in its early stages, but its lessons point to inclusive and transparent local governance procedures as tools to substantially improve the local government performance and encourage greater citizen participation. However, the in-depth and crucial reforms needed in the operating modes of local political or social institutions require significant investments in time and capacity building to ensure ownership and sustainability of the process. The need for local reforms is why the state's strong political commitment is essential to institutionalize these mechanisms and to provide financial support to local authorities engaged in their implementation.

Advocacy based on the results in Fissel and elsewhere is needed, and this could start by supporting similar pilot experiences in Senegal and other West African countries and by organizing workshops and forums at a national or subregional level to share experiences and discuss mechanisms for their dissemination. These meetings would bring together decision makers, members of parliament, training and research institutions, CSOs, community representatives, local government, and development partners. It is this kind of strong advocacy that can encourage other local authorities to incorporate citizen control mechanisms and thereby create a critical mass that can influence policy making.

ANNEX

Table 2.A.1 Criteria for the Decision-Making Process in the Fissel Rural Council

Criteria	Weaknesses	Strengths
Frequency of rural council meetings	• Difficulty in convening rural councilors • Responsibility of each councilor for own transport and food • Difficulty in watering horses when traveling by cart • Dissension within rural council • Late notice of meetings • Difficulty in achieving quorums • Difficulty in reaching agreement due to political differences	• Decisions documented • Decisions in accordance with texts • Decisions often well thought out • Decisions based on everyone's ideas • Councilors well-informed about decisions
Councilor participation in meetings	• Several functions for some councilors • Distance from certain villages • Uncovered attendance-related expenses	• Understanding of procedures and deliberations • Development of decision-making capacities

(Table continues on the following page)

Table 2.A.1 (continued)

Criteria	Weaknesses	Strengths
	• Uncertainty of councilors about roles and responsibilities • Lack of motivation • Silence of some councilors at meetings • Tardiness in sending information or meeting notices • Absenteeism among certain councilors • Varying educational levels among councilors • Interest in only certain activities by some councilors • Underestimation by some councilors of their potential impact • Lack of knowledge about rights and responsibilities	• Expression of attendee points of view
Number of development partners	• Conditions demanded by some partners not in accordance with rural council's capacities or means • Difficulty of mobilizing financial resources from local people • Poor financial management capacity	• Better training of local people • Diversification of development programs • Development of local economy
Existence of planning and management tools	• Lack of means • Few development partners • Decentralization of responsibilities not matched by decentralization of means • Lack of transportation • Inaccessibility of existing materials to some councilors • Inadequate coverage of all competencies in existing materials • Lack of importance accorded to national languages	• Existence of a functional office • Equipment for organizing meetings • Planning skills of some councilors • Availability and initiative of rural council president • Availability of certain materials
Existence of means to disseminate information	• Lack of financial resources • Lack of transportation • Distance of villages	• Existence of a community radio station • Existence of weekly markets

(Table continues on the following page)

Table 2.A.1 (continued)

Criteria	Weaknesses	Strengths
	• Low levels of literacy • Irregular access or attention to community radio	• Availability of community secretary • Existence of documented decisions
Management of financial resources	• Distant holding of local government authority funds • Ponderous decision-making procedures • Lack of grassroots community involvement in monitoring management of rural council resources • Financial management training not extended beyond councilors • Need for more training of councilors	• Actions in accordance with decisions • Councilors generally well-informed about decisions • Transparency of decisions
Availability of materials publicizing decisions	• Difficult access to documents recording the decisions • Limited range of materials for disseminating information • Lack of translation of informational materials from French to national languages • Local people unaccustomed to seeking information	• Existence of extension agents • Posting of several decisions • Dissemination of several decisions via community radio
Nature and diversity of available resources	• Limited possibilities for generating resources at local level • Isolation of area, with few agencies operating there • Lack of natural resources to exploit • Low level of rural tax recovery	• Support from the state and partners • Local efforts to train local people on revenue generation • Actions to protect environment

Source: Guèye 2005.

NOTES

1. Formerly the Sahel Program of the International Institute for Environment and Development (IIED).
2. The rural council is an elected body in charge of the commune's management. It is composed of representatives of villages sr groups of villages and a president. Members

are elected by universal suffrage for five years, and all lists of candidates who wish to participate in the election must be presented by a political party. Independent candidates are not authorized in local elections.

3. Town planning, natural resources, state property, education, health, culture, youth and sports, land use, and planning.

4. In 2006, results of budget implementation were presented at the subzone scale. The rural community was divided into four subzones, each with an average of seven villages. Each village had 10 representatives.

5. Ndiaganiao is a rural commune supported by IED Afrique for the implementation of the participatory budgeting process. The process is similar to the Fissel experience.

REFERENCES

Dioh, Mohamed. 2007. "Le budget participatif, outil d'amélioration de la gouvernance locale? Cas de la communauté rurale de Fissel." Thesis, National School of Applied Economy, Dakar.

Guèye, Bara. 2005. *Participatory Evaluation and Budgetary Processes.* London: International Institute for Environment and Development.

Ngaidé, Moustapha. 2006. "Aspects juridiques liés au genre et à la décentralisation au Sénégal: Une contribution au Projet de Réforme de l'Administration Locale." Study prepared for the Making Decentralization Work program of IED Afrique. IED Afrique and United Nations Development Fund for Women (UNIFEM), New York.

CHAPTER 3

CIVIC PARTICIPATION IN POLICY AND BUDGETARY PROCESSES IN ILALA MUNICIPAL COUNCIL, TANZANIA

Renatus Kihongo and John Lubuva

This case study illustrates the experiences of urban civic participation in the Ilala Municipal Council (IMC) in Tanzania, which set the stage for a new type of relationship between citizens and their governing authorities based on mutual trust. It evaluates the extent to which such a relationship could be fostered through the process of participatory budgeting, and demonstrates how this led to increased IMC effectiveness and a 53 percent increase in tax-based revenues for the municipality in just three years.

The 2003 participatory budgeting process cost less than $20,000, with proposed projects totaling $12 million. In 2004, the IMC executed 63 percent of the projects proposed by the community.

Important to this success story were a conducive national political and administrative context; a favorable local social and economic context; extensive support from an exceptionally wide range of institutions; and a flexible, innovative, and persistent process that achieved greater success through trial and error. Yet challenges persist, including the urban setting, inadequate funds for all the identified needs, some conflict, and impediments to reaching the most disadvantaged.

LAYING THE GROUNDWORK FOR INCREASED
CIVIC PARTICIPATION

Tanzania began to encourage civic participation in the 1960s by creating new structures to support subnational community initiatives. By 1975, the country had transferred key functions for development planning, coordination, and management to regional and district levels and had established village councils to strengthen grassroots participation.

Government's relationship with civil society organizations (CSOs) and the overall strength of democracy play a significant role in the quality of participatory processes. Tanzania cultivated good relations with citizens during the *Ujamaa* (African socialism) era in the late 1960s, and government has since maintained a liberal attitude toward participation, allowing a fairly open society even under the previous one-party rule. Political liberalization has created an environment that is conducive to the establishment of CSOs, and a strong partnership has developed between government and CSOs in the areas of advocacy; public education; program implementation in poverty reduction, HIV/AIDS, gender mainstreaming, and the fight against corruption; and, in local government, legislative and other sector reforms.

Tanzania has 21 administrative regions and 114 districts and Local Government Authorities (LGAs). The government structure penetrates deep into the grassroots, facilitating engagement of civil society at various levels. The central government comprises national, regional, district, and divisional levels of administration, and the LGAs comprise wards, subwards, village governing councils, and rural hamlets.

However, the LGA structure presents some challenges (Clifford and Meijer 2001). For example, it is not clear which of the subentity levels constitute "communities." The LGAs contend that "wards" are primarily communities in practice, but the wards' population size (up to 40,000, in some cases) make it difficult to have all groups' views adequately represented at that level. In its participatory budgeting initiatives, the IMC defines communities as subwards and villages, in which the law grants citizens the right to attend public meetings for decision making.

Ilala Municipality was established in 2000 following the decentralization of the Dar es Salaam city administration into three autonomous municipalities for Ilala, Kinondoni, and Temeke districts. The long-term Strategic Urban Development Plan (SUDP) for Dar es Salaam was developed in 1992 through a citywide consultation process of the Sustainable

Dar es Salaam Program (SDP) of the post-Rio Sustainable Cities Initiatives on Environmental Planning and Management. Based on a city environmental profile, consensus was reached on nine priority objectives around which nine working groups of stakeholder representatives were formed to develop strategic plans for implementation. The SDP process that guides city development turned the city around by popularizing participatory planning procedures to improve living conditions.

The ruling party, Chama Cha Mapinduzi, won the 1995 and 2000 elections on the platform of good governance. When President Benjamin William Mkapa took office in November 1995, he declared good governance to be the priority of his presidency. Therefore, strong political will on governance issues, including civic participation, facilitates participatory budgeting in Ilala. All ministries with sector reform responsibilities— including local government, civil service management (public sector reforms), planning and privatization (economic sector reforms), and a new ministry of state for good governance—are in the president's office. The prime minister's office coordinates government activities concerning the good-governance commitment.

After developing a Poverty Reduction Strategy Paper (PRSP) in the late 1990s, Tanzania embarked on a multifaceted set of budget and public administration reforms, including decentralization of service delivery responsibilities to LGAs, the introduction of performance budgeting, and a performance management system for public services. In addition, local government capacity has been built through the ongoing Local Government Reform Program (LGRP). Regulatory frameworks for central-local administrative and fiscal relations were reviewed to increase the LGAs' autonomy and decision-making authority, to foster good governance, and to improve the accessibility and quality of public service delivery.

Tanzania's budgets are derived from annually updated Medium Term Expenditure Frameworks (MTEFs), which protect expenditures on priority poverty-reduction sectors from in-year cuts. The government also has issued framework guidelines on sectoral, regional, and district medium-term development plans for the implementation of Vision 2025.

The constitution and Local Government Acts Nos. 7 and 8 require LGAs to consult citizens in annual budgeting and planning processes, and the LGRP guidelines instruct LGAs to hold stakeholder consultations at least during the diagnostics stage and in developing the strategic plan. The IMC decided to implement a participatory planning and budgeting program to conform to government policy directives and legislation and in response to citizens' concerns. When IMC councilors took office after the October 2000 elections, they expressed popular concerns and complaints about top-down, technocratic budgets and plans that failed to address community priorities.

WHY ILALA IS WELL-SUITED FOR PARTICIPATORY BUDGETING

The IMC generates about 50 percent of its revenue from its own sources, but most LGAs depend on the central government for most of their revenues. These revenues are allocated as conditional grants based on statements of objectives, strategies, and targets, and on reports showing progress on performance indicators.

A new, formula-based system of allocating conditional block grants has been adopted for education and health programs, which account for 88 percent of all transfers. These formula-based allocations will add predictability and equity to the grants system. However, the IMC has its own relatively robust revenue base that gives it enough financial autonomy to sustain participatory budgeting despite the risks inherent in central government transfers.

With own-source revenues (in Tanzania shillings) of T Sh 16 billion ($16 million) in 2002, expenditures on all municipal functions, including staff salaries, totaled only T Sh 30,000 ($300) per capita. There is stiff competition among communities for scarce public resources, which along with poor-quality services, spurred citizen interest in how resources are allocated and motivated them to participate in the municipal budgetary decision-making process when the opportunity was presented to them. Awareness of the gap between IMC financial resources and needs gave citizens further incentive to contribute resources and to ensure value for money.

The main source of livelihood in Ilala is self-employment, mainly in the informal sector that accounts for 40 percent of adult employment. The Tanzania Household Budget Survey for fiscal 2000/01 recorded mean per capita monthly income of T Sh 40,767 ($41), with wide income disparities across gender and educational levels (NBS 2002). The most educated earn 10 times more than the least educated, and the income of men is nearly twice that of women. Ilala's incidence and depth of poverty is much less than Tanzania's, with 7.5 percent of people (versus 18.7 percent nationally) below the food poverty line and 17.6 percent below the basic needs poverty line (versus 35.7 percent nationally). Absolute poverty—which breeds frustration, despair, and apathy among citizens preoccupied with their next meal—does not impede participation in Ilala.

Ilala's level of access to basic services is also better than the national average, as table 3.1 indicates. The quality of services, however, leaves much to be desired. The ratio of households with access to piped water declined from 93 percent in fiscal 1991/92 to 85.7 percent in 2000/01. Primary school facilities are overcrowded from shortages of 21 schools and 1,132 classrooms. The desire to improve service delivery and quality only added to the motivation for civic participation in Ilala.

Housing and tenure systems present both opportunities and constraints to civic participation in the municipality. That only 31 percent of houses are owner-occupied means that a large proportion of the population who rent housing is transient, with little incentive to participate in local issues. Property owners in planned and surveyed land have regular title to the land. About 60 to 70 percent of houses are built in unplanned, unsurveyed, and underserviced settlements. Tanzania's land law, however, recognizes such tenure rights except for obviously hazardous land or public property such as road and utility reserves. This broad-based security of tenure facilitated the IMC's participatory budgeting initiatives because secure tenure stimulates the community spirit that bonds urban dwellers around common interests.

"Freedom and Unity" was the rallying call of the main preindependence political movement, the Tanganyika African National Union, which fostered peace. The postindependence government took deliberate steps to eliminate potential causes of conflict, such as abolishing traditional, tribal-based leadership and making the state a secular institution. Tanzania has

Table 3.1 Comparison of Service Levels between Ilala and Tanzania, FY2000/01

Service indicator	Ilala	Tanzania
Mean distance to primary school	0.8 km	1.8 km
Mean distance to health center	0.7 km	3.9 km
Percentage of households within 6 km of a health center	98	75
Percentage of households connected to the electric grid	59	10
Percentage of households with access to piped water	86	39

Source: Tanzania Household Budget Survey 2000/01 (NBS 2002).

since stood out as a peaceful society with a stable government. The absence of tribal, religious, political, or other forms of armed conflict enables communities to live harmoniously with mutual respect for each other and government, which strengthens the government-citizen relations that are essential for civic participation.

The urban character of Ilala means that its communities are culturally diverse and the traditional systems of social capital that, in rural Africa, normally develop along clan and tribal lines are absent. Ilala's cultural diversity presents both advantages and disadvantages to community participation. Diversity generates a richer mix of ideas and experiences, in turn creating a wider range of possible actions to solve local community problems. Also, income levels are generally higher in urban areas, enabling greater financial contributions to community projects. Those who cannot afford the cash payments can make in-kind contributions such as voluntary labor.

On the other hand, varying lifestyles often make it difficult to bring community members together in the urban context. Salaried workers and others who commute to earn a living find it difficult to make time for local community meetings. They either send representatives to attend meetings on their behalf or they have to abide by the decisions that are reached without their representation. In addition, most of the urban residents are first-generation rural-to-urban migrants who maintain strong links with their ancestral villages, to which they often must contribute for social and economic reasons. This divided loyalty diverts potential resources that could be directed toward community projects.

Overall, however, despite its diverse culture, Ilala residents have been able to interact constructively with each other and with the IMC in the participatory planning and budgetary processes. Social capital formation largely revolves around community-based organizations (CBOs) that develop group-based capacity to solve problems or address government systems, especially in underserved, spontaneous urban settlements. The HIV/AIDS pandemic, urban insecurity, widespread unemployment of women and youth, low wages, and the predominance of the informal sector economy have inspired a wide range of CBOs. These organizations include advocacy groups, community policing initiatives, cooperative societies, credit associations, petty trading associations, and women's income-generation groups. They provide material benefits from community initiatives in infrastructure and social services development or self-employment activities that improve livelihoods.

The rich variety of CBOs provided channels for the IMC to reach some, but not all, of the disadvantaged groups in its participatory budgeting processes.

THE IMC PARTICIPATORY POLICY AND BUDGETING PROCESS

Not long after its formation in 2000, the IMC saw the need for participatory budgeting—as an obligation to government policy, as a necessity for meeting legislative requirements to involve people in decision making, and as a means for achieving sustainable development in the municipality. First, the IMC focused on sensitization of subward leaders and on raising awareness for the participatory budgeting and planning process in 2001. However, the first attempt to produce a participatory budget and plan for fiscal 2002 failed and was abandoned because expectations were unrealistically high: up to T Sh 40 billion ($40 million) in requests for development expenditures against T Sh 5 billion ($5 million) of own-source revenues. Furthermore, the community priorities were not clearly articulated.

The participatory planning and budgeting process began again early in July 2002 to allow key players to be trained. The IMC developed a tailored training program on urban participatory planning and budgeting in collaboration with the University of Stuttgart's Institute of Regional Development Planning. Residential and field training sessions were conducted for IMC extension staff, ward executive officers, and NGO and CBO representatives from each ward. The training covered the participatory planning process using PPA (participatory poverty assessment), PRA (participatory rural appraisal), and Opportunities and Obstacles to Development (O&OD) tools. The IMC management team received three days, and the 22 ward councilors one day, of training. The focus was on planning, budgeting, and advocacy skills as well as on role assignments for all stakeholders.

The participatory planning and budgeting process begins when the IMC management team provides revenue projections and indicative figures of the amounts available for participatory decision making. Communities use the O&OD tool—a simplified model for environmental scanning similar to a strengths, weaknesses, opportunities, and threats (SWOT) analysis. Men, women, and marginalized groups participate equally in public meetings, which all community members are encouraged to attend at the *Mitaa* (local government) level. Community members identify their social and economic problems and possible solutions, and rank and prioritize development projects.

Project proposals are then submitted for discussion and approval of the ward development committee before being forwarded to the council. The council management team compiles the ranked priorities into sector plans and submits them to the council standing committees for consolidation into the municipal annual budget and development plan that the full council later approves at its budget meeting. For the projects proposed at the community level, resource allocation comes from four sources: government grants, own-source revenue, community contributions, and donor funds.

Following the initial round of IMC training to prepare for the participatory planning and budgeting process, the participatory budget for fiscal 2003 was more realistic and the priorities were much clearer than they had been the previous year. This time, 60 percent of the projects that were implemented originated from the community, and 40 percent of the projects were implemented to address cross-cutting issues and to meet national PRSP targets.

IMC planning and budgeting follows the three-year cycle of national MTEFs. The value of all project budget requests from communities ranked as top-five priorities was T Sh 12 billion ($12 million) over three years. During the first year, the IMC financed implementation of projects worth T Sh 3 billion ($3 million)—equivalent to 50 percent of all proposed projects—mainly from Ilala's own-source revenues of T Sh 6.2 billion ($6.2 million). With projected increases in own-source revenues of about 15 percent per year from 2000 to 2003, larger resource contributions from communities and other stakeholders were expected due to improved relations with the IMC. With access to unconditional grants, the IMC would finance the remaining projects over the next two years.

In 2003, IMC established 22 community-level planning and budgeting support (CLP) teams—10 people on each team, one team per ward—to build community capacity for participatory planning and budgeting. An effort was made to ensure the teams were apolitical, gender-balanced, and inclusive of vulnerable groups.

CLP team members were trained in participatory mechanisms and technical planning and budgeting skills, which considerably improved the quality of grassroots plans and budget proposals. In the interim January–June 2004 budget, for example, the IMC executed 26 of the 41 new projects (63 percent) proposed by communities through the participatory process. Participatory budgeting in fiscal 2005 allocated a minimum of T Sh 50 million ($50,000) for each ward to ensure that all communities benefit from the process. The IMC also set aside a fund of T Sh 60 million ($60,000) to support community-driven development (CDD) projects as a way to encourage citizens to tackle their own problems more actively by collectively initiating, financing, and managing projects. In fiscal year 2006, the IMC set aside T Sh 125 million ($125,000) and in 2007, T Sh 300 million ($300,000).

The participatory planning and budgeting process, including training—at a cost of T Sh 18,732 ($18,732)—represented less than 1 percent of the resulting projects' value (T Sh 3 billion, or $3 million) implemented in fiscal 2003. Community participation brought increased satisfaction with services, far outweighing the cost.

The combined costs of training and budgeting processes for the January–June 2004 period and for the 2005 fiscal year were T Sh 22.5 million ($22,500). As the need for training decreases, the costs were expected to decline considerably in the future.

ORGANIZATIONS THAT MAKE PARTICIPATORY BUDGETING POSSIBLE

A wide range of organizations must provide various forms of complementary support if a participatory budgeting process can be possible, let alone successful. These groups include the media, CSOs, political parties, businesses and other private sector organizations, the people at the grassroots level, central government entities, and international agencies.

The media were instrumental in disseminating public information to create awareness and educate citizens about participation, particularly at the national level. Territory-based CSOs, mainly CBOs, helped to identify and prioritize the local social, economic, infrastructural, and environmental concerns of communities. The CBOs also mobilized community resources for service delivery and other projects.

Thematic and sector-based CSOs contributed quantitative and qualitative information from field experiences as well as mobilization and advocacy skills. They also mobilized additional resources for community projects through their national or international associates.

Labor-based CSOs are not very active at the subnational level, but they participate in annual consultations with CSOs on national budget priorities.

Faith-based CSOs are highly active on the local scene, where they provide a wide range of affordable social services, especially in health and education, supplementing the IMC's service delivery efforts. Their other main contributions are in advocacy against HIV/AIDS, crime, and other social ills, and in building consensus across religious lines.

Women's organizations, including women's wings of political parties, provide a gender-related perspective, both at the municipal level of consultations and in lower entities. They focus particularly on health and other social services, self-employment for women, and safety and security.

Political parties participate in policy and budgetary consultations at the national and municipal levels, helping to build consensus on important public issues across political lines. Experience has shown, however, that political differences can be divisive at the grassroots level, where partisan interests tend to divert community focus away from common objectives and toward narrow political party interests and rivalries.

The good intentions normally associated with the ruling party are deliberately misinterpreted and portrayed negatively by opposition parties. For example, community water schemes in two Ilala wards have collapsed for lack of maintenance because the opposition party that won local government elections ousted the popularly elected water committees and took over the schemes—then diverted the revenue collected from water sales to their political party. Partisan roles are therefore discouraged at the grassroots level by ensuring, for example, that the selection of CLP teams is apolitical and by continually educating communities on the government's nonpartisan role in service delivery.

Private sector organizations provide financial and managerial support to various community initiatives, though often from a spontaneous philanthropic standpoint as opposed to a more structured, constructive approach based on sustainable corporate social responsibility. Business organizations have also influenced municipal tax policy in favor of fair, broad-based taxes that encourage compliance. In addition, these organizations have been influential in determining the costs of services that the IMC has outsourced to them, such as solid waste management.

The people's direct involvement in grassroots meetings to discuss and prioritize community problems, and to propose projects for the IMC's budgetary resource allocation, underpins and legitimizes the annual IMC participatory planning and budgeting process. People contribute material and in-kind resources to service delivery and other projects, and with their presence on the ground, they monitor and evaluate ongoing programs and projects through physical inspection.

Monitoring is done by continually comparing a project's resource inputs with outputs. Communities also are equipped with the capacity to apply accountability tools for monitoring and evaluation, namely the Community Scorecard, which brings together beneficiaries, leaders, and service providers to evaluate the performance of service delivery organizations. Another monitoring tool is the requirement for monthly, quarterly, and annual reports. Monitoring and evaluation are also accomplished through regular performance review meetings that involve committee members and the technical staff responsible for service delivery.

In addition, the people have played an important role in generating local information, especially evidence-based information through the PPA, to supplement government and IMC data.

The central government created a conducive institutional and regulatory environment for the entire process by expanding the IMC's decision-making and budgetary mandates, by providing technical and managerial capacity development training of staff and councilors, and by financially supporting IMC surveys and consultation meetings with the LGRP. Regional and district administrations assisted the IMC in interpreting government policy and legislation on good governance, in monitoring and evaluating feedback on the participatory initiative, and in resolving religious or political conflicts. Parliamentary revision of laws created an enabling environment for LGAs to involve people in policy and budgetary decision making and to focus on inclusion of women in decision making processes. Several presidential commissions on issues of national interest— including corruption, land laws, political party organization, and legal reforms—collected public opinion to reach national consensus in a manner that raised public awareness about the civic role in government affairs.

International agencies, including the Bretton Woods Institutions (the World Bank and the International Monetary Fund), encouraged and pressed for integration of good governance and civic participation in poverty-reduction initiatives, making such integration a condition for access to foreign aid and eligibility for debt relief. This led developing country governments to open up to civic society, unleashing immense opportunities for subnational, participatory, budgeting processes. Many international agencies provide technical and financial support to the IMC participatory budgeting process and for project execution.

THE IMPACT OF INCREASED CITIZEN PARTICIPATION

Civic participation has had many positive impacts on the structure and effectiveness of the IMC budget and development plans, including the following benefits to communities and the IMC.

Increased effectiveness. Civic participation increased the number of projects implemented by communities with the IMC. Employment creation in solid waste management also increased solid waste removal by the CSOs and local enterprises engaged in waste management. In addition, good performance in implementing the Primary Education Development Program guaranteed an uninterrupted flow of central government grants.

Greater sustainability. Civic participation increased the sustainability of local-level development projects. For example, in the construction of water projects in Ilala ward where communities fully participated in planning and implementation, decisions on water pricing based on affordable user fees were agreed-upon for operation and maintenance, thus contributing to project sustainability.

Increased community capacity. The participatory process increased community skills to analyze and prioritize problems and to design and execute community projects. The process also increased community involvement in monitoring and evaluating projects during implementation and service provision.

Improved citizen-government relations. IMC budgets and development plans better addressed community concerns. Increased participation of women and youth in decision making and council resource allocations created a focus on social services and these groups' employment needs. The increase in participation and inclusion improved relations with civil society and brought a new spirit of cooperation in all municipal programs and projects. Official recognition of private and civil society contributions to community projects that are now incorporated into the council budget and development plan encourages greater contributions of private resources and gives hope to citizens who are concerned about poor services. Citizens now have increased interest in IMC affairs.

Improved accountability. Participatory budgeting increased transparency and equity in allocating scarce public resources among communities, especially between the previously neglected inner city and the periphery. It led to better IMC performance in national benchmarking for good governance. It also improved the accountability of CSOs whose projects are incorporated into the IMC budget and development plan. More positive taxpayer attitudes resulted in increased revenue from taxes, service user charges, and cost recovery. Although it might not be the only reason, the community accountability that emerged from participatory planning and budgeting contributed to the increase of own-source, largely tax-based revenue from T Sh 4.3 billion ($4.3 million) in 2002 to T Sh 6.6 billion ($6.6 million) in 2005, an increase of 53 percent in three years.

FACTORS OF SUCCESS

A large number of factors combined to make the IMC participatory budgeting process successful.

National political and administrative context. The national political environment was conducive to the participatory budgeting process. The central government provided enduring political will and steadfast support to civic involvement at the central and local levels of government. It also fostered an institutional and regulatory environment that allows for LGA autonomy and direct citizen participation at the grassroots levels of administration. In fact, numerous laws *require* citizen participation in policy and budgeting processes as well as surveys on satisfaction with service delivery.

Local economic and social context. The local context was also favorable. Ilala had sufficient own-source revenues to make participatory budgeting worthwhile. Ilala citizens generally were not that poor and had secure-enough tenure to have the incentives and capacity to participate. There was relatively little conflict and a tradition of cooperation among Ilala's many diverse groups.

Previous experience with participatory initiatives. Many citizens had some previous experience with participatory processes, either in Ilala or their previous residences. There had been the 1992 citywide consultative process to develop the city environmental profile, the 2000 service delivery user satisfaction surveys, the two stakeholder consultations for the MTEFs, and the PRSP consultations. Furthermore, some of these consultations, such as the PPA and the International Labour Organization labor study, provided useful data in addition to the experience (Mjema and Shitundu 1996). Institutionally, Ilala was fertile territory for piloting a participatory budgeting process.

Institutional support. The participatory budgeting process received extensive support from an exceptionally wide range of institutions. Ilala had a rich variety of CBOs with experience in participatory processes that could, and did, support the budgeting process. CSOs, mainly CBOs, helped to identify and prioritize community concerns; mobilized community resources; and contributed quantitative and qualitative information, mobilization, and advocacy skills. Faith-based CSOs helped to build consensus across religious lines, and political parties helped to build consensus across political lines.

The central government and parliament created an enabling policy environment, and regional and district administrations helped to interpret government policy and legislation on good governance. The media helped to educate and sensitize citizens. Private sector organizations provided financial and managerial support. And international donors encouraged and pressed for integration of good governance and civic participation in poverty reduction while also providing technical and financial support to the IMC participatory budgeting process.

Process factors. The participatory budgeting process itself contained numerous factors contributing to its success. These include a clear definition of communities along the boundaries of local government structures and careful identification of key stakeholders to ensure broad-based representation of all sections of society, including disadvantaged and vulnerable groups.

Other important factors include extensive, continual public awareness and education efforts; sensitization of staff, councilors, and local community leaders regarding the bottom-up processes; and training of IMC councilors, management, extension staff, and CSO representatives in the use of participatory mechanisms and planning and budgeting tools. Another major factor in ensuring the quality of participatory plans and budgets was deliberate community empowerment through the establishment and training of CLP teams to build their capacity for community organization and to equip them with technical tools and skills for analysis, planning, and budgeting.

CHALLENGES TO SUCCESS

The IMC also faced several problems and many constraints in executing the participatory budgeting process, including those explained below.

The urban setting. Although many people want to participate, the degree of participation was low because most people are at work during the day, when meetings are held. The IMC is addressing this problem by encouraging communities to hold grassroots planning and budgeting discussions and meetings after working hours or during weekends at times that would be convenient to many community members. Where this approach has worked, it has added the advantage of encouraging skilled community members to participate so they can provide advice on technically complicated infrastructure issues, thus saving on hiring consultants.

CLP team members who are not permanent residents may move from one ward or district to another, and the IMC frequently had to pay for training replacements. The IMC ensures that CLP teams are largely constituted by permanent residents of the localities, and the IMC reviews CLP-team membership regularly to fill any vacancies before starting the annual planning and budgeting process.

Inadequate funds. Financing from the IMC and the central government affects the consistency of most CDD projects and other community initiatives. The IMC has sensitized and trained its staff on improving efficiency and cost-effectiveness in project implementation to leverage the IMC's limited financial resources and to forge partnerships with private sector organizations that contribute resources to support community-initiated projects.

Lack of skills. The urban social and economic infrastructure is costly and technically complicated, making it difficult for communities with low skill levels and resources to initiate and design projects, thereby increasing dependence on government.

Political conflict. Political differences and conflicts sometimes arise within communities in which a loss of solidarity and community cohesiveness takes place, affecting citizens' participation in planning and budgeting or even stalling the process.

Exclusion of vulnerable groups. Previous development initiatives in Dar es Salaam, including Ilala, demonstrated that communities are willing and able to contribute resources to improve services. However, inclusion of the most disadvantaged in such schemes remains a major challenge. Mobilization in these initiatives requires substantial skill and support of community development workers and depends to a large extent on unsustainable donor funding. How and how much the extremely poor—those with impaired abilities, the elderly, and other minority groups—participate in decision making is not yet clear.

In the Mtambani subward, a PPA also revealed that youth feel excluded from decision making processes at all levels—from the community to the national level—and that their interests are not addressed. In addition, the elderly and people with disabilities who can work feel excluded from access to credit and training for various skills that are made available to other social groups in the community. The IMC continues to seek ways to reach the vulnerable and excluded sections of society.

LESSONS AND CONCLUSIONS

The factors that have contributed to the success of the participatory budgeting process hold three overarching lessons.

First, extensive experience with participatory processes facilitates the process. Experienced leadership and facilitation makes people more willing and able to participate. Even so, additional training and technical assistance, especially by the CLP teams, is also critical for effective participation and development of high-quality budget plans.

Second, a wide range of institutions, especially CBOs and CSOs, is vital to success. The process involves not only citizens and local government but also higher levels of government, the private sector, the media, political parties, and international donors. Together, all these institutions provide the support that keeps the process going. They create space and provide civic participation forums; public awareness and mobilization; participatory and technical skills; training in planning and budgeting; sensitization of council staff and decision makers on bottom-up decision-making approaches; and administrative and financial support. They generate and analyze data from surveys, records, and reports; disseminate information; and allocate funds from their budgets to execute decisions reached in the participatory process.

Third, management staff and elected decision makers must be flexible, innovative, and persistent in responding to citizen demands and have the will to change procedures to ensure the process's effectiveness and sustainability. At first, citizen priorities were not clear, and their proposed budgets were unrealistic considering the available resources. With additional rounds of the participatory budgeting process, and more training, budgets became more realistic and priorities much more clear. While the financial costs were not high, it took substantial human resources from all parties involved to make the IMC participatory budgeting process a success.

REFERENCES

Clifford, Kate, and Sonja Meijer. 2001. "Dar es Salaam: Strategies for Development." Consultancy report prepared for the Development Planning Unit, University College of London, and Buro Happold.

Mjema, G. D., and J. Shitundu. 2002. Draft document survey (1996) for the ILO (International Labour Organization) Office for East Africa, Jobs for Africa Programme. In *Investment for Poverty Reduction Employment in Tanzania*. Dar es Salaam: ILO.

NBS (National Bureau of Statistics Tanzania). 2002. *Tanzanian Household Budget Survey 2000/01*. Dar es Salaam: NBS. http://www.tanzania.go.tz/hbs/HomePage_HBS.html.

CHAPTER 4

TRACKING THE GHANA DISTRICT ASSEMBLIES COMMON FUND

Charles Abbey, Vitus A. Azeem, and Cuthbert Baba Kuupiel

Over the past few decades, Ghana has received billions of dollars of overseas development assistance to support its economy and development. Currently, close to 40 percent of Ghana's annual domestic budget comes from external sources. It is becoming imperative for civil society to be actively involved in budget formulation, implementation, monitoring, and evaluation at both the central government and local government levels. The challenge, however, is civil society's inability to make its voice adequately heard and to hold the authorities and themselves accountable.

To improve development effectiveness and facilitate local participation in budgeting and planning, the central government decentralized power and resources to more than 100 district assemblies (DAs). The District Assemblies Common Fund (DACF) was created in 1993 to provide adequate and reliable funds for DAs. As one outcome of a 2002 World Bank and British Department for International Development (DFID) workshop on public resource management and social accountability, a number of nongovernmental organizations (NGOs) committed to promote civil society participation in public resource management and to monitor and evaluate public expenditures, focusing on the DACF.

The DACF tracking initiative revealed major weaknesses in DACF administration, including delays in allocations and disbursements to DAs, lack of transparency in selection of projects and contract awards, and political and central government interference in the use of the fund. It also found that the DACF disbursement formula favored wealthier districts and that community members often were not consulted in the selection of DACF projects.

On the positive side, the tracking initiative was highly participatory and brought together local stakeholders who had not known about DACF and had never before seen themselves as part of the solution. It brought the community closer and developed its capacity in terms of knowledge and the ability to meaningfully engage local government authorities in policy dialogue. As a result of the initiative, civil society organizations (CSOs) are now motivated to participate in DACF and Poverty Reduction Strategy Paper (PRSP) monitoring and evaluation. The government also has begun to modify the budget process.

The expenditure tracking exercise has not been repeated, however, and a one-time exercise may not have any lasting impact or benefits.

This chapter discusses how civil society can be empowered to play a critical role in social accountability in Ghana. It focuses on two studies conducted in tracking the DACF and independent budget analysis. It describes the tools that were used in both initiatives, the target audience, the main findings, and the lessons learned.

POLITICAL AND ADMINISTRATIVE CONTEXT

Ghana is a multiparty parliamentary democracy based on the 1992 constitution. It provides for an executive president and a unicameral 200-seat parliament. Since 1992, there has been a gradual deepening of democracy. In 2000, for example, there was a peaceful election and transfer of power from a president and the National Democratic Congress party, which had been in power for nearly 20 years, to one of its chief opponents, the New Patriotic Party.

Ghana has decentralized central government administration to the local government level. There are regional coordinating councils for each of the 10 administrative regions, and 138 metropolitan, municipal, and district assemblies (MMDAs) that involve local communities in the formulation and implementation of government policies and general development.

The 1992 constitution guarantees freedom of association. This has contributed to the healthy environment for civil society formation and operations in Ghana. The past decade and a half, in particular, has seen exponential growth of CSOs in Ghana. They have grown in numbers and range of activities as well as in response to the challenges and opportunities of reducing poverty, promoting human development, and strengthening democratic governance. The proliferation of CSOs, however, also has brought some organizations that misuse and misappropriate resources; generated technically weak projects funded primarily to showcase donor activities; and increased mutual mistrust between government and civil society.

Public forums, press conferences, and press releases promote evaluation of public services. There is media freedom and pluralism with more than 20 public and private radio stations and four television stations in the national capital, Accra. There are many public and private newspapers, especially in Accra, and circulated throughout the country. There is no control over what these stations broadcast and what the numerous newspapers publish although there is a media commission that mediates in disputes.

According to recent reports from the Ghana Integrity Initiative and the Center for Democratic Development Ghana, Ghana suffers from a high level of corruption. The reports mentioned corruption in the judiciary, security services, civil society, and the private sector. The perception among the population is that the central government, while professing to champion the rule of law, is doing little to fight corruption.

With an annual per capita income of about $300, Ghana is a poor country. Unsuccessful efforts at poverty reduction are blamed on poor macroeconomic performance and inadequate focus on poverty and non-export agriculture, especially in poor, remote regions. The underlying causes of this poor performance include poor planning and implementation of government budgets and policies; weak linkages between policies, strategies, and programs for employment and poverty reduction; and insufficient capacity to implement the programs.

Ghana's decentralization process involves the transfer of responsibilities for services and infrastructure from the central government to the MMDAs. Decentralization requires the transfer of resources to local authorities because most of them cannot generate sufficient funds. These resources include the DACF, a statutory fund for the transfer of central government resources to local authorities; the Heavily Indebted Poor Countries (HIPC) Account, created for the administration of HIPC debt savings; and the Ghana Education Trust Fund, created for education expenditures. These resources are earmarked for basic infrastructure and service delivery, particularly for health, education, water and sanitation, and income-generating activities.

There been no serious assessment of the efficiency and effectiveness of the use of these substantial resources or of their impact on poverty reduction. Moreover, the general public has complained about financial improprieties in the use of these resources.

THE DISTRICT ASSEMBLIES COMMON FUND

In 1993, Ghana's Local Government Act created 110 assemblies (later increased to 138) at the metropolitan, municipal, and district levels to be the seats of local administrative and development decision making. Among each assembly's powers is its planning authority in the district, including responsibility for preparing and implementing development plans and budgets. The assembly also is expected to mobilize resources, develop local infrastructure, and promote the development of local productive activities with the help of central government institutions (also decentralized) to operate as part of the DAs as a whole.

The DAs reflect the government's commitment to decentralization as a mechanism for bringing government closer to the governed. The goal is to improve public administration by empowering local authorities to be the planning and decision-making bodies, thereby facilitating local participation.

To ensure that DAs have adequate, reliable revenue sources, the DACF was established to serve as the mechanism for transferring resources from the central government to the local authorities (the MMDAs). One of the purposes of the DACF was to prevent severe imbalances in the regional distribution of wealth and development that decentralization might create, because the resources of local authorities are often unequal. By law, 5 percent of Ghana's total revenue should go to the DACF for distribution to MMDAs, mainly to undertake development projects and specific programs. Despite this requirement, the MMDAs have limited sources of revenues for carrying out their activities. These include the DACF, grants, transfers, ceded revenues, external credits, land rates, mineral royalties, and other internally generated funds.

The Ministry of Finance and Economic Planning (MFEP), the Ministry of Local Government and Rural Development (MLGRD), and the Controller and Accountant General's Department (CAGD) are involved in the disbursement and supervision of the DACF. The administrator of the DACF must propose the sharing formula within six months of his or her appointment and within three months of the end of each fiscal year. However, both the MFEP and the MLGRD determine aspects of district budgets that can be financed from the DACF.

As a response to Ghana's Poverty Reduction Strategy (PRS), the current formula has been made more pro-poor with more attention to health, education, and water and sanitation. The DACF ceiling is based on budget revenue projections for the year, and after the parliamentary approval of the formula, the district allocations are announced. Districts must submit supplementary budgets proposing the use of funds before DACF allocations are released to them. When the assembly approves projects, they are awarded on the advice of the district tender board. The General Assembly must provide the final approval before the contract is awarded. Projects are monitored by project monitoring teams, but project consultants may prepare payment certificates. The district coordinating director and the district finance officer are signatories for payment.

The DAs face considerable problems, including limited capacity and lack of appropriate skills for financial management, budgeting, and program and project implementation. This situation is exacerbated by inadequate supervision and weak oversight. Because of the DAs' prominent role in rural development, several communities are seeking new districts—a situation that could be exploited for political gains. In addition, audit reports on the DACF have shown several common improprieties, including misuse of funds, failure to deduct the 5 percent withholding tax on contract payments, questionable payments for incomplete projects, overdue loan repayments, and goods paid for but not delivered.

In addition to the generally slow decentralization process, Ghana faces several other major problems regarding fiscal decentralization, in particular:

- The lack of reliable and timely flow of funds to the districts hampers development, especially in the poorer districts.
- MMDAs' ability to generate their own resources for development projects and service delivery is hampered by huge leakages in revenue collection and accounting.
- The reluctance of central government agencies to decentralize the ministries and their proper integration at the district level creates structural problems, including payments for contracts executed at the district level.

- The generally poor capacity of DA members and officials, local CSOs, and much of the population to deal with budget issues has been used as an excuse for withholding funds from the DAs. As a result, the DAs are plagued by complaints, misuse of public resources, alleged political interference, and similar problems.

The DACF has faced additional problems that affect DA performance. Some MMDAs fail or refuse to follow guidelines for the use of the DACF. The Regional Coordinating Council and the central government are partly to blame for this failure because they sometimes issue directives for the MMDAs to release monies for activities that are not directly their responsibility.

However, the DACF's main problem concerns frequent delays in disbursing the fund to the DAs. There have been delays of more than one year, resulting in the failure to disburse funds to the MMDAs despite the constitutional requirement to pay funds into the DACF. Thus, DA complaints center on delays in releasing their shares or their full allocation. There are even complaints about the MLGRD interfering with the disbursement of the DACF. This affects DA budgeting, especially if the DAs have to divert funds from budgeted projects to unbudgeted expenditures, leaving contracts unpaid for long periods. Complaints also have surfaced from the general public and in media reports about alleged misapplication and financial malpractice in connection with the disbursement and use of DACF proceeds.

The effectiveness of monitoring and evaluation, especially by civil society, depends on the ready availability of the necessary information from national and local government. It is crucial that civil society take steps to track the flow of resources, not only from the central government to the MMDAs but also from local revenue sources to these assemblies. It should be possible to trace the flow of resources from origin (the Consolidated Fund) to destination (the DA) and determine the location, scale, and anomalies (if any) of disbursed funds. Expenditure tracking highlights both the use and abuse of public money and provides insights into resource capture, cost efficiency, and accountability.

INDEPENDENT BUDGET ANALYSIS

The overall goal of independent budget analysis (IBA) is to enhance public resource allocation and to better address the needs of the poor and socially marginalized. It covers national and local government budgets, focusing primarily on the social sectors: health, education, social welfare, and water and sanitation. Special attention is paid to public policies in these sectors (as contained in both the national and MMDA budgets) to ensure that they are pro-poor. IBA seeks to accomplish these goals:

- Demystify economic decision making and budgets through economic literacy campaigns and creating awareness. This goal particularly entails demystifying the highly technical and inaccessible budgets often left to technocrats at the Ministry of Finance and Economic Planning and to bringing debates and issues related to the formulation and implementation of budgets to a wider audience.
- Analyze national and local authority budgets to influence them. Public participation promotes transparency, effectiveness of the legislature, and social accountability.
- Study and use alternative budget and planning models such as the Distributive Effects of Economic Policies (DEEP) model for analyzing budgets and development policies.
- Collaborate with partners in disseminating research findings and budget information to all stakeholders and the public.
- Influence the budget process through evidence-based research and analysis, lobbying, and working with networks and partnerships.

More specifically, the IBA initiative seeks to address the following accountability problems:

- Lack of equity in the generation and allocation of public resources
- Waste, corruption, and inefficiency in the use of public resources
- Lack of a voice for the poor and marginalized
- Domination of policy design and budgeting by external players, leaving little space for local players

IBA also recommends ways to fill budget gaps based on the goals below. These recommendations empower civil society groups and other stakeholders to engage in the budget process through the creation of public awareness while also equipping these groups and stakeholders with necessary skills. The IBA aims to determine the extent to which Ghana's national and local budgets ensure that the following goals are achieved:

- Allocate adequate resources for poverty reduction
- Ensure that most citizens have increased access to basic social services
- Adequately address equity concerns in resource allocation

- Expand democratic space through greater civil society involvement in governance
- Increase participation in the budget process to ensure better prioritization
- Consider alternative policy priorities to ensure that the best policies are adopted

TRACKING DACF DISBURSEMENT

"Tracking the Disbursement of the District Assemblies Common Fund" was a pilot study conducted to promote participation in managing public resources and monitoring public expenditures (King and others 2003). The study represents a form of civil society involvement in public expenditure monitoring and participatory mechanisms for social and public accountability in Ghana in light of the importance of the PRS and the role of the DAs in implementing it. The following CSOs supported and produced the study: the African Development Programme (ADP), the Integrated Social Development Centre, Friends of the Nation, the Muslim Relief Association of Ghana, and the Centre for the Development of the People, in collaboration with DFID and the World Bank.

The DACF was selected for study because DAs are in close contact with people, and the DAs' activities most directly affect the lives of the poor. Furthermore, the largest source of funding for most of the MMDAs is the DACF, which comes from the Consolidated Fund into which every Ghanaian contributes. The efficient use of the DACF is, therefore, in the interest of all Ghanaians, whether or not they stand to gain personally from it.

The DACF disbursement-tracking study was an outcome of a three-day workshop conducted by the Ministries of Finance and Economic Planning and Regional Integration, in collaboration with DFID and the World Bank. More than 50 participants from government agencies, CSOs, and donors attended the workshop, which deliberated on concepts and practices in public and social accountability, public expenditure management, the Ghana PRS, and plans for a national monitoring and evaluation system for the PRS.

Resource persons, including donor representatives, emphasized that effective progress on the PRS depended on civil society. Civil society, as the beneficiary of PRS programs and projects, is in a privileged position to monitor and evaluate PRS implementation. Therefore, CSOs called for a unified approach to accounting and reporting to avoid overburdening the system and to make it easier for civil society to undertake its monitoring and evaluation role. They spoke about areas of analysis of public resources management, including participatory budgeting, demystifying the budget process, expenditure tracking, surveys on the quality and delivery of public services, and the key outcomes of public expenditures.

At the end of the workshop, various civil society groups and individuals agreed to act, over the following 12 months, to advance participation in public resource management and public-expenditure monitoring and evaluation. A Decentralization Group, formed at the end of the workshop, offered to track DACF disbursement in selected DAs. Tracking the DACF started as a pilot exercise in 2003 in four districts and was extended to cover 10 more districts.

The targets of the study were parliamentarians, traditional authorities, security services, market women, religious leaders, DA officers and staff, regional coordinating committees, teachers, youth, and drivers unions. The study recommended improvements in the administration and use of the DACF and specifically sought to determine whether

- DACF guidelines were followed in the allocation and use of the fund.
- Resources allocated by the DACF administrator were fully released to the MMDAs.
- Funds received by the MMDAs were used for their intended purpose.
- Disbursement processes were transparent and followed established procedures.

METHODOLOGIES AND TOOLS FOR IBA AND DACF TRACKING

The Centre for Budget Advocacy (CBA)[1] was not the first organization in Ghana to conduct IBA or similar analysis of economic policy instruments, but it was the only organization to have focused specifically on publishing budget analysis and using it for advocacy.[2] The CBA combined eight kinds of analysis, conducted continuously throughout the year: budgetary process analysis, general economic analysis, budget expenditure analysis, sector-specific analysis, analysis of effects on different population groups, revenue analysis, advancement of budget literacy and provision of budget training, and evaluation of public services and programs. This section describes how the CBA used each of these kinds of analysis for the IBA initiative in Ghana.

Budgetary process analysis. The CBA began its IBA initiative by commissioning a paper on Ghana's budgetary process as a basic tool for identifying the process's various stakeholders, processes, and legal framework. This analysis assessed the knowledge of and general transparency surrounding the budgetary process, including access to budget information and the extent of the legislature's participation in budget decisions. The CBA sought to assess how easily public information can be accessed at the regional and district levels. The paper also outlined the basic administrative steps involved in formulating, approving, and implementing the budget (Azeem and Adamtey 2004).

General economic analysis. This analysis is usually divided into four main parts: (1) review of the previous year's budget performance, (2) overview of the current budget's macroeconomic framework, (3) analysis of the revenue measures to generate the required funds to execute the budget, and (4) analysis of the expenditure allocations, with special focus on the social sectors.

Budget expenditure analysis and sector-specific analysis. The initiative combined budget expenditure analysis with sector-specific analysis, focusing on the budget's implications for health and education. Expenditure analysis examines the details of expenditure allocations and compares planned expenditures with the actual budget of the previous year. It also analyzes discrepancies in the implementation of the budget. Related to this is an analysis of the potential effects of the budgets on different population groups, particularly the poor, the vulnerable, women, and children. The CBA also examines the policy implications of budgets for human rights.

Distributive effects of economic policies. To further enhance efforts to assess the effects of economic policies, particularly pro-poor policies, the CBA has been working on its economic model, DEEP, to forecast the impact of intended policies and thereby guide policy makers. This model is in its final stages and would enhance the CBA's budget analysis because it could present evidence to support its analysis.

Revenue analysis. Civil society groups working on budgets tend to focus on expenditure allocations alone, ignoring the most important part of the budget: revenue mobilization. Revenue analysis is important not only because the budget is useless without revenue but also because the methods for such revenue generation have serious implications.

The revenue analysis assesses the microeconomic and macroeconomic effects of tax increases or cuts, the tax collection capacity of the government, and new policy initiatives in this area. The CBA published a booklet, *Taxation in Ghana Made Simple*, to help citizens understand the tax system (Azeem 2002).

Advancement of budget literacy and budget training. Since its inception, the CBA has advanced budget literacy and budget training targeted at civil society groups, the media, legislators, and members of the executive branch, with an emphasis on DA members and staff. The training of local government staff, legislators, and civil society groups on pro-poor planning, budgeting, and policy analysis equips stakeholders to analyze the budget and to improve their budget making process (in the case of budget staff and legislators) and their advocacy work (in the case of civil society and advocacy groups). The aim is to provide accessible materials and training on budget-related issues. The initiatives have been influential in building capacity among DA staff and members, civil society, and the general public, and have led to greater accountability around the budget, especially at the DA level.

Evaluation of public services and programs. The CBA organizes annual public forums and press conferences on the annual budget in all 10 regions of Ghana and disseminates its analyses without government interference. These public forums start the analysis process, are open to all citizens, are widely advertised, and attract the general public and experts who make presentations. The reports of these public forums are published in at least two newspapers and are sent to the president as an open letter. However, many Ghanaians view budgets as technical documents and policy instruments that cannot be easily understood. Attendance at these forums is low, especially among poor and illiterate citizens.

The tracking of the DACF and other central government transfers to local authorities involves the poor and other stakeholders through focus group discussions on resource flows, their use and usefulness, and measures to improve their effectiveness. The community assessment involves community meetings to assess service delivery and interface meetings with service providers to discuss the results of the assessment. During the community meetings, citizens are made aware of their rights, what resources have been earmarked for them, and what they should expect and demand from service providers. At the interface meetings, they also have the opportunity to raise their concerns with service providers and DA officials.

The service providers explain policies to the communities, thus building their capacity and sensitizing them on local development issues. However, this community assessment exercise has been undertaken only on a pilot basis.

Generating public interest in budgets and getting public officials to accept civil society intervention and inputs into the budget process has not been easy. Most people think the budget statement is too technical for easy comprehension. There are high levels of economic illiteracy and public apathy. Documentation on the DACF and projects undertaken with the fund is either not available or not easily accessible. And community members have little knowledge about the guidelines, disbursement, volume, and use of the DACF. This limited information and knowledge, in turn, limits citizens' ability to demand accountability from district authorities in charge of the disbursement of the fund.

In addition, public officials have been part of the challenge because they are reluctant to accept and work with civil society. Long-standing mutual mistrust between the government and civil society is the underlying problem.

MAIN FINDINGS ABOUT THE DACF

The records at the Office of the Administrator, the Controller and Accountant General's Department, and the DAs—in addition to the one-to-one interviews and focus group discussions—showed major weaknesses in DACF administration. These weaknesses included delays in allocations and disbursements to DAs, lack of transparency in selection of projects and contract awards, and political and central government interference in the use of the fund.

The study's most important finding was that, during the four-year period (1999–2002), the MFEP never released the full allocation to the administrator of the Common Fund. Table 4.1 shows the DACF disbursements. Previously, allocations had been equal to or more than the statutory 5 percent of tax revenue. More worrying is the fact that the government was not even able to disburse the amount that it declared as the transfer to the DACF, which suggests that there might have been diversions to other uses. Furthermore, the MLGRD had no means of verifying or challenging the MFEP on the amounts declared as the statutory allocation of 5 percent of total tax revenue to the fund.

Table 4.1 Disbursements to DACF, 1999–2002
cedis billions

Fiscal year	Total tax revenue	5% of tax revenue[a]	Projected MFEP release to DACF[b]	Actual MFEP release to DACF
1999	3,116.9	154.5	165.0	126.3
2000	4,414.7	220.7	211.5	192.3
2001	6,556.9	327.8	296.6	296.7
2002	8,132.0	406.6	367.9	109.7

Source: Ghana Controller and Accountant General's Department.
Note: MFEP is the Ghana Ministry of Finance and Economic Planning. DACF is the District Assemblies Common Fund.
a. By statute, 5 percent of tax revenue is allocated to DACF.
b. Amount declared by the government to be transferred to DACF.

Second, the study discovered multiple delays throughout the disbursement process, starting with the submission of the proposed guidelines to parliament, getting parliamentary approval for the guidelines, making the allocations, disbursing the funds to the MMDAs, and finally, receipt of the funds by the DAs. Furthermore, the study found large delays between releases by the MFEP, transfer by the CAGD, and payment by the Bank of Ghana. However, these gaps have decreased significantly since 2001.

The delays in disbursements to DACF occur for several reasons:

- The government may lack funds or have too many competing demands on resources (for example, paying debt savings into the HIPC account to meet donor conditionalities at the same time that the DACF allocation is due).
- The formula for disbursement must be approved every year; a delay in parliamentary approval of the proposed allocation formula also delays disbursement.
- Government fiscal and monetary policy concerns may result in withholding disbursements to help control money supply.
- Some DAs fail to meet deadlines for submitting supplementary budgets and reports on use of previous allocations—both of which are required for new disbursements.

The late release of the fund is a major constraint on the districts' development efforts because most MMDAs depend on the fund for development projects, poverty alleviation loans, and service delivery.

Late disbursement potentially increases DACF project costs and also disrupts DA budgeting and planning.

A third major finding is that the DACF is far in arrears. Since 1999, DACF disbursement gradually fell behind schedule and reached its nadir in 2002. By April 2003, the allocation disbursements for the first quarter of 2002 were still being made in installments.

The amounts the DAs received agreed with the figures released from the office of the Administrator of the Common Fund. However, the DAs released the amounts contained in the administrator's letters of allocation instead of the amounts they actually received. These figures did not agree with the figures released from the MFEP. One reason for this discrepancy is that some releases for the year were made in subsequent years. However, the main reason is that the central government deducted various amounts from the assemblies' DACF disbursements, including these general deductions:

- Two percent for the Institute of Local Government Studies for DA staff training expenses
- Bulk purchases
- Annual contributions to the National Association of Local Authorities of Ghana
- Other deductions determined on an ad hoc basis—for example, required contributions to the Sister City Program conference held in Ghana for those DAs that participated in the program

In addition to making its own deductions, the central government issues directives and guidelines with the DACF releases concerning how to use the disbursements. The DA's entitlement is divided into two categories: those determined by the central government and those decided by the DA. The central government mandates the following allocations:

- *Productivity improvement and employment generation fund* (20 percent) for credit to micro-, small-, and medium-scale enterprises in each district
- *Self-help projects* (10 percent) to support community-initiated projects
- *District Education Fund* (2 percent) to provide scholarships or repayable loans to needy students in the district
- *Establishment and strengthening of substructures of the assemblies* (5 percent) to provide offices, furniture, and equipment for the DAs' area councils, zonal councils, and unit committees

- *District Response Initiative* (1 percent) for HIV/AIDS
- *Malaria prevention fund* (1 percent)

After allocating these mandatory expenditures, the DA is left with only 61 percent of the DACF disbursement for its own priorities. Even then, the law requires that these priority areas include addressing the needs of vulnerable groups and promoting income generation. Specifically, the law requires that expenditures target the following areas:

- *Social services*: education, health, electrification, water supply, housing, sports, and recreation
- *Environment*: sanitation, drainage systems, waste management, and environmental protection
- *Economic ventures*: energy, markets, industry, agricultural services, roads, streets, bridges and culverts, information and communication technology, private sector support, and counterpart funding
- *Administration*: human resource management, office facilities, equipment, and project management

Fourth, the study also had major findings about the DAs. In general, the DACF was seen as a suitable mechanism for providing resources to the districts for basic infrastructure. The DACF has increased governmental resources and services at the district level. The problem is that both community and assembly officials view the formula for DACF disbursement as favoring wealthier districts, which widens the gap between rich and poor districts. This bias was reinforced by the disbursement of the HIPC Account to the MMDAs in 2002, when the metropolitan assemblies received the largest share, followed by the municipal assemblies, while the 103 district assemblies received smaller shares. However, the formula has become more pro-poor over time.

Generally, project selection was based on the guidelines for use of the fund. However, community members often were not consulted in the selection of DACF projects, which in most cases led to the selection of projects they felt did not meet their needs. This can undermine the sustainability of projects. However, in some cases, the people were consulted about DACF project selection. In Suhum, for example, the planning committee met with stakeholders at the executive and subcommittee levels to select projects, which the DA then approved.

Political patronage can also jeopardize the disbursement and efficient use of the DACF at the district and community levels. There was a general lack of transparency in tendering procedures and contract administration. This reduces the ability of DA members to monitor projects in their communities. The DA assesses the quality of projects undertaken with the DACF through a monitoring and evaluation team.

CONCLUSIONS AND LESSONS LEARNED

The CBA initiative (administering the questionnaire and the public forums) brought together district stakeholders who had neither known about the DACF nor saw themselves as part of the solution. These included market women, youth and religious leaders, members of the security services, traditional authorities, drivers, and teachers. As a result of the initiative, CSOs are now motivated to participate in DACF and PRSP monitoring and evaluation. The problem is lack of funding to mobilize and train the communities and the remaining districts.

Participation of the poor was facilitated because the researchers involved community institutions in administering the questionnaire and the focus group discussions. The initiative brought the community closer and developed its capacity in terms of knowledge and the ability to meaningfully engage local government authorities in policy dialogue. Indeed, the initiative had strong mobilizing and empowering elements. The danger was that it risked being captured by politicians who might see such initiatives and social accountability tools as threats.

This initiative has not been institutionalized. The ADP, CBA, and their partners see themselves (and others) as institutions that are ready to continue the linkages established with parliamentarians, communities, government, media, market women and traders, security servicemen, and others. The expenditure tracking exercise has not been repeated. How, then, can the people hold their leaders accountable more meaningfully, such as through this social accountability initiative? A one-time exercise may not have any lasting impact or benefits.

Regardless, both case studies—the pilot study involving the several international groups and the CBA's independent budget analysis of the DACF—demonstrated some positive results. They found, for example, that the 1992 constitution of the Republic of Ghana had guaranteed a conducive environment for CSOs that enabled the CSOs to undertake their activities without fear or intimidation. Civil society must work hard to protect and defend its constitutional rights.

The willingness of the NGOs to be involved in the case studies demonstrated they were willing to take on such work under challenging circumstances. These and other CSOs must be empowered to undertake similar activities in the remaining districts and train local organizations to engage more meaningfully with local authorities. Donors and development partners need to support more of the CSOs' confidence-building measures and flexible funding strategies. Sometimes, CSO representatives felt humiliated by the delays and donor impositions before funds were released.

The primary outcome of the case studies was the increasing interest of many citizens in the DACF and IBA initiatives. An improved budget system, however, is less assured. The government has now decided, in response to civil society activities, to have parliament approve the budget before the beginning of the fiscal year. The government is now soliciting public views on budget policies during budget formulation. Ghana's continued dependence on external financing and accompanying policy prescriptions constrain government's acceptance of CSOs' policy recommendations

Except for inputs from a few research and academic institutions that undertake analysis for academic purposes, there is a general lack of knowledge and awareness of budget processes in Ghana, even among legislators and other public officials involved in it. As a result, an intensive budget literacy campaign among civil society is necessary if pro-poor budgets are to be achieved. There is also a need for collaboration among CSOs in Ghana and with international groups doing budget work. The international groups can provide important information about donor programs and conditions, which are not easy to obtain in-country. They can also arrange meetings with donors and other power brokers to enable CSOs to voice their views on policy reforms.

During the DACF studies, a strong relationship developed between the government, development partners, and the study team. The involvement of the government and communities in the study right from the beginning helped ensure that their perspectives would be taken into account and would facilitate the team's work. Having people from all sectors and backgrounds involved in the study was invaluable.

Finally, the tendency to underestimate the knowledge and contributions of people from the grassroots must be overcome. It is still the case that the people most affected by the outcome are left out of discussions on policy development, implementation, monitoring, and evaluation. Every effort must be made to change this situation.

NOTES

1. The CBA is part of the Integrated Social Development Centre (ISODEC). http://www.inter nationalbudget.org/groups/ghana.htm.
2. The Institute of Social, Statistical and Economic Research, the Centre for Policy Analysis, and the Institute of Economic Affairs have conducted economic analysis over the past decade.

REFERENCES

Azeem, Vitus. 2002. *Taxation in Ghana Made Simple*. Accra: ISODEC.

Azeem, Vitus, and Nicholas Adamtey. 2004. "Ghana's Budgeting Process: Who Is Involved?" Paper prepared for ISODEC (Integrated Social Development Centre). ISODEC, Accra.

King, Rudith, Vitus A. Azeem, Charles Abbey, Samuel Kwaku Boateng, and Donkris Mevuta. 2003. "Financing Decentralised Development: How Well Does the DACF Work? A Pilot Tracking of the District Assemblies Common Fund in Four Districts." Study conducted by civil society organizations led by ISODEC, in collaboration with the British Department for International Development and the World Bank offices in Ghana. ISODEC, Accra. http://www.icsw.org/doc/DACF%20Report.doc.

CHAPTER 5

ENHANCING CIVIL SOCIETY CAPACITY FOR ADVOCACY AND MONITORING: MALAWI'S POVERTY REDUCTION STRATEGY BUDGET

**Dalitso Kingsley Kubalasa and
Limbani Bartholomew Elia Nsapato**

Without active citizenship, democracy will be the monopoly of big men in fancy suits spouting buzzwords. "The people" will be treated as passive recipients of fertilizer, maize, schools, bridges, and other necessities but not real power to influence decisions.

—Dr. Edge Kanyongolo (2007)

Malawi has adopted a number of policies to combat poverty, disease, and ignorance, including the Statement of Development Policies. While these have continued to exist on paper, the reality and implementation usually have not matched the rhetoric. The situation changed considerably following the country's shift to a democratic multiparty state in 1994, which ushered in the adoption of a Poverty Alleviation Program as the operative development philosophy. This was subsequently complemented by the longer-term Malawi Vision 2020, developed after allegedly extensive public consultations. Then Malawi adopted its Poverty Reduction Strategy (PRS) in 2002 before moving on, in 2006, to the second-generation PRS: the Malawi Growth and Development Strategy (MGDS). However, none of these initiatives has been made fully operational with a fundable action plan, and all have been plagued with implementation challenges.

In exploring the role of an active and critical citizenry from a civil society perspective, the importance of the link between general economic literacy and PRS budget monitoring is vital. A society that better understands the basics of the economy and the development agenda has a stronger knowledge base to effectively demand its rightful entitlement from government. This is achieved through, among other things, monitoring economic and development progress. A critical citizenry can understand and be aware of the indicators to monitor the poverty reduction agenda as well as of the outputs and impacts to expect for any given development agenda.

This case study recounts an interesting success story in empowering a critical citizenry. As a civil society organization (CSO) coalition dedicated to promoting pro-poor participatory economic governance in Malawi, the Malawi Economic Justice Network (MEJN) recognizes that its strength and future is in its ability to build capacity, increase knowledge, and develop advocacy skills among its members. MEJN recognized, at the outset, that economic literacy needed to be developed if CSOs in Malawi were to constructively participate in economic governance issues. This chapter focuses on how civil society's involvement in the nation's economic governance developed, its capacity increased, and its image improved. It describes the main methods the initiative used, its impacts, the challenges it faced, and the lessons learned.

THE ENVIRONMENT FOR CIVIL SOCIETY

Malawi has historically been poor. Nature plays a role in this, but the many reasons for this also include economic management and the external environment. The country's politics have not necessarily been pro-poor, just as they have not inspired the expected development. Public administration has not been as efficient and effective as hoped in addressing poverty in Malawi, and poverty reduction efforts since the country's independence in 1964 have been largely disappointing.

After the political transition from a one-party system to a multiparty system in 1994, Malawi has been transforming from a closed society, with considerable government control over many aspects of daily life, to a more open and democratic society. Political governance has tended to dominate economic governance. The decentralization process pursued by the government since 1998 has created yet another set of challenges to the work of nongovernmental organizations (NGOs) and civil society in general. Nevertheless, decentralization is understood to have the potential to create more space for CSOs to become more involved and more influential. In addition to individual CSOs' advocacy on specific issues, there has also been rapid growth of CSO coalitions and networks to support the people's voice, particularly from the grassroots.

Despite civil society's historical weakness and near-nonexistence for most of Malawi's history, it has shown great resilience and stature in playing a vibrant part in the quickly maturing democracy. Donor support in the mid-1990s made resources available, even to organizations without the capacity to deliver, creating numerous "briefcase NGOs" that affected even NGOs with legitimate claims to representativeness. Exceptions stood out, including churches, faith-based institutions, and other organizations that made good efforts to sustain their grassroots memberships. These efforts include the advocacy that has continuously emerged to monitor the development and policy formulation and implementation processes, including the efforts of MEJN and similar networks.

THE PRO-POOR PARTICIPATORY ECONOMIC GOVERNANCE INITIATIVE

MEJN emerged out of a modest but important November 2000 meeting of about 27 CSOs. Ever since its inception, MEJN has established itself as a major civil society voice on issues of economic governance in Malawi, with the central focus being the formulation and implementation of the PRS. It has been involved in coordinating and facilitating increased civil society and community participation in the national budgeting process and the Poverty Reduction Strategy Paper (PRSP) in addition to undertaking a leading role in advocacy and lobbying policy makers and the donor community. MEJN has provided critical information to parliament (especially the Budget and Finance, Public Accounts, and other key sectoral committees), civil society groups, the donor community (especially those that are part of the Common Approach to the Budget groups), and the general public through focused and thematic briefings.

MEJN, whose national secretariat is based in the capital city, Lilongwe, has extended its network structure to the community level through the consolidation of district-based CSOs and NGOs, associations, local assembly officials, traditional leaders, and religious leaders. These MEJN participants are coordinated by representative committees called MEJN district chapters. The district chapters average 10 to 14 members from institutions representing different socioeconomic groups. They operate with minimum core support and are largely voluntary.

The goal of the coordination program is to strengthen the operations of civil society as an effective alternative voice to government and other stakeholders by promoting civil society participation in shaping development policy and practice, with a specific focus on those policies that directly affect poverty. The purpose is to increase civil society coordination and understanding of economic policy and to create a civil society advocacy coalition on national economic development. The program has the following key objectives:

• Decentralize civil society networks to involve communities at the regional and district level
• Enhance coordination among civil society networks
• Link civil society to decision makers such as parliament, government, and other partners
• Enhance CSO technical capacity to offer credible alternatives
• Document and disseminate civil society work

With support from Development Cooperation Ireland (now Irish Aid), MEJN piloted the coordination of CSO networks to push for division of labor in civil society while maximizing opportunities for synergy. Expectations have grown much faster than capacity. The core partners in MEJN's coordinated effort have been the Civil Society Agriculture Network (CISANET), the Civil Society Coalition for Quality Basic Education (CSCQBE), the Malawi Health Equity Network (MHEN), and the organizations under MEJN's own broader umbrella. The project ensures a unified voice for civil society. MEJN has continued to renew and strengthen its relations with the Council for Non-governmental Organizations in Malawi through joint programming efforts in organizing several joint activities and campaigns, including NGO Week, the Global Call to Action against Poverty, and the Millennium Development Goals (MDGs) campaign, among others.

The Economic Literacy Project

With initial support from the Open Society Initiative for Southern Africa (OSISA) in 2002 and later from the Canadian International Development

Agency (CIDA) through the CIDA Project on Economic Governance (CIDA-PEG) in 2003, the Economic Literacy Project was conceptualized and incorporated into one of MEJN's earliest programs. Its objectives were to increase civil society's awareness, skills, and knowledge about the economy, more specifically to

- Improve the knowledge of community and civic leaders in economics and public finance
- Enhance civil society technical capacity to plan and design projects to facilitate sound economic governance
- Empower communities with knowledge and advocacy skills on economic governance and rights
- Build community capacity to monitor key policies relevant for poverty reduction in agriculture, health, and education
- Influence and expand the impact of debt relief and the PRS by improving civil society capacity to engage government and international financial institutions
- Enhance pro-poor policy reforms at the national level

The initial project targets were leaders in civil society, communities, and government officials at the central and local assembly levels. The creation of MEJN district chapters to act as both information conduits and platforms for discussing economic governance issues grew out of the Economic Literacy Project. This project has grown into a deeper and wider initiative that includes budget literacy (known as the Budget Participation Initiative), trade literacy, and trade justice (known as the Trade Weather Stations). These have all remained central to the significance of MEJN as a champion for pro-poor participatory economic governance in Malawi and beyond.

The Civil Society Budget Training Manual

Among the most important activities implemented through the MEJN Economic Literacy Project was the development and publication of a user-friendly Civil Society Budget Training Manual that member CSOs have used for training since MEJN kick-started the initial training. MEJN developed this manual in September 2003 drawing upon existing materials on public financial management and civil society applied budget work.[1] It provides detailed insights into the key issues and processes of the Malawi national budget to enable civil society stakeholders with an interest in economic governance to participate meaningfully in the process. It describes the framework, content, and general processes of the national budget as the policy tool the government uses to facilitate investment, employment, trade, and economic growth.

The manual adopts a user-friendly approach to highlight a general picture of public budgets and citizen roles. It identifies primary stages of the Malawi budgetary process, clearly outlining entry points for civil society to influence pressure points in the system. It also focuses on the most important aspects for civil society, emphasizing essential topics such as gender budgeting and budget advocacy.

The Budget Participation Initiative

In 2003, the project's overall objective was extended from the national level to increasing civil society and local assemblies' knowledge and skills, with an emphasis on policy implementation. The extension of the Economic Literacy Project to the Budget Participation Initiative (BPI) was designed to enhance public dialogue on the budget among civil society and communities, the legislature (parliament), and the executive branch. Project activities included CSO training needs assessments, development of a training manual on budgeting processes, identification and training of local facilitators, and facilitation and conducting of training workshops.

At first, the training workshops were conducted at the regional level in the three main regions of Malawi (northern, central, and southern). A sectoral approach was adopted in targeting comprehensive coverage of leaders and beneficiaries in the three most prominent sectors: education, health, and agriculture. More than 79 CSOs took part in these training workshops during the first year of implementation.

Submissions were developed during the training workshops, and they formed the basis for follow-up project activities such as budget monitoring based on contributions at the national and regional levels to the budgetary formulation process. By popular demand, the training was extended to the district level and was held in several districts. In all of these training sessions, gender was seriously considered in all processes to advance capacity-building objectives and ownership. The process of ensuring local ownership of the budget participation initiative by CSOs and government implementing agencies at the district level (district assemblies) continued with the MEJN secretariat's identification and training of local facilitators.[2] During

2004, 15 facilitators were identified and trained, of whom 6 were women, to conduct training sessions when needed.

As a result, MEJN has been eager to train more local facilitators to expand the impact of training throughout Malawi. The MEJN Secretariat has been developing a special focus on facilitating and coordinating tripartite civil society submissions for dialogue with people in decision-making positions. Targets include members of parliament and government officials at the community, district, and national levels. These challenges and expectations have all been consolidated in the MEJN Programme Support Document (PSD), in which BPI activities have been combined with the Economic Literacy Project, creating a MEJN core program called Budget and Economic Literacy.

Tools for Monitoring Government Commitment to Poverty Reduction

The programs described above to increase economic literacy, increase public dialogue about the budget, and train CSOs to facilitate and support MEJN's Budget and Economic Literacy program have achieved synergies that collectively drive MEJN's overall citizen empowerment effort to achieve pro-poor participatory economic governance in Malawi.

Along the way, MEJN developed several important tools that have been among its most significant contributions: the Service Delivery Satisfaction Survey, independent budget analysis, MPRS annual reviews, and the Public Expenditure Tracking Survey (PETS).

Service Delivery Satisfaction Survey (SDSS). In 2001, MEJN began coordinating civil society efforts to monitor the implementation of Protected Pro-Poor Expenditures (PPEs) as part of government's commitments in the Malawi Poverty Reduction Strategy (MPRS). To achieve its goal, MEJN carried out three Service Delivery Satisfaction Surveys (SDSSs) covering the government's performance in fiscal years 2003, 2004, and 2005 (MEJN 2006). The SDSS findings provide useful platforms for interaction with government officials, parliament, donors, and other key stakeholders. The Ministry of Economic Planning and Development (MEPD) has formally recognized the SDSS as a tool for qualitative monitoring, and the SDSS results informed the development of the MPRS annual review reports. From then onward, MEJN has continued to strengthen its efforts to monitor the government's MPRS commitments, using several approaches described below.

The SDSS uses a mixed approach of quantitative and qualitative monitoring of MPRS implementation. It assesses citizen satisfaction with the quality of the public services provided by the Malawi government. The data are obtained using a closed-ended questionnaire with ordered choices to capture the opinions and perceptions of the respondents. The questionnaire asks questions about people's access to services, their satisfaction with the quality of services, and the commitment of the staff at the facilities.

The questionnaires were pretested as a part of the enumerators' training before data collection. Data collection is completed over three weeks with the help of the enumerators drawn from MEJN district chapter member institutions, as a way of building their capacity and facilitating ownership from the beginning. The sampling procedure was designed with expert advice and oversight from the National Statistics Office (NSO).

The survey findings have been quite instrumental in the popular debate about national budget formulation, allocations, and execution. The reports formed the basis for civil society interaction with government officials as well as other CSOs. In time, the results became available to inform parliamentary deliberations (among others) on the budget because they provide suggestions for improving the focus of allocations toward pro-poor priority expenditures. In addition to production of the reports, a detailed advocacy and dissemination campaign based on the results has been carefully choreographed to ensure that all the relevant stakeholders are kept abreast of the findings and that implementation of the PRS budget is in line with what the people want.

After carrying out the surveys, the draft report is sent to principal stakeholders for comments, quality control, and data verification. For example, feedback sessions were conducted for all MEJN members from the district chapters, including the enumerators and supervisors who took part in SDSS I, II, and III. The draft reports are then presented to all key parties—especially government ministries and departments—after which a final report is released for widespread dissemination by the media.

The project also reflects gender sensitivity in the SDSS by obtaining gender-balanced perspectives in the household sampling at the village level. As a matter of principle for MEJN research, every other household deliberately has a female respondent to capture gender perspectives. This has also been built into the MEJN PSD as reflected in the MEJN Strategic Plan.

Independent budget analysis. Independent budget analysis (IBA) has been another significant MEJN contribution. Immediately after the finance minister presents budget statements in parliament, MEJN commissions a quick but thorough analysis of the previous budget and the proposed budget to highlight the salient issues to be considered before passing the budget. IBA reports help civil society, parliamentary committees, and other primary stakeholders obtain an in-depth understanding of each year's national budget.

The IBA reports' main objective is to assess the degree to which the budget incorporates activities identified in the overall government's development policy for funding. Second, it assesses the amount of the resources devoted to pro-poor priority expenditures in comparison with the resources devoted to nonpriority poverty expenditures. Third, it reviews implementation and identifies strengths and weaknesses from a pro-poor perspective before offering a synopsis of votes in parliament. MEJN submits the IBA report's recommendations to parliament's Budget and Finance Committee for inclusion into its submission to the national assembly in addition to general circulation and dissemination of the report to all members of parliament and other stakeholders.

This approach ensures that the contributions from civil society find their way into the national assembly debate on the budget. So far, it has been one of MEJN's greatest successes. In general, MEJN budget analysis has been instrumental in revealing most anomalies worth correction and further clarification. The IBA findings have made for some of the most interesting parliamentary debates in recent years. Funding and support for this advocacy effort has come from several partners, including the National Democratic Institute for International Affairs, OSISA, the Joint Oxfam Programme in Malawi, and CIDA-PEG.

MPRS annual reviews. Another complementary contribution for ensuring transparent and prudent use of public resources has been an annual review of MPRS implementation compared with the PPEs' performance. A specific submission was made after MEJN commissioned a study that revealed the MPRS was being implemented piecemeal and that the PPEs were not getting enough protection, as became evident when unnecessary diversions of funds were not proportional to overexpenditures in non-poverty-reducing areas.

All of these observations were presented to government and parliament. Specific submissions formed the core in addition to MEJN's overall presentations and input to the MPRS annual review process. This process underscored the significance of MEJN as a key part of the government committee responsible for MPRS reviews in collaboration with other stakeholders. The MPRS annual review effort has led the MEPD to spearhead an initiative to resuscitate its PRS Support Group. This group has championed implementation of the government-led PRSP Monitoring Master Plan by creating a roadmap for linking the MPRS (both first- and second-generation) to MDG monitoring.

Public Expenditure Tracking Surveys. MEJN has continued carrying out its own Public Expenditure Tracking Surveys (PETS) as part of its efforts to follow the money allocated in selected votes of interest in addition to being a part of the Malawi government team driving the PETS. For example, the government commissioned a pilot initiative, through the MEPD's monitoring and evaluation division, to track how government funds were used in fiscal 2003/04. This was one of the most significant outcomes of the first phase of the SDSS dissemination, whose findings went to the MEPD and the Ministry of Education. A survey management team was put in place comprising representatives from most key stakeholders, including donor agencies, coordinated by the MEPD's monitoring and evaluation division. MEJN, in collaboration with CSCQBE, took the lead in coordinating civil society input into the process.

This project benefited from the expertise of the World Bank-supported Financial Management, Transparency, and Accountability Project (FIMTAP). In 2004, the pilot focus was the education sector. The tracking survey was conducted in several districts of the biggest education zones in Malawi, with technical support coordinated by the NSO in conjunction with the MEPD. After the PETS report was released, MEJN, in collaboration with CSCQBE, moved on to streamline some of the pertinent issues from the report for its own advocacy and lobbying.

Another example of CSO government monitoring is the PETS commissioned by MEJN concerning one channel of the public resource allocations for decentralization, the Constituency Development Fund. Four institutions were analyzed: members of parliament, district assemblies, project implementation committees, and area development committees (ADCs). MEJN hopes the report will inform the government's review of the Constituency Development Fund, which is expected to evolve into a Local Development Fund, according to the most recent government reports about its development plans.

ADVOCACY FOR ECONOMIC JUSTICE

Since its formation, MEJN has conducted advocacy in parliamentary budget sessions, government trade negotiations, and economic reforms, to mention a few. It has devoted its efforts toward advocacy of pro-poor budget analysis and fair trade positions and against privatization of essential services. MEJN meets with relevant stakeholders, including parliamentary committees and key government departments, and engages the media to disseminate the civil society position along with the government's. In its few years of existence, MEJN has concentrated its advocacy efforts as highlighted below.

Popularization and Simplification of Key Policy Documents

MEJN has launched several initiatives related to building government social accountability in the budgeting process. As part of developing tools for its projects (all of which are interlinked), MEJN has commissioned simplifications of most of the technical materials—such as the national budget, the Malawi PRSP, and other policy documents—for popularization and dissemination.[3] These materials have been widely disseminated in local languages to district chapters, member organizations, members of parliament, government officials, and other stakeholders, including donors. It is important to note that Chichewa, the vernacular language of Malawi, has been used in documents distributed throughout Malawi to strengthen citizen participation in advocacy related to promoting participatory economic governance.

These popularized documents have been further distilled into leaflets disseminated to the main newspapers: *Weekend Nation* and the *Malawi News*. MEJN also conducted radio programs on popular state radio and television stations (MBC radio stations 1 and 2 and Television Malawi) and private radio stations such as Capital FM and FM 101. In addition, MEJN conducted workshops in all districts as part of sensitization on popular documents. There were separate sessions for community members and traditional authorities, local assembly councilors, district executive committees, and members of parliament. These sessions have proven to be quite useful because the policy documents are new to many participants, even among members of parliament and local government officials whose work was made easier by not having to read long, technical documents.

The Fair Trade through Trade Justice Project

Because Malawi is an import-oriented economy with a negative trade balance, the country is vulnerable to exploitation by its trading partners, multinational corporations, and even wealthy Malawians who benefit from skewed trading arrangements. MEJN has developed a project to promote trade justice and fair trade as well as to enhance civil society knowledge based on trade. Christian Aid, a London-based NGO, provides funds for this project.

By the end of 2004, MEJN had conducted training needs assessments through nationwide consultations during which civil society and local government assembly officials provided input on the campaign's core issues. One need that emerged was a compilation of all trade agreements and protocols that Malawi has with its trading partners, with a view toward assessing the agreements' advantages and disadvantages for poor people. The compilation was completed in 2004 in addition to a research report titled, "Effects of Liberalization on Local Communities." Based on the research findings, awareness workshops will be conducted to begin the process of ensuring trade justice in Malawi.

The Civil Society Manifesto

MEJN has been developing a Civil Society Manifesto (MEJN 2004) or People's Manifesto (as it was renamed for the 2009 elections [MEJN 2009]) as a blueprint containing civil society issues that parliamentary and presidential candidates should address in their campaign promises. The manifesto was developed with citizen input through MEJN's decentralized structures, soliciting citizen's submissions on the priorities they want candidates to address. The manifesto has then been used as an important advocacy tool, having aggregated the people's needs and aspirations into policy demands that have been further verified and validated by people in the districts before being simplified into user-friendly versions and translated into Chichewa.

The manifestos have been unveiled during launches that target political parties and their leadership as well as key civil society representatives, traditional leaders, and MEJN district chapter members. The documents are developed well in advance, prior to the parties' own manifestos, to influence the parties' positions and policy agendas—a phenomenon that has worked quite well in both elections. These versions have been disseminated widely through public roundtable discussions with aspiring candidates and key stakeholders, district workshops, and radio and television programs preceding the general elections.

An innovative example of the manifestos' dissemination was a music album produced by MEJN, to which eight popular Malawian artists contributed songs for the elections. The album, *Mfundo patsogolo* (*Policies First, not Personalities*), emphasized the need for content-based elections and not those based on mere personalities. The manifesto, cassettes, and CDs were distributed to political parties and candidates as well as through the National Initiative for Civic Education (NICE) district offices and other organizations under MEJN district chapters. After presenting the manifesto to candidates, MEJN embarked on a comprehensive nationwide initiative to bring the manifesto to the electorate through community workshops involving influential stakeholders, who in turn disseminated the manifesto more broadly.

The manifesto was acknowledged to have been quite timely in the more than 20 districts visited. Candidates reportedly had been focusing their campaigns more on personality—projecting irrelevant gestures and using scathing attacks and unnecessary innuendo, devoid of policy content, to prejudice the electorate against their opponents. Notably, after the civil society manifesto campaign, some candidates adopted the manifesto, shaping their campaigns around some of the key civil society positions. The more issue-oriented campaigns and materials gave voters a chance to make an informed choice among the candidates in the wake of isolated cases of candidates who were allegedly trying to buy votes.[4]

PARTICIPATORY BUDGET MONITORING PROBLEMS AND CHALLENGES

Although many of MEJN's initiatives have succeeded, substantial challenges and constraints remain. The challenges themselves, however, often contain the seeds of opportunity for even greater success.

These challenges include the persistent issue of balancing poverty reduction and economic growth; the need to maximize synergies among both stakeholders and programs; the weak link of MEJN's data and findings with the government policy machinery; the challenges posed by decentralization, including increasing needs for transparency and accountability as well as constraints specific to local governance; the need for greater institutional support and sustainable capacity; inadequate financial resources; and inadequate technical capacity.

Balancing Poverty Reduction and Economic Growth

As an officially endorsed blueprint for reducing poverty in Malawi, the PRS continued to serve as a key instrument and framework for holding government accountable through commitments made in the national budget. During the PRS transition to a more growth-oriented strategy—the Malawi Growth and Development Strategy (MGDS)—the main challenge for all stakeholders, including civil society, has been to achieve the proper balance between social sector and productive sector support to reduce poverty while also generating economic growth. In addition to the good governance agenda, it continues to be important to effectively monitor the PRS's impact on poverty reduction to determine whether these were appropriate government policies and programs.

Maximizing Synergies

Participatory governance is costly, but it can also be cost-effective for both civil society and government. It can ensure consistency by creating space for verification and cross-checking of data for tripartite comparison of monitoring findings. For the government, this has been quite challenging because of its piecemeal, disjointed approach to rolling out implementation of the Monitoring and Evaluation Master Plan. Nonetheless, there has been a growing desire for cementing relations among the Government Monitoring Master Plan's key players, particularly its leadership, which has been strengthened.

For civil society, the primary challenge has been to manage the complexities of member organizations' different institutional interests, constraints, capacities, monitoring mechanisms, and frameworks. MEJN addressed this concern through a joint monitoring initiative that MEJN started in collaboration with other networks. Although still small in scale, this initiative has helped reduce the animosity and rivalry that had been hampering progress, although capacities still remain constrained by the minimal resources available to the overall network compared with the huge expectations it is raising.

Weak Data Links with Government Policy

The limited scope of civil society's interaction with monitoring and evaluation mechanisms for government policies (such as the PRSP and the

MGDS) has been another challenge, particularly regarding how to link data and findings with the government policy machinery. CSO capacity in research, monitoring, and evaluation must be enhanced to generate information for meaningful engagement with government, donors, and other stakeholders on a consistent, ongoing basis.

Opportunities and Challenges of Decentralization

As deconcentration and devolution advance through increased budgetary control at the district assembly level, the districts will have greater responsibilities for the efficiency and efficacy of public financial management—for example, in the Constituency Development Fund. This shift of responsibility further underscores the need for greater transparency and accountability through diligent monitoring. Decentralization also means that more avenues are being opened for community participation in monitoring.

Constraints of Local Governance

Local governance structures (the village development committees, ADCs, and district executive committees), although in place with clear mandates, appear limited in their capacity and understanding of conditions for true participatory governance. Many actors still view civil society's role as in implementing policies, with decision making and policy formation still occurring at a considerable distance from the people most affected. In addition, pending local government elections (overdue since 2005), some local governance structures are still not operational; they exist only on paper.

Institutional Support and Sustainable Capacity

MEJN has seen its capacity tested at its national secretariat and at the regional and district levels, so it must urgently strengthen and sustain its structures to continue monitoring key central and local government operations, most of which are not yet fully devolved. MEJN has continued making progress in establishing a decentralized system, both at the national level (with other networks' national secretariats) and at the regional and local levels (through its regional coordinators who link up with the district chapters). Internally, MEJN has not received adequate financial and technical support to achieve its vision. MEJN must comprehensively and critically examine and fine-tune its two parallel structures of representation and clarify and refine how the chapters feed into the policy, positions, and overall direction of the network.

Inadequate Resources

Obtaining sufficient funds to support core administrative functions (such as overhead costs and institutional development) has posed a large challenge to the smooth delivery of almost all of MEJN's programs and activities. Growing demand to produce and disseminate books, policy papers, and other technical papers explaining economic literacy and the government development agenda and strategy has strained its limited resources.

Inadequate Technical Capacity

Lack of capacity remains a big challenge and contributes to civil society's inability to deliver and match high expectations—in part because poor remuneration, among other factors, has caused high staff turnover. This lack of capacity requires the network to nurture its institutional memory, coordination skills, and knowledge about social accountability tools (for example, the Citizen Report Card and Citizens' Jury).

RESULTS AND IMPACTS

MEJN's impact and results are grounded in its solution-based approaches to program development and problem solving. In the course of establishing itself as a major civil society voice on economic governance issues in Malawi, MEJN has stressed the importance of pursuing realistic, balanced advocacy and of keeping its criticism constructive.

The ways in which MEJN has advanced social accountability fall under the categories of enhancing civil society status, strengthening and increasing CSO budget monitoring, increasing public awareness, and developing local capacity.

Enhanced Status of Civil Society

CSOs are now seen as important partners instead of as troublesome, provocative, and confrontational. They now have a much sharper, more organized, and more professional sense of direction and a strategic programming approach grounded in evidence-based advocacy. These advancements in both status and capacity have facilitated CSOs' engagement with government and other stakeholders in helping to craft and implement policies and programs.

The growing expectations and demand from MEJN members and other CSOs confirm the relevance of the network initiative, the budget and economic literacy modules, and MEJN's tools and methodologies—all of which were once viewed as too technical and only for senior government officials. Participatory budget monitoring encourages community members to increase their skills and knowledge about socioeconomic issues because these are major prerequisites to their effective participation.

Proliferation of CSO Budget Monitoring

At least 10 notable CSOs in addition to those in the MEJN have added economic literacy to their key program areas. These include Action Aid International in Malawi; the Catholic Commission for Justice and Peace; the Malawi Council of Churches; the Association for Progressive Women; the Women's Voice, Church, and Society Programmes of the Livingstonia Synod (Northern Malawi), Nkhoma Synod (Central Malawi), and the Blantyre Synod (South) of the CCAP Church (Church of Central Africa Presbyterian); the Active Youth Initiative for Social Enhancement; the Malawi Human Rights Youth Network; the Childrens' Research, Information and Documentation Centre; and selected offices of NICE.

In addition, other civil society networks that have closely collaborated with MEJN now have fully operational efforts to track and monitor government's use of public finances in their respective sectors. These include CISANET, MHEN, and CSCQBE. MEJN district chapters are strengthening and sustaining local-level community mobilization for social accountability.

Increased Public Awareness

MEJN's budget analyses have catalyzed public interest, access, and understanding of budget documents. This interest and understanding, in turn, has helped to popularize budget debates and other key economic bills in parliament. The bills' sudden newsworthiness has increased the demand for economic and budget literacy training and for simplification and popularizing of key policy documents.

MEJN has conducted media advocacy campaigns, such as the "Budget and You" television program (during parliament's budget session); the *Phungu* (member of parliament) television program (emphasizing public knowledge of their members of parliament and their philosophies of representation versus development); and live radio debates and phone-in programs. Demand for all these programs is high, based on public requests for rebroadcasts of the programs and demand to hold more educational, interactive, and entertaining programs on issues of national importance previously regarded as unsuitable for popular participation.

Development of Local Capacity

Although still at an early stage in their development, the MEJN district chapters have carried out a wide range of activities, some initiated by the MEJN secretariat and others at the chapters' own initiative. These include trainings, research, awareness raising, and advocacy targeted at local authorities and political leaders. Despite a number of challenges faced by chapters in this work—including transportation, capacity, time, and information resources—the impact of this work is apparent.

By raising MEJN's profile in their districts and stimulating public debate on critical developmental issues, MEJN chapters have contributed to overcoming the culture of silence and fear that lingered as a legacy of the Banda era. In attempting to institutionalize their participation in local governance through involvement in local assembly structures, chapters are providing a channel for community concerns, analyses, and aspirations because they are accepted as key players at the district level and as part of the executive committees of the district assemblies.

LESSONS LEARNED

As a success story, MEJN's experience holds important lessons for other CSOs involved in social accountability initiatives: the importance of evidence-based advocacy, the value of constructive criticism, the need to maintain good rapport with parliament, the value of strategic alliances, the priority of capacity-building training, and the need for ongoing media advocacy on the budget.

Importance of evidence-based advocacy. MEJN's success is attributed largely to evidence-based advocacy, as seen in the dissemination of the research reports, the SDSS, and budget analyses—all of which call for evidence-based policy making by all stakeholders, especially the government. Prominent stakeholders, including government ministries and members of parliament, have grown to rely on and look forward to these analyses for their own policy decisions. Sustaining these policy briefs and evidence is critical to civil society's influence on policy.

Value of constructive criticism. Constructive criticism that offers alternative solutions and a balanced approach to resolving problems encourages the good working relationship that civil society is eager to nurture with government, parliament, corporate partners, and other stakeholders. This is one of the basic ingredients for cementing trust, earning respect, and gaining a fair hearing.

Maintenance of good rapport with parliament. MEJN has developed a good rapport with members of parliament through the parliamentary committees and parliamentary staff—to the extent that committees and staff even look forward to MEJN's support on national budget and economic governance issues. For example, the parliamentary committee for health asked MEJN to analyze the health sector budget when MHEN was undergoing restructuring to ensure that health issues were not left behind during parliamentary debate. The Budget and Finance Committee also asked for continual in-depth analysis of policy issues to enrich their budgetary debates in parliament.

Value of strategic alliances. The MEJN initiative uses a multisectoral, multistrategic approach of involving a larger number of member organizations and representatives at all levels through the division of labor among networks. This distributed the workload, created broader alliances, and took advantage of the knowledge and skills of more specialized organizations.

Prioritization of training. The demand for budget and economic literacy training is widespread as reflected by the increased demand from districts, faith communities, chiefs, councilors, and other local stakeholders. The general public and members of civil society recognize the MEJN's role in capacity building on economic governance issues and national budgeting processes. MEJN needs to prioritize budget training to groups that can offer higher multiplier effects.

Need for ongoing media advocacy on the budget. MEJN tries to conduct prebudget consultations and ongoing media advocacy with the general public through radio, television, and print media. Radio programs, particularly those on community radio or with large audiences, are good avenues for disseminating and getting feedback from the general public because they promote dialogue. The programs also benefit people who may not have access to the training workshops.

NOTES

1. Information sources for the manual, all referenced and credited therein, include the World Bank's online resources on covering budgets and public spending and additional material from publications by the Commonwealth Secretariat, the International Budget Partnership, the Institute for Democracy in South Africa, the International Monetary Fund, and the Government of Malawi.
2. These are individuals who belong to the MEJN member institutions vested with the responsibility to anchor the BPI and manage the training sessions at the local level.
3. For example, the simplified materials have been used in the Budget Participation Initiative, the Economic Literacy Project, and the Budget Monitoring Project.
4. Vote buying was raised as a concern in the 2004 general elections. The 2009 general elections were hailed as having been peaceful even though the people's vote greatly surprised all the commentators, who had predicted different results.

REFERENCES

Kanyongolo, Edge. 2007. "People, People, The People." *Sunday Times*, Blantyre, Malawi, April 22.

MEJN (Malawi Economic Justice Network). 2003. *Civil Society Budget Training Manual.* Lilongwe, Malawi: MEJN.

———. 2004. *Content-Based 2004 Elections: A Socio-Economic Framework-Civil Society Manifesto.* Lilongwe, Malawi: MEJN. http://www.sarpn.org.za/documents/d0000756/ P846-MEJN_CS_Manifesto.pdf.

———. 2006. "Delivering the Promises: Making Public Services Accessible to the People." MEJN report of Service Delivery Satisfaction Survey III. MEJN, Lilongwe, Malawi. http://www.ansa-africa.net/uploads/documents/publications/Delivering _promises_MEJN_2006.pdf.

———. 2009. *The People's Manifesto: Elections 2009.* Lilongwe, Malawi: MEJN. http:// community.eldis.org/.59c15535/MejnManifesto.pdf.

CHAPTER 6

GENDER-SENSITIVE AND CHILD-FRIENDLY BUDGETING IN ZIMBABWE

Bob Libert Muchabaiwa

This chapter seeks to flag lessons—in terms of context, processes, and results—for possible replication and further learning by policy makers, practitioners, and technocrats on two social accountability initiatives in Zimbabwe: (1) the Child-Friendly National Budget Initiative being coordinated by the National Association of Non Governmental Organisations (NANGO), and (2) the Gender Responsive Budgeting Project by the Zimbabwe Women's Resource Centre and Network (ZWRCN).

NANGO is the umbrella body of nongovernmental organizations (NGOs) operating in Zimbabwe. Over the years, it has become the premier coordination body of more than 1,000 local and international NGOs. Its mission is to create space and identify opportunities for NGOs to pursue their missions and visions and to facilitate the building of members' capacities, resource bases, and synergies. ZWRCN was established in 1990 by a small group of like-minded women who wanted to develop a space dedicated to the collection, analysis, discussion, publication, translation, and distribution of information about the lives of women across Zimbabwe.

Gender-sensitive or child-friendly budgeting does not refer to separate budgets for women or children. Rather, it is an analysis of the government's budget that measures its varying impact on women, men, boys, and girls regardless of religion, political affiliation, ethnicity, social and physical status, or geographical location (Muchabaiwa 2009). Fundamentally, a gender-sensitive budget is about mainstreaming gender issues and ensuring that they are integrated into all national policies, plans, and programs rather than setting women aside as a special interest group.

Broadly classified as independent budget analysis, although recently incorporating aspects of participatory budgeting, both initiatives are based on the right of citizens to participate in development processes—particularly in the allocation and use of national resources—and to demand accountability from the government for its performance. While traditionally the focus was on the supply side of service provision, these recent developments show a trend toward the demand side (Muchabaiwa 2009). Through systematic and participatory methodologies and tools, citizens should be empowered and enabled to demand accountability for delivery of services by state agencies.

For years, budget formulation, implementation and analysis in Zimbabwe have been the preserve of government technocrats under the leadership of the Ministry of Finance. The author of this paper argues that a series of national and local budgets, supposedly informed by national development interests (especially after 2000), failed to achieve economic growth with equity. Hardly any evidence shows that national budgets in Zimbabwe, particularly between 2000 and 2008, address the underlying causes of poverty, marginalization, and exploitation or the needs of vulnerable groups, particularly women and children.

Civil society interest in budget analysis and advocacy arose from the need for more diagnosis and prognosis of the development challenges bedeviling the country. The budget analysis and advocacy work by NANGO and ZWRCN since 2002 was therefore, in the same vein, not only an attempt to find lasting solutions to structural causes of poverty but also, and equally important, an attempt to institute mechanisms of holding the government accountable for its policies and actions. The conceptualization, design, and implementation of NANGO's and ZWRCN's interventions are inspired by the key principles of participation, empowerment, fairness, equality, transparency, and accountability.

GOVERNMENT, POVERTY, AND BUDGETS IN ZIMBABWE

Zimbabwe is a constitutional democracy with a multiparty parliament. The country is currently presided over by a Government of National Unity that was birthed through the Southern Africa Development Community (SADC)-brokered Global Political Agreement signed by the three main political parties—the Zimbabwe African National Union Patriotic Front (ZANU PF) and the two Movement for Democratic Change (MDC) formations—after nearly a decade of political stalemate, economic regression, and deepening poverty.

Although there is some semblance of economic stabilization after the formation of the Government of National Unity, the nation is still entrenched in a political stalemate, torn by poor economic performance, and reeling from the effects of regional and international isolation. The country is therefore enmeshed in multifaceted and multilayered problems on all fronts—social, economic, and political—that render most of the people, particularly women and children, vulnerable and destitute.

The Governmental and Legal Environment for NGOs

NANGO contends that the operating environment for NGOs remains hostile as the government continues to exert control through a combination of restrictive measures and political interference. Suspicion and mistrust is still entrenched between NGOs and the government (NANGO 2009b). There is continuous harassment of human rights defenders alongside deliberate efforts to curtail civic activities. The political environment has remained highly polarized and paranoid as the major political parties, the ruling ZANU PF, and the opposition MDC jostle for power. Fear is still the order of the day (NANGO 2009b).

NANGO further argues that the legal environment, cited by many civil society organizations (CSOs) as a major threat to their operations, has invariably remained disabling. Notable cases include the widely discredited Public Order and Security Act, Access to Information and Protection of Privacy Act, and the Miscellaneous Offences Act. It has become increasingly difficult for citizens to freely assemble, associate, and express themselves in the face of such restrictive laws (NANGO 2009a). For example, the Public Order and Security Act requires that every gathering or public meeting first be cleared by the police.

State of the Economy and Poverty

Economically, budget deficits, shortages of foreign currency, depressed productivity, unemployment, and corruption have become commonplace. In the 10 years between 1997 and 2007, cumulative inflation reached nearly 3.8 billion percent, and the living standards of Zimbabweans fell by 38 percent (Hanke 2008).

The 1995 Poverty Assessment Study indicated that in 2002, 69 percent of the Zimbabwean population was living below the poverty line (Government of Zimbabwe 2003). As the economy collapsed, poverty deepened. For instance, the 2002 National Nutrition Assessment Study estimated that 11 percent of the children in urban areas and 26.5 percent of children in rural areas were malnourished. Meanwhile, the Government of Zimbabwe National Action Plan for Orphans and Other Vulnerable Children (2006) estimated that there are approximately 780,000 AIDS orphans in Zimbabwe. The Joint United Nations Programme on HIV/AIDS (UNAIDS) reports that approximately 2,500 people die of AIDS per week (Government of Zimbabwe 2004).

Slow Progress toward Participatory Budgeting

The political and macroeconomic challenges characterizing the political economy of Zimbabwe, particularly since 1999, therefore have imposed significant financial pressure on households and on the nation as a whole, making budgeting difficult.

Since 1991, when parliament ratified the Convention on the Elimination of Discrimination against Women (CEDAW), progress toward achieving national gender benchmarks has been painfully slow. Parliament remains a patriarchal institution; fewer than 20 percent of its members are women, falling below the SADC target of at least 30 percent.

In 2002, however, CSOs seized the opening up of the multiparty parliament to the public, through the portfolio system, as an opportunity to influence the budgeting process in favor of women, children, and the poor majority. Through public hearings, policy makers can elicit oral evidence from citizens and civil society to inform budgeting. Through these reforms, the budget-making process has become more participatory to improve government accountability and responsiveness by making public budgets more transparent (Muchabaiwa 2007).

BUDGET INITIATIVES FOR WOMEN AND CHILDREN

The Child-Friendly National Budget Initiative (CFNBI) and Gender Responsive Budgeting Project (GRBP) are based on the premise that the national budget is a vital social accountability tool to advance human development, spur administrative reform, and truly measure the state's commitment to women and children. Through the budget, policy makers can facilitate the fair redistribution of national income in a way that fosters both economic growth and equity. Both projects were precipitated by slow progress in achieving women's and children's rights even though Zimbabwe was a signatory to a set of international conventions, including CEDAW and the United Nations Convention on the Rights of the Child.

A series of consultative workshops and studies on the situation of women and children, conducted separately by ZWRCN and NANGO, revealed inequalities, inequities, and injustices affecting women, men, boys, and girls in resource allocation, distribution, and use. Children's and women's concerns, needs, and perspectives were missing not only from the public avenues that inform how national public resources are allocated and spent but also from the discourse around the national budget itself. Not surprisingly, therefore, the national budget was not responsive enough to the needs and expectations of women and children. CFNBI and GRBP were born as civil society responses to this glaring reality. Their objectives are as follows:

- Increase citizens', policy makers', and budget makers' understanding, through economic research, of the effects of budgets and socioeconomic policies on women, men, girls, and boys
- Influence policies in favor of child-responsive and gender-sensitive budgeting
- Influence resource allocation and use for the benefit of women and children
- Develop the capacity of women and children, policy makers, and other stakeholders to be effectively involved in budgeting processes

The Gender Responsive Budgeting Project (GRBP)

ZWRCN began developing the GRBP in 2001 as a follow-up to a study on the extent to which economic policies and national budgets were responsive to the needs and expectations of women (ZWRCN 2002a). The study revealed painful gender-related disparities in national resource allocation, distribution, and use. The slow progress in achieving women's social, economic, and political rights was largely the result of how national resources are allocated. The study further showed that women's gains are being eroded primarily in three areas: access to education, social protection (including unpaid care), and health.

Another study on unpaid-care work, conducted by ZWRCN, observed that women's contributions to the care economy remain unaccounted for and uncounted (ZWRCN 2003). Following the study on unpaid-care work, ZWRCN launched a workshop series to advocate for the recognition of unpaid-care work in collaboration with women; other women's organizations; home-based care (HBC) organizations; and policy makers, including parliamentarians, parliamentary portfolio committees, sector ministries, and other stakeholders. One session, a capacity-building workshop, targeted women's organizations involved in HBC in collaboration with the United Nations Development Fund for Women (UNIFEM), which had been working in three other SADC countries.

To follow up the study about unpaid-care work, ZWRCN decided to strengthen women's understanding of unpaid-care work and to build the capacity of women leaders and organizations to lobby for the recognition of women's contributions to the economy. Other workshops were held to train policy makers about care work and its impact on women. This led to debate in parliament about care work and ways to lessen the burden on women. ZWRCN later broadened the scope of its work to influence economic policies and budgets in favor of women. In 2003, ZWRCN developed the Shadow Gender Budget Statement in consultation with women's organizations, UNIFEM, grassroots women, and other stakeholders about what they would like to see in a gender-sensitive budget. The statement was a position paper outlining the budgetary demands of women and focusing on social sectors. It formed the basis for lobbying and advocacy in the early days of the project.[1]

ZWRCN focuses primarily on women in rural areas—among the poorest and most marginalized of Zimbabweans—to help them articulate their concerns to policy makers. Outreach to women in Harare, the capital city, is achieved primarily through monthly Gender and Development discussions about topical gender-related issues, as well as through the ZWRCN Documentation Centre, which disseminates information on gender and development issues.

Since its inception, the GRBP has consistently provided a gender-responsive perspective on each year's budget (based on its wide-scale consultations with grassroots women) and independent budget analysis, sometimes with the help of consultants.

The Child-Friendly National Budget Initiative (CFNBI)

CFNBI, coordinated by NANGO, is a child rights–centered idea conceived in 1999 as a partnership project of nine child-focused organizations in Zimbabwe, including Save the Children Norway and UNICEF. The initiative began in 2000 after the production of a comprehensive research report that focused on the situation of children in Zimbabwe (Save the Children Norway Zimbabwe 2000). The report showed how children's rights could be more effectively upheld by changing national budget expenditure patterns in social sectors such as education, health, and general child welfare, including the effects of HIV and AIDS. The report—widely distributed among government ministries, local government bodies, parliament, and child-focused organizations—included the following recommendations:

- Improve government macroeconomic policies to generate resources to benefit children.
- Design mechanisms to protect children from economic hardships and the humanitarian crisis.
- Democratize the budget formulation process.
- Restructure the budget with greater allocations for social sectors to improve children's welfare.

CFNBI seeks to benefit and involve children from rural and urban areas and all social classes. In recent years, the project has focused on orphans and other vulnerable children (OVC). The CFNBI principles of inclusion, participation, equity, and equality have ensured that the issues it has raised with, and for, children and young people reflect all of their concerns, regardless of whether they are orphaned, living with HIV and AIDS, have disabilities, are from rural or urban areas, or are living on the street.

Participatory Budgeting and Independent Budget Analysis in Both Initiatives

The ZWRCN and NANGO interventions seek to catalyze women's and children's involvement in analyzing and influencing local and national budgets, thus helping to make those budgets responsive to the needs of women and children. Both initiatives also significantly contribute to the democratization of budgeting processes, transparency, and accountability in the allocation and use of local and national resources.

The initiatives place special emphasis on independent budget analysis, to be done by children and women themselves, the results of which are used to influence future budgets. Over the years, the approach has also shifted toward increased representation of women and children in public hearings to give oral and written evidence to policy makers and budget makers. The submissions outline the situation on the ground as it relates to women and children. They identify priority budget issues and specific fiscal recommendations to achieve gender-sensitive and child-friendly budgeting.

Noting that parliament has limited research capacity, ZWRCN and NANGO contribute to parliament's oversight role by providing research and budget analysis from gender-related and children's perspectives. The GRBP helps the government to close the gender gap and ensure that public money is spent more effectively. It helps to improve compliance with international conventions and to promote transparency and accountability to people, especially women, who are generally more marginalized than men in decision making about public money.

To ensure ownership of the program, stakeholders from multiple areas are involved in the projects, including people at the grassroots level who are represented by community-based organizations (CBOs) and NGOs in both the women's movement and the child welfare sector. Women in decision-making positions in government; policy makers (from the parliamentary portfolio committees and women's parliamentary caucus); regional organizations[2] working on gender-sensitive and child-friendly budgeting as well as economic policy advocacy; academic institutions (particularly the University of Zimbabwe); and other research institutions are involved. These research institutions complement NANGO and ZWRCN by strengthening their capacities to collect and analyze data relating to budget work.

Both initiatives derive legitimacy from the consistent and inclusive involvement of women, children, civil society, central and local government officials, and parliamentarians in analyzing and influencing fiscal policies and budgets in favor of women and children. The value of the two initiatives lies in their potential to democratize budgeting processes, make budgets more responsive to issues affecting women and children, and to hold state and nonstate actors to account for their decisions and actions.

STRATEGIES, METHODOLOGIES, AND TOOLS

The CFNBI and the GRBP employ similar strategies, methodologies, and tools. The main strategies are action-oriented research, independent (and usually participatory) budget analysis, lobbying and advocacy (including information dissemination and media liaison), capacity development, and stakeholder participation and partnership development. Each strategy is characterized by distinct methodologies and tools that collectively explain the success of the two initiatives. This section provides a detailed description of each of the main strategies as well as the methodologies and tools that each strategy uses.

Action-Oriented Research

For assurance that lobbying and advocacy issues are relevant and that there is baseline information to assess the impact of the initiatives, periodic research is conducted. This research takes various forms with different objectives, as described below.

Situation analyses and impact assessments. These are usually conducted on selected subjects to ascertain the status of women or children to measure realization of rights or the long-term impact of projects. These usually take the form of surveys or desk studies from work done by research institutions such as the Central Statistical Office.

Multistakeholder consultative workshops. These bring together project beneficiaries (mainly women and children), policy makers and budget makers, CSOs, research and academic institutions, local leaders (mostly chiefs and councilors), and private companies. Facilitated by NANGO and ZWRCN, the workshops are conducted at the national, provincial, and district levels. These consultations aim to elicit the views and expectations of this broad array of stakeholders with regard to gender-sensitive and child-friendly budgeting.

Focus group discussions with women and children. To help women or children to speak up (especially those from remote areas or in vulnerable circumstances who are easily intimidated by men or adults, respectively), focus group discussions are held with similar objectives as those listed above. The results of these discussions, along with other research findings, are used to prepare reports to inform the policies and budgets of key government ministries (particularly the Ministries of Finance and Economic Development; Health and Child Welfare; Education, Sports, and Culture; Higher and Tertiary Education; Youth Development; Gender and Employment Creation; Public Service, Labour and Social Welfare; and

Agriculture). The discussions also provide background information for the development of training materials for budget and economic literacy workshops.

Rapid assessments. If there are limited resources but urgent issues to be addressed, useful information and statistics pertaining to women and children can be obtained through rapid assessments. These assessments use short questionnaires, focus groups discussions, and literature reviews. An example of this type of research is the 2004 Rapid Assessment of Gaps and Opportunities in Service Delivery to Orphans and Vulnerable Children by NANGO; UNICEF; and the Ministry of Public Service, Labour and Social Welfare (UNICEF and others 2004).

Independent Budget Analysis

The essence of budget analysis—whose results are shared with policy makers, government officials, and other stakeholders—is to identify gaps and opportunities in local and national budgets to improve the situation of women and children in Zimbabwe. The analysis is done independently of government, hence the term "independent budget analysis." While such analyses traditionally are done by consultants and economic experts, the recent trend is toward participatory analysis (Muchabaiwa 2009). Consultants and experts then play the role of facilitators. The effect has been the demystification of the budgeting process. Analysis by ZWRCN and NANGO has the three distinct components listed below.

1. *Policy and program analysis* entails the analysis of policies, laws, and programs aimed at benefiting women and children from a rights-based perspective. The motivation is to ensure that budgets reflecting women's and children's priorities remain consistent with society's choices and in line with sustainable and growth-oriented economic and fiscal policies and strategies. The fundamental questions are which policies, strategies, or programs informed a given budget and whether they reflect the aspirations, needs, and experiences of (different classes of) women and children.
2. *Budget inputs, outputs, and outcome analysis* involves detailed analysis of resource allocations (budget inputs), including prioritization, adequacy, equity, efficiency, effectiveness, and results. This analysis explores the link between inputs and outcomes of budgets. Other issues include trend analysis of resource allocations and an analysis of service delivery

bottlenecks. The fundamental questions are how much has been allocated to programs or activities targeting various categories of women, men, boys, and girls, and whether the allocations have adequately taken into account their different vulnerabilities, needs, and stages of development. It is important to know who ultimately benefits from a given budget and whether there are gender-related or other forms of discrimination in the allocation, distribution, and use of resources.

3. *Budget process analysis* looks at how budgets are developed and implemented. Issues include levels of citizen participation (especially women's and children's), transparency, and accountability. The fundamental questions are who was involved, why, and at what stages in the formulation and implementation of a given budget.

Each year, the independent budget analysis produces position papers, which are then used as lobbying tools. To influence the allocations, the analysis is done before the national budget is crafted and after the budget statements have been presented. Post-budget analysis workshops— attended by grassroots-based CSOs representing women and children, budget makers, the media, and academic and research institutions—have become common. Post-budget analysis workshops help to identify, plan, and implement additional action-oriented research and advocacy activities. Parliamentarians, policy makers, and budget makers within the government are invited to participate so that they hear for themselves the undiluted views of women and children.

Lobbying and Advocacy

The CFNBI and the GRBP employ various strategies to lobby for and advocate child-responsive and gender-sensitive budgeting, using information from independent budget analysis and situation analysis reports. The following paragraphs describe the specific strategies employed.

Dissemination of research findings. Research findings are shared with parliamentarians, government officials, the media, the private sector, NGOs, and the general public to influence policies, resource allocations, and resource use. Dissemination is done through meetings and workshops; promotional material such as posters and flyers; press releases and newspaper supplements; and circulation of documents through electronic newsletters, mail, and other means.

The lobbying work relies heavily on, and is strengthened by, findings from research carried out by other organizations, particularly CSOs. For example, CFNBI used the following two research reports: (a) "The Situation of Children Living in Institutions" (ZNCWC 2004)[3] and (b) the "Basic Education Assistance Module Evaluation," conducted jointly with the Ministry of Education, Sports and Culture and the Ministry of Public Service, Labour and Social Welfare, in cooperation with the World Bank (Government of Zimbabwe 2004).

In 2006, NANGO-sponsored research, "Trends on the Level and Impact of Budgetary Allocations to Orphans and Other Vulnerable Children in Zimbabwe," influenced the 2007 national budget (Muchabaiwa 2007). The research made a strong case for the Ministry of Finance to prioritize OVC issues in the national budget by laying bare the statistics on education, health, food, and access to justice. As a result, the 2007 budget statement acknowledged the need to mobilize more resources for OVC protection and care (Muchabaiwa 2007).

Mass mobilization and coalition building. NANGO and ZWRCN make deliberate efforts to mobilize various stakeholders—especially CSOs, women, children and young people, academia, and churches—to come together and form strong coalitions for child-responsive and gender-sensitive budgeting. Coalition members further sensitize and involve their constituencies and also lobby public officials with whom they work. Ideas are shared on how stakeholders can better participate in monitoring the national budget.

Both initiatives value the critical role that communities can play in holding the state to account for its decisions and actions. To tap this vital resource, communities are mobilized to participate in the discourse on budgetary matters, both before and after budget formation, through meetings and workshops on the community and district levels. These meetings provide space for women, children, and the broader civil society to highlight budgetary priorities and raise concerns on past budgets and processes. That the two organizations have decentralized their operations is an indicator of the effort to mobilize grassroots organizations to participate in budgeting processes. This effort is complemented by public dialogues and debates about the ways in which allocations of national resources should prioritize women and children.

Engagement of policy and budget makers. In lobbying and advocacy, the support of policy makers and relevant government officials is critical. Both NANGO and ZWRCN make oral and written submissions and hold meetings with government officials and policy makers to share specific recommendations on issues that will make the national budget more responsive to the challenges facing women and children. This interaction has helped develop the mutual confidence and trust necessary for effective lobbying. As a result, the two organizations, by virtue of being active in budgeting issues and as officially recognized umbrella bodies, are always consulted by parliamentarians and line ministries. NANGO's and ZWRCN's relations with parliament and government officials developed organically and have matured over the years through sustained dialogue. The trust and cooperation between the government and NANGO and ZWRCN can be attributed to several factors, especially that children's issues are not perceived as political and that both organizations have remained objective and nonpartisan in their advocacy work.

All research reports and position papers are shared with parliamentarians and government officials. NANGO and ZWRCN have received several letters from parliamentarians and ministries acknowledging the two organizations' valuable contributions in promoting the rights and welfare of women and children. ZWRCN, for example, facilitates prebudget advocacy visits to parliament and portfolio committees by representatives of grassroots women's and men's organizations. This gives communities the opportunity to meet directly with members of parliament and to express their concerns about the budget.

Community-level capacity development in budget analysis. A key advocacy strategy is to organize and hold workshops with stakeholders at the local levels to develop their capacity for budget analysis and advocacy and to demystify the budget. For NANGO, these workshops have been held in more than 12 districts, while ZWRCN has concentrated its efforts in 6 other districts and Harare.

The workshops are designed to build consensus and sensitize local authorities to how they can help in the formulation of child-friendly and gender-sensitive budgets. This is in line with the decentralization thrust of the government of Zimbabwe. Members of parliament, ministers, senior government officials, and chiefs have often participated in the workshops and fully support the need for child-responsive and gender-sensitive budgeting (NANGO 2006). The CFNBI and the GRBP continue to receive numerous requests from different districts to hold these workshops.

Documentation and dissemination. Information collection, analysis, collation, and dissemination have proved to be integral components of communication and advocacy. Considerable time is spent on packaging research reports into reader-friendly flyers, newsletters, posters, and news articles. Several research reports, position papers, brochures, pamphlets, banners, and posters giving background information on the budget and encouraging popular participation in the debate have been produced and circulated to stakeholders. This information is used by policy makers and budget makers, parliamentary portfolio committees, researchers, CSOs, relevant government departments such as the Zimbabwe Revenue Authority, and individual citizens.

Media campaigns. Both initiatives recognize the power of the media in influencing society's perception of reality. Therefore, the initiatives use the media (both print and electronic) to campaign for adequate allocation and distribution of national resources to benefit women and children. Both initiatives produce press statements, news bulletins, and television programs—all of which carry strong messages for policy makers to put children first and mainstream gender when formulating national budgets. Media practitioners have become a common feature at budget workshops organized by NANGO and ZWRCN.

ZWRCN contends, however, that an ongoing challenge is that the Zimbabwe media often report in a gender-biased way, frequently sensationalizing and portraying women in a negative manner. Efforts have been made to collaborate with organizations such as the Federation of African Media Women in Zimbabwe and the Media Institute of Southern Africa to discuss gender-sensitive reporting and to train children and women's organizations on how to work with the media. One avenue might be to mainstream gender-related concerns into the curriculum of media studies.[4]

Exhibitions and other public events. A final basic lobbying and advocacy strategy is to participate in public relations activities such as the NGO Exposition, trade and book fairs, and agricultural shows. Such events help raise public awareness and mobilize support on advocacy issues.

Capacity Development

One sustainable way of influencing budgeting processes is through comprehensive capacity-development programs that enhance understanding and appreciation of the role and importance of budgets. NANGO's and ZWRCN's capacity-development programs include budget literacy and analysis training workshops that use a "trainer of trainers" approach; participants are expected to pass along the skills they learn to other people.

The organizations also use "non-training" capacity-building methodologies, including training manuals, information, and education material that government officials, civil society, and other development actors can use independently.

In addition, workshops are conducted for the public and for members of parliament, the Women's Parliamentary Caucus, and government policy makers. ZWRCN has developed testing and training materials in economic literacy for use by policy makers and budget makers (on the supply side) and for citizens and CSOs (on the demand side).

Stakeholder Participation and Partnership Development

Broad stakeholder participation strengthens the voice and capacity of communities, especially as women and children become involved in issues that affect them and learn to demand responsiveness and accountability from public officials. To ensure that the debate on the national budget reaches a wider audience, the initiatives have adopted a decentralized, community-level approach. This approach has seen women, children (see box 6.1), traditional chiefs, local authorities, provincial governors, and senior citizens actively contribute to budget debates and raise concerns that need to be addressed through the budget. Some primary methods of ensuring the participation of various stakeholders are workshops, meetings, and opinion-seeking sessions. Through these forums, ideas are solicited on how public and private expenditures can better promote the interests of women and children (Muchabaiwa 2009).

To derive strength and comparative advantage in partnership and coalition approaches, ZWRCN has developed a strong base of women researchers and activists who understand economic theory, which allows them to question and change the status quo while developing the capacity of those men who inform the economic decision-making process to do so from a gender-sensitive perspective.

Box 6.1 Children's Participation in Budgeting Processes

NANGO values children's participation as both a means and an end in its work, and it encourages and enables children to make their views known on issues that affect them. Put into practice, participation entails listening to children in all their varied ways of communicating. Participation ensures their freedom to express themselves and takes their views into account when making decisions that affect them. Engaging children in dialogue and exchange allows them to learn constructive ways of influencing the world around them. Children's participation, therefore, must be authentic and meaningful—starting with children and young people themselves, on their own terms, within their own realities, and in pursuit of their own visions, dreams, hopes, and concerns.

NANGO, through the CFNBI, facilitated the establishment of different Children's Clubs, run by children. The Children's Club in Bulawayo held a Children's Convention in May 2004 to promote dialogue with policy makers in the province on budgetary matters. The Chitungwiza Junior Council, through support from the CFNBI, held a Children's Gala, which the local member of parliament attended, to sensitize other children on how budgets could be used to alleviate child poverty.

The media also have proven to be crucial partners and instrumental tools in championing children's concerns and priorities. Through collaboration with the IN-TV Citizen Child program, children have participated in the budgeting process by airing their views about national resource allocation on national television and radio. (IN-TV is a Zimbabwean production company whose primary objective is to ensure children's participation in development activities through radio and television).

In a landmark achievement, with NANGO's help, children from all over Zimbabwe formed the Zimbabwe Child and Youth Budget Network (Z-CYBN) to find ways of enhancing their participation in budgeting processes. Z-CYBN got its start at a CFNBI-organized capacity-building workshop, held in April 2006 in Harare, for child legislators and other child-led groups. Z-CYBN was born out of the realization that even though children and young people have the potential to influence development processes that affect them, there was no effective child and youth participation in budgeting processes. Although children have been actively participating in issues such as HIV and AIDS campaigns, reproductive health discussions, talent shows, and other such activities, their views were not being deliberately and adequately sought and captured in policy and budget processes. Z-CYBN seeks to address this gap by giving voice, space, and capacities for all young people to participate meaningfully in budgeting processes.

In 2006 the Z-CYBN held a National Children's Conference on the Budget attended by the speaker of parliament, the UNICEF country representative, the director of budgets within the Ministry of Finance, and the Save the Children Norway country director, among other distinguished delegates. Children continue to actively engage policy makers and budget makers on issues that affect them. With support from the CFNBI, children are developing and implementing annual plans informed by their strategic plan.

Source: NANGO 2006.

Similarly NANGO, to augment the already diverse founding members of the CFNBI, is working with research institutions—primarily the Institute of Development Studies, the National AIDS Council, the National Action Plan for Orphans and other Vulnerable Children, UNICEF, and many other local and international children's rights organizations—to influence policies and budgets in favor of children (NANGO 2006).

In rolling out their strategies, both NANGO and ZWRCN collaborate and network with several governmental and nongovernmental organizations. Strategic partnerships have been developed with grassroots organizations, parliamentary portfolio committees, research institutions, and the media. Ultimately, the sustainability of the CFNBI and the GRBP resides partly in the capacity developed in local and national state and nonstate actors who have the potential to carry forward NANGO's and ZWRCN's work. To broaden the scope and depth of participation in the GRBP, gender is presented as a cross-cutting economic justice and rights issue that can be the subject for engagement across a wide range of sectors.

Networks have been formed with organizations such as the Zimbabwe Coalition on Debt and Development, Practical Action, the Zimbabwe National Chamber of Commerce, the Confederation of Zimbabwe Industries, and many others. These networks have proved valuable, especially in consultations with portfolio committees, by enriching position papers through the diversity of coalition members. For example, in 2002, ZWRCN held a meeting with organizations working on economic justice. The outcome of this meeting was the formation of a Gender and Economic Justice Network to carry out a number of empowerment projects for women (ZWRCN 2002b).

RESULTS AND IMPACTS

Although the initiatives continue, ZWRCN and NANGO have already made some notable impacts. By emphasizing the need for equitable distribution of resources, they have highlighted debate around these crucial issues. Both organizations have built expertise in reading and analyzing budgets from a gender-sensitive and child-friendly perspective among national legislators, local government officials, CSOs, and other development practitioners. The results of the two initiatives can be categorized as increased transparency, accountability, and decentralization in policy making and budgeting processes; increased budget allocations;

expanded participation and coalition building; and improved policies
(NANGO 2007).

Increased Transparency and Accountability

The ultimate aim of most social accountability initiatives is to increase
transparency and accountability throughout the budget life cycle if budgets are to be responsive to people—in this case, to women and children.
Gradually, the budget process is becoming more transparent with the
increased involvement of women, children, and civil society.

A classic example is the government's new policy to publish financial
statements on how the National AIDS Trust Fund is used. It is now common for a newspaper to run a full-page list of quarterly beneficiaries of these
funds. During 2002 and 2003, NANGO, ZWRCN, and other AIDS service organizations mounted a strong campaign for increased transparency in
the distribution and use of resources set aside for HIV and AIDS.

The CFNBI and GRBP initiatives also strengthened the national and
local budgetary processes by identifying important weaknesses in procedures, such as the need to ensure that the budgeting process responds to
the policy framework, to provide clear guidance on implementation, and
for the budgeting process to feed information into the policy process so
that resource constraints can be assessed. Other outcomes of the two initiatives include the following:

- Improvement in the quality of parliamentary debates on gender and
  public finance
- Increased participation of women and children in budget making, decision making, and economic policy formulation
- Institutionalization of gender-sensitive budgeting in the Ministry of
  Finance and Economic Development through establishment of a gender focal person who, among other responsibilities, would assess the
  degree to which bids from line ministries will be gender-sensitive
- Increased ability of parliament, women, and men to track and monitor
  government expenditure to ensure accountability. Budget tracking,
  though at a nascent stage, has been done with the help of consultants. For
  example, a 2004 evaluation of the Basic Education Assistance Module
  (BEAM) was an attempt to find out whether resources allocated for educational assistance, as a social protection strategy, actually reach the
  intended beneficiaries.

Decentralization and Democratization of Budget Debates

The continued demand by women's and children's organizations (under CFNBI and GRBP) to participate in issues that affect them has resulted in the budgeting process being reviewed and democratized to ensure that different stakeholders take part in the process and that fiscal discipline is exercised. One example is the establishment of parliamentary portfolio committees, including the budget committee that reviews submissions of line ministries and stakeholders on policy issues and allocations.

While parliament and government ministries have discussed budget issues in major cities at best, the CFNBI and GRBP successfully piloted the decentralization of budget debates to both urban and rural communities. District consultative workshops have been held in more than 15 districts in Zimbabwe. These district workshops are the first of their kind to facilitate public debate on the national budget and have been hailed by local authorities as a landmark achievement in empowering communities to participate in the budgeting process. Some districts have set up children's forums and committees to stimulate community interest.

Increases in Budgetary Allocations

One of the direct results of the consistent and robust advocacy under the CFNBI and GRBP has been the steady increase in budget allocations for issues that benefit women or children directly. These allocations indicate greater prioritization of children's and women's issues in the national budget. In some cases, new budget line items were introduced, such as the Children in Difficult Circumstances line item under the Ministry of Public Service, Labour and Social Welfare. The following issues, as reflected by corresponding increases in budgetary allocations, also resulted directly from the CFNBI and GRBP (NANGO 2007):

- Increased focus on orphans and other vulnerable children, as shown by a nearly 50 percent increase in budget line items such as BEAM, Children in Difficult Circumstances, public assistance, and other social protection programs as a percentage of the total national budget
- Gender and HIV/AIDS mainstreaming within government, including setting aside resources for gender focal persons and gender awareness campaigns

- Increased attention to child sexual abuse and domestic violence, which affects mainly girls and women. Efforts by ZWRCN in partnership with other women's organizations resulted in enactment of the Domestic Violence Bill in 2007.

ZWRCN is now advocating a quota system in sector ministries, obligating them to allocate a certain percentage of their budgets to gender-sensitive programs, although not much progress has been achieved so far.

Capacity Development of Parliament, Civil Society, and Citizens

The CFNBI and GRBP have strengthened parliament's role in shaping budget priorities and holding sector ministries accountable. Members of parliament now use research findings to highlight gaps and opportunities in budgets to help achieve women's and children's rights. The members obtain this information through the capacity-building workshops held before and after the budgeting process.

Transparency and parliamentary participation in determining public spending have increased. Members of parliament and policy makers have now started debates around gender-sensitive budgeting. At the launch of the National Gender Policy in 2004, a number of members of parliament agreed that this important policy cannot be implemented without being adequately financed and that gender-sensitive budgeting is the core issue in the whole discussion surrounding gender equity (ZWRCN 2004).

Moreover, the budget is being demystified for ordinary women and men through the budget and economic literacy training workshops. Women and children can now use economic terms and concepts with confidence. One example is the ability of women to now understand the annual budget statement and budget estimates. As a result of economic and budget literacy training, a strong cadre of women and children has been created who can effectively articulate their concerns to policy makers. A prime example is the formation of Z-CYBN under the banner of the CFNBI and its plans to embark not only on participatory independent budget analysis but also on expenditure tracking. In response to these efforts, a number of portfolio committees are now recognizing the importance of gender equality and empowerment.

Policy Improvements

On the policy front, achievements include the following:

- Introduction of the Public Finance Management System to manage expenditures as a result of the call for fiscal discipline through effective monitoring of government budgets
- Elevation of early-childhood (preschool) education to formal status by the Ministry of Education, Sports, and Culture, thus making preschool education an integral part of primary-level education
- Decentralization of the registration of births and issuance of certificates to assist orphans and other vulnerable children (OVC)
- Review of taxation policies with a view to lowering the value added tax on sanitary pads

KEY PROBLEMS AND CHALLENGES

Although the CFNBI and the GRBP have made great strides in spearheading budget discourse in Zimbabwe, they continue to face several challenges.

Contentious Government-Civil Society Relations

Increasingly, the political context under which most NGOs operate makes advocacy work difficult, all the more so because Zimbabwe is in election mode every two or three years. The acrimonious, often intolerant relations between the two main political parties mean that NGOs (most of them viewed as "opposition NGOs" by the government) must tread carefully.

These tensions could also mean tighter scrutiny of NGO activities by local authorities and ruling party activists eager to ensure that the opposition party does not reach the rural electorate through NGO programs. Already, NGOs are often denied entry into most rural areas and spend much time and money seeking clearance for projects from the local authorities (NANGO 2009a). For example, it took ZWRCN eight months to get approval to conduct the GRBP in Rusape, thereby affecting reporting and program implementation. Legislation restricting NGOs—such as the Public Order and Security Act, the Access to Information and Protection of Privacy Act (AIPPA), and the NGO Bill that the president of Zimbabwe refused to sign in 2005—also creates a legally challenging environment. As of this writing, the old Private Voluntary Organizations Act is still the law governing NGOs.

The strategies and methodologies employed by ZWRCN and NANGO have sometimes not been well received by the government. Although there is overall cooperation between the government and child-focused organizations (at least relative to organizations whose core business is human rights, democracy, and governance), some lobbying and advocacy efforts are perceived as confrontational. The government has castigated some revealing research and position papers as representative of the views of western countries bent on effecting regime change in Zimbabwe, especially when the papers expose corruption and malfeasance (NANGO 2007).

Limited Information Availability and Accessibility

Gender-disaggregated statistics are scarce in Zimbabwe, making advocacy work difficult because there is little data to substantiate the work. It is therefore important to ensure that information is as disaggregated as possible. Disaggregated data would make it easier to report factually on the implications of policies and programs for women, men, boys, and girls.

In addition, the suspicion and mistrust between NGOs and government make it difficult for the latter to take advantage of crucial information, especially relating to expenditures (NANGO 2009b). The government's fear is that NGOs may use this information, should anomalies be found, to expose or discredit it. AIPPA has failed to facilitate free access to information on revenue and expenditure issues (NANGO 2009b).

Limited Role and Capacity of Parliament

Parliament continues to redefine its role and responsibilities, particularly its oversight function. Unfortunately, in many instances, the voices of reason are too few and often sacrificed for political expediency. Members of parliament have no choice but to rally behind the position of their party, especially now given the deepening polarization.

Parliament's somewhat irregular sitting calendar also makes it difficult to set meetings and appointments. Last-minute changes or cancellations were an irksome feature of the 2005–08 period, not just for ZWRCN but also for other civil society groups. The growing power of the executive further limits the extent to which parliament can fulfill its constitutional mandate to represent the public interest in scrutinizing policies and demanding accountability for expenditures. According to ZWRCN, the diverse skills, capacities, and expertise of members of parliament are therefore underused.[5]

Although parliament tends to rubber-stamp the budget, its oversight role should not be underestimated. Oversight by portfolio committees, which conduct their work through public hearings, must be emphasized because they monitor sector ministries and can hold them accountable. The Committee on Health and Child Welfare stood out as an example of excellence between 2002 and 2008. The main contributory factors include the personalities and background of committee members as well as good leadership. This committee has been able to hold pre- and post-budget analysis workshops every year and successfully advocated increased access to HIV and AIDS treatment. In fact, the entire committee publicly went for HIV and AIDS testing to help break the stigma and reduce discrimination (ZWRCN 2006).

Less positively, the Committee on Youth Development, Gender and Employment Creation is somewhat stagnant and a disappointment to women's groups. This work is hampered by the scarcity of women in decision-making positions in government and in parliament, hence the importance of working with and training such groups as the Parliamentary Women's Caucus.

Economic Decline

Among the other major challenges that the projects face are Zimbabwe's negative economic growth, chronic foreign currency shortage, massive unemployment, corruption, and severe distortions in the economy. The result has been a serious shrinkage in national resources, recurrent budget deficits, and a trend toward supplementary budgets. Apparently, poor economic performance negates all the gains made by CSOs in recent years as Zimbabwe is surviving on a shoestring budget.

Inadequate Civil Society Capacity to Engage in Budget Advocacy

Skilled resources, particularly in the NGO sector, are constantly on the move in Zimbabwe. As a result, NGOs, particularly national and local ones, are continuously training people who then move on, often to mainstream or international organizations. Tracking budget allocations and expenditures is a highly technical and time-consuming exercise that requires specialized personnel, resources, and capacity building.

LESSONS LEARNED

A number of lessons have been learned and recommendations can be drawn from the work of NANGO and ZWRCN that NGOs may find useful:

- NANGO, as the umbrella body of NGOs operating in Zimbabwe, should open up dialogue on government-CSO relations to improve ways of working together.
- Seize the opening up of parliament through the portfolio committee system as an opportunity to provide continuous input into ministry consultations, taking advantage of processes such as the mid-term fiscal and monetary policy reviews to provide input. The Ministry of Finance now often invites stakeholders to make oral and written submissions before and after the formulation of policies and budgets.
- Take advantage of respected organizations, piggybacking on their credibility to make gender and children's concerns heard.
- Make capacity development in budget literacy and analysis an ongoing process feeding into the broad social accountability strategy, not an isolated workshop. This is important so that policy makers and other stakeholders can better internalize the concepts and apply them practically to their sectors.
- Focus on the organizational level, not on individuals, to institutionalize the process and lessons learned so that the project continues if staff changes.
- Lobby for an increase in the number of women in decision-making positions and in parliament as a strategy to push through issues relating to women.

Since the inception of the CFNBI and GRBP, NANGO and ZWRCN have also learned the additional lessons described below concerning the budget advocacy process (NANGO 2006).

Link Budget Analysis to an Advocacy Plan

Independent analysis without efforts to influence policies, attitudes, and actions through communication and advocacy becomes a mere academic

exercise. For NANGO and ZWRCN, budget analysis has a specific purpose: to hold government accountable and to form the basis for policy dialogue and engagement. Therefore, budget analysis must include advocacy
or partnership with advocacy organizations to advance the interests of
women and children.

Improve Information Availability and Accessibility

Budget analysis—by its very nature and its emphasis on policy documents,
budget statements, and other information—makes a strong case for a
national framework that enhances the accessibility and availability of relevant and timely information for comprehensive and objective analysis.
Better information laws can enable this accessibility (Streak 2003).

Build Capacity for Economic Analysis

Budgeting is largely perceived as a technical process requiring economic
analysis acumen. Through systematic capacity development, actors from
both the supply and the demand sides of service provision become better
informed to engage on budget issues. Had it not been for the capacity
development of women, children, and CSOs on the one hand, and legislators and budget makers on the other, meaningful debates on the budget
would have been difficult to achieve. There is a definite need to continuously educate and mobilize communities.

Build Networks, Strategic Alliances, and Coalitions

The diversity and complexity of social accountability initiatives requires
civil society to establish and nurture sustainable partnerships, networks,
and coalitions for lobbying and advocacy. The power of partnerships,
networks, and coalitions lies in their potential to harness greater
resources, information, and knowledge than individual organizations
could achieve alone. With greater numbers comes greater strength.

Use the Media

The media play a critical role in influencing the development agenda by
shaping public opinion. The media can make or break an issue. CSOs
must develop media strategies that enhance outreach to policy makers, citizens, and other stakeholders and capitalize on the opportunities created

by the media. NANGO and ZWRCN successfully used both print and electronic media to influence budgeting processes.

Advocate for Enabling NGO Environment

NGOs' effectiveness depends upon an enabling operating environment supported by the legal and policy framework. The continued blacklisting of NGOs as agents of imperialism and consequent suspicion and mistrust between NGOs and government is unhealthy. For social accountability initiatives to be effective, cordial working relationships for dialogue and engagement are critical.

Institute a Sound Monitoring and Evaluation Framework

Organizations involved in social accountability initiatives should put in place a sound monitoring and evaluation framework supported by a coordinated data collection and knowledge management system. This is crucial to facilitate learning and replication of good practices.

NOTES

1. Interviews with former ZWRCN program officer for the GRBP.
2. The regional organizations include, for example, UNIFEM, the Institute for Democracy in South Africa (IDASA), the African Network on Debt and Development (AFRODAD), and MWENGO (an acronym based on the Kiswahili expression "Mwelekeo waNGO," which translates to the direction or vision of NGOs).
3. The report's author, the Zimbabwe National Council for the Welfare of Children (ZNCWC), is a member of the CFNBI advisory committee.
4. Interview with ZWRCN GRBP staff members.
5. Interview with ZWRCN GRBP staff members.

REFERENCES

Government of Zimbabwe. 2003. "1995 Poverty Assessment Study Survey." Report of survey conducted by the Ministry of Public Service, Labour and Social Welfare, Social Development Fund. Government Printer, Harare.

———. 2004. "Zimbabwe Millennium Development Goals: 2004 Progress Report." Government Printer, Harare.

Government of Zimbabwe; Ministry of Education, Sports and Culture; and Ministry of Public Service, Labour and Social Welfare. 2004. "Basic Education Assistance Module Evaluation." Internal report, Government of Zimbabwe, Harare.

Hanke, Steve H. 2008. "Zimbabwe: From Hyperinflation to Growth." Development Policy Analysis 6, Center for Global Liberty and Prosperity, Cato Institute, Washington, DC. http://www.cato.org/pub_display.php?pub_id=9484.

Muchabaiwa, Bob Libert. 2007. "Trends on the Level and Impact of Budgetary Allocations to Orphans and Other Vulnerable Children in Zimbabwe." Report prepared for the Child-Friendly National Budget Initiative of the National Association of Non-Governmental Organisations (NANGO), Harare.

———. 2009. *Child Friendly Budget Analysis Handbook.* Harare: NANGO.

NANGO (National Association of Non-Governmental Organisations). 2006. "Child Friendly National Budget Initiative: Lessons Learned." Internal report, NANGO, Harare.

———. 2007. "Evaluation Report of the Child Friendly National Budget Initiative." Internal report, NANGO, Harare.

———. 2009a. "Early Warning System." Report for October 2009 to February 2010, NANGO, Harare. http://www.nango.org.zw.

———. 2009b. "Security Scoping Study." Report for NANGO. http://www.nango.org.zw.

Save the Children Norway Zimbabwe. 2000. "Situation of Children in Zimbabwe." Internal report for Save the Children Norway Zimbabwe, Harare.

Streak, Judith. 2003. *Monitoring Government Budgets to Advance Child Rights: A Guide for NGOs.* Cape Town: Institute for Democracy in South Africa.

UNICEF (United Nations Children's Fund), NANGO, and the Zimbabwe Ministry of Public Service, Labour and Social Welfare. 2004. "Rapid Assessment of Gaps and Opportunities in Service Delivery to Orphans and Vulnerable Children." Research report, Harare.

ZNCWC (Zimbabwe National Council for the Welfare of Children). 2004. "The Situation of Children Living in Institutions." Research report for ZNCWC, Harare.

ZWRCN (Zimbabwe Women's Resource Centre and Network). 2002a. "Gender-Based Budgeting Scoping Study." Research report for ZWRCN, Harare.

———. 2002b. "Workshop Report of the National Consultative Workshop on Economic Justice." Unpublished report. Cresta Oasis Hotel, Harare, September 13–15.

———. 2003. "Unpaid Care Work." Research report for ZWRCN, Harare.

———. 2004. "Workshop Report at the Launch of the National Gender Policy." Unpublished report. Crown Plaza Hotel, Harare, October 6.

———. 2006. "Annual Progress Report to Donors and Stakeholders." Annual report for ZWRCN, Harare.

CHAPTER 7

THE NIGERIA EXTRACTIVE INDUSTRIES TRANSPARENCY INITIATIVE AND PUBLISH WHAT YOU PAY NIGERIA

Dauda S. Garuba and John G. Ikubaje

> *The African Union estimates that corruption costs Africa about $148 billion annually or 25 percent of Africa's official GNP. Certainly revenue from extractive industries, which dominates the economy of most African countries, is a major contributor to this monumental and preventable loss. The popular "paradox of poverty in the midst of plenty" is a daily experience in many African countries rich in oil, gas, and minerals. Transparency, accountability, and commitment to democratic deployment of resources can prevent conflicts, waste, and devastation.*

—Olusegun Obasanjo (2006)

> *NEITI is the revenue side of the Obasanjo administration's due process mechanism.*

—Obiageli Ezekwesili (2006)

Contemporary discourse on natural resource governance reveals extremes of wealth and poverty and of power and disempowerment. Ordinarily, countries with abundant natural resources would seem unlikely candidates for poverty and poor economic performance. However, the reality of many resource-rich countries in the developing world is that, because of systemic corruption, highly prized natural resources do not necessarily translate into development.

In Nigeria, corruption facilitated by abundant oil wealth has compromised national development, contaminated the people's morality and values, distorted national planning, and destroyed collective integrity and discipline—just as it has also destroyed the country's foundation of creativity, innovation, competition, and democratic culture (Obasanjo 2006). The result is that Nigeria is worse off today than it was at independence in 1960, when oil did not dominate government revenue. Of more than $400 billion that Nigeria has earned from oil in almost 50 years, it is estimated that $50 billion to $100 billion of the export revenues have been lost through corruption and fraud (Lubeck, Watts, and Lipschutz 2007).

It was the desire to reverse this trend and to ensure that Nigeria's oil wealth and other long-neglected natural resources are managed sustainably that led to the launch of the Nigeria Extractive Industries Transparency Initiative (NEITI) and Publish What You Pay (PWYP) Nigeria in February 2004.[1] NEITI and PWYP Nigeria work in tandem for transparency and accountability in the financial management of the extractive industry. Both initiatives are subsets of the Extractive Industries Transparency Initiative (EITI), the global coalition of governments and civil society organizations (CSOs) that calls for the mandatory disclosure of extractive companies' payments to national governments and governments' receipt of such payments.

NEITI's achievements in the past five years are impressive and have earned Nigeria worldwide recognition for being one of the two countries leading the global EITI. By 2007, NEITI had saved Nigeria about $1 billion. Even so, an estimated 70 percent of Nigeria's oil wealth was stolen or wasted in 2003, a loss that fell to only 40 percent in 2005. The initiative's impact extends beyond the oil and gas sector to other natural resource sectors and to agencies dealing with oil and gas. For its part, PWYP Nigeria has been vital in publicizing NEITI and pushing it forward.

This chapter examines the NEITI and PWYP Nigeria social accountability initiatives and analyzes their achievements and impact, problems and constraints, strategies and approaches, success factors and lessons learned.

CONTEXT AND BACKGROUND OF NEITI AND PWYP NIGERIA

Since independence from the United Kingdom in 1960, Nigeria has had a troubled history of development and governance, arising from the challenge of how to structure and run the country so that all citizens—regardless of ethnic, religious, or cultural identity—see themselves as major stake-holders. This challenge of federalism, often referred to as the "national question," has precipitated repeated state and local government creation (Momoh and Adejumobi 2002). This is evident in the sharp increase in the number of Nigeria's regions—from 3 at independence to the pres-ent-day 36 states—and in the number of local governments, from 131 in 1963 to the current 774.

Nigeria is known to be rich in oil, gas, and mineral resources.[2] However, the rise of oil and gas as the foundation of the modern economy and the sub-stantial rents and revenues they attract have prompted the complete neglect of other natural resources and agriculture, which used to be the mainstay of the country's economy, at least until the early 1970s. Nigeria is estimated to have earned more than \$400 billion in oil exports since 1958. Production has increased from 5,100 barrels per day (bpd) in 1958 to 2.1 million bpd in 2005. The government expects to increase oil production to 4 million bpd, and proven reserves to 40 billion barrels, by 2010. Nigeria also has proven natural gas reserves estimated at 184 trillion cubic feet (International Crisis Group 2006).

Nigeria is a classic example of the "paradox of plenty" that has placed oil wealth distribution at the heart of the country's politics and corrup-tion. The quest to control oil profits has precipitated coups, military dic-tatorship, creation of states and local government councils (all of which have become economically unviable), political ambitions, and election rigging. Despite the huge revenue accruing from oil—estimated to con-stitute 50 percent of gross domestic product, 85 percent of national rev-enue, and 95 percent of foreign exchange—socioeconomic conditions reflect a crisis in resource governance manifested by worsening poverty, unprecedented corruption, and violent conflict (Garuba 2007).

Human development in Nigeria has been at a virtual standstill at best—in a tailspin at worst—as these indicators show:

- Economic growth averaged just 2 percent between 1980 and 2002.
- Real income per capita is only one-third of the level attained in 1980.
- Agricultural and mineral exports are virtually moribund (Lewis 2004).
- The proportion of households surviving on less than the United Nations' dollar-per-day absolute poverty line grew from 27 percent in 1980 to 66 percent in 1996 and to 70 percent in 2006 (International Crisis Group 2006).
- While rural areas have been the most affected, the incidence of poverty in towns and cities has risen from 17 percent to 58 percent.

- Although Nigeria's richest 10 percent controls 40 percent of the country's wealth, the poorest 20 percent shares a paltry 4 percent of the wealth (Christian Aid 2003).
- The global average for malnutrition in children under age 5 is 27 percent; in Nigeria, the rate is 38 percent, and 43 percent of the population lacks access to safe drinking water.
- Nigeria's infant mortality rate remains among the worst in the world (International Crisis Group 2006).
- The country's population has an average life expectancy of 51 years.
- Close to half of Nigeria's population is illiterate.

Development indicators are even more damning in the Niger Delta region where the oil is located, as the following examples show:

- Regional per capita gross national product is below the national average of $280.
- Seventy-two percent of the region's households live below the poverty line.
- Only 27 percent and 30 percent of the region's households have access to safe-drinking water and electricity, respectively, less than the national average (Fayemi 2005; Garuba 2006).
- The ratio of patients per doctor is estimated at 132,600 to 1, more than three times worse than the national average of 39,455 to 1.
- Many areas lack infrastructure, have poor transportation (especially for communities in the riverine arteries), and have inadequate or no medical facilities.
- Primary school enrollment is 30 percent, well below the national average of 76 percent (Fubara 2002).
- The human development index (HDI) is 0.564 (1 being the highest score) relative to other countries with similar oil and gas resources, such as Indonesia (0.697), Kuwait (0.844), Libya (0.799), República Bolivariana de Venezuela (0.722), Saudi Arabia (0.800), and the United Arab Emirates (0.849) (UNDP 2006).
- Environmental degradation and pollution in the region further diminish the quality of life.

Women's roles and representation have been minimal because of inhibiting factors that include deliberate efforts to hold them down (Ibrahim and Salihu 2004). The lack of adequate representation and relegation to minor roles make women the most politically and economically vulnerable and marginalized social group in Nigeria. They can neither be major investors in the extractive industries for lack of financial means, nor continue their small-scale fishing and agricultural activities owing to the devastating environmental impact of large companies, which has crippled their livelihoods. However, the marginal increase of women in public office since 1999 has provided them space to influence public policy in their favor. At the North-Central Road Show on NEITI held in Abuja in May 2006, the chairperson of NEITI, Madam Obiageli Ezekwesili, observed that it is not by coincidence that President Obasanjo appointed women in strategic positions to oversee the country's economy.[3]

Indeed, the stark reality of oil in Nigeria is this: in many respects, the nation was better off 50 years ago, when it had just gained its independence and oil revenue had not yet taken over its economy and its government. Nigeria has been pillaged by its criminal oligarchy, past military dictators and their civilian cronies, and politicians (today often called "militicians.")

Corruption and fraud have sapped between 12 percent and 25 percent of Nigeria's oil wealth since 1958, some national observers have estimated. Moreover, the situation has only worsened with time. Nigeria's former anticorruption czar, Nuhu Ribadu, was reported as saying that 70 percent of the country's oil wealth was stolen or wasted in 2003; anticorruption initiatives have reduced the loss to only 40 percent by 2005 (Lubeck, Watts, and Lipschutz 2007). In addition, a report by Global Financial Integrity estimates that illicit financial outflows from Nigeria amounted to $58.5 billion between 1970 and 2008 (Kar and Cartwright-Smith 2010). These figures point to a causal link between Nigeria's oil resource abundance and the corruption, authoritarianism, and violent conflict that cause rent-seeking behavior. The Nigerian state, whose military rule has cast a long shadow of authoritarianism and institutionalized corruption and ineptitude, has failed to serve the interests of the Nigerian people.

This is the context in which the NEITI and PWYP initiatives emerged and in which Nigerian government and civil society seek to reverse decades of secrecy, neglect, and corruption that have characterized the management of oil and other natural resources. While still facing the complex challenges of the transition from military rule to democracy in 1999, civil society and government are also united on the principles behind the global campaign for transparency in the management of oil, gas, and mining revenues. Both NEITI and PWYP Nigeria are based on the shared conviction that prudent management of natural resource wealth will provide the basis for transforming public financial management, reducing corruption, promoting good governance, and achieving sustainable development.

NIGERIA EXTRACTIVE INDUSTRIES TRANSPARENCY INITIATIVE

The global EITI originated at the World Sustainable Development Summit in Johannesburg, South Africa, in October 2002. The following year, former President Olusegun Obasanjo committed Nigeria to being part of the process, and NEITI was launched in February 2004. In September 2007, after NEITI published its first audit report for the period 1999–2004, Nigeria became an EITI Candidate Country, meaning that it met certain indicators toward achieving resource revenue transparency.[4]

The Obasanjo administration's sense of urgency to sign on to EITI was based on the findings of a 2000 World Bank study, commissioned by the president, that revealed disturbing declines in crude oil output and sales, discrepancies in fund inflows and outflows, weak institutional capacities, and ineffective management of extractive industry revenues.[5] These findings set the stage for the creation of a 28-member National Stakeholders Working Group (NSWG) as a platform for formulating policy and implementing the country's EITI initiative.[6] Under the NEITI Act 2007, the NSWG has been reduced to 15 members, comprising an executive secretary and 14 other members drawn from government, the six geopolitical zones, oil companies, labor, civil society, and the media. The NSWG, coordinated by a secretariat, comprises five teams:

1. The Technical Evaluation Team evaluates all tenders for NEITI assignments and reports its findings to the NSWG.
2. The Legislative Team defines the legislative framework (that is, the NEITI Bill) for the initiative.
3. The Focal Team designs and oversees technical assistance programs.
4. The Civil Society Team directly engages broader interest groups such as trade unions, professional bodies, nongovernmental organizations (NGOs), and community-based organizations (CBOs).
5. The Media Team ensures wider dissemination of the NSWG's work.

NEITI is responsible for developing an extractive industry that will become a global model in transparency and investor friendliness, with policies and regulations that maximize value sustainably for the government. Through the NSWG, NEITI seeks to achieve the following objectives (NEITI n.d.):

- Conduct an independent audit of Nigeria's extractive industries (EI)
- Codify NEITI principles and objectives to ensure continuity beyond the current administration
- Build the capacity of civil society and government agencies relevant to EI revenue management
- Develop and implement a communication strategy to engage the public, particularly Nigerian CSOs and community groups, to ensure that Nigerians know that EI resources belong to them
- Develop and implement a mechanism for the disclosure, investigation, study, oversight, and publication of EI revenues and public expenditures to give Nigerians the information they need to hold the government accountable

The NEITI objectives correspond with the core principles and objectives of the global EITI (McPherson 2005):

- Ensure that resource revenues are properly accounted for and contribute to sustainable development and poverty reduction
- Provide guidelines to stakeholders on auditing, reporting, and disseminating information about resource payments and revenues
- Facilitate transparency and accountability in support of EITI implementation

The Nigerian government demonstrated a strong commitment to NEITI by initiating a bill that makes NEITI mandatory rather than voluntary. The bill went through the usual legislative processes, was passed into law, and was signed by President Obasanjo on May 28, 2007 (the evening before his tenure ended).

Since then, NEITI has engaged stakeholders through in-country meetings, presentations, and training. The government has accepted international support through the EITI Trust Fund and the World Bank-supported Sustainable Management of Mineral Resources Project. President Obasanjo pledged that Nigeria will support its African neighbors in their EITI implementation as well.[7] For example, in August 2008, the Nigerian government, in collaboration with the Economic Community of West African States, hosted the West African EITI.

PWYP NIGERIA

NEITI, as previously described, is a government initiative to bring about the transparency in extractive industries that will help change public perceptions of the industry. PWYP Nigeria represents the civil-society driver of that process. Deliberate mainstreaming of CSO participation, as a distinctive feature of NEITI implementation, has helped to deepen this understanding.

PWYP Nigeria seeks to engage core institutions and stakeholders within the extractive industry regarding the need to publicly disclose what companies pay to the government (bonuses, royalties, profit taxes, production shares, government sales of crude oil, domestic market allocation, and other taxes and charges) and to publish the government receipts for public scrutiny. Driving this initiative is the belief that, although the Nigerian government bears the responsibility for managing natural resources (including oil wealth), extractive companies are also culpable in the mismanagement and embezzlement of the revenues when they fail to be transparent about their dealings with the government.

PWYP Nigeria, like its counterparts in other countries, actively engages both the Nigerian government and extractive companies operating in Nigeria. It collaborates with other country chapters to press for global and comprehensive frameworks that incorporate international accounting standards and mandatory disclosure rules for security markets, export credit agencies, international financial institutions and donor countries, oil-backed loans from banks, and the host country.

PWYP Nigeria set out the following objectives in its operational document (PWYP Nigeria 2004):

- Build a dynamic, competent civil society coalition to engage with federal, state, and local governments; the extractive industry; international financial institutions; donors; and other relevant stakeholders to improve transparency and accountability in the reporting and management of natural resources revenue
- Actively and independently monitor NEITI implementation by providing constructive analysis of how natural resource revenues are disclosed, reconciled, and reported publicly, and by building and maintaining open and productive dialogue with the NSWG and the NEITI Secretariat
- Promote the mass mobilization and sensitization of the Nigerian people, especially among host communities of oil-producing regions, to the PWYP campaign, NEITI, and related efforts

- Build CSO capacity and skills to monitor the disclosure and expenditure of natural resource revenues through advocacy activities and applied budget analysis
- Work with civil society partners throughout Nigeria, Africa, and the world to ensure that international financial institutions (including the World Bank and International Monetary Fund) and other multilateral and bilateral donor agencies promote revenue transparency in a systematic and comprehensive way by making company and country-level support conditional on revenue transparency

The General Assembly of PWYP Nigeria—consisting of representatives from about 120 member organizations (including grassroots groups and women's organizations) that work on a wide range of sociocultural and economic issues—is the most powerful part of the organizational structure.[8] A steering committee is responsible for policy formulation, and a secretariat oversees day-to-day operations of the campaign. In 2006, the steering committee was restructured in response to an independent committee's review of PWYP Nigeria's activities during its two years of operation.[9] Under the new structure, the steering committee was broadened from 11 to 13 member organizations, representing Nigeria's six geopolitical zones and five thematic areas (gender and community participation, research and documentation, administration and finance, and media and advocacy).[10] In December 2008, another effort to restructure PWYP Nigeria retained the General Assembly as the highest power in the governance structure; a seven-member executive committee (six of whom represent member institutions of the country's geopolitical zones), headed by a national coordinator, replaced the steering committee. The executive committee runs the affairs of the campaign in coordination with staff of the secretariat.

The PWYP Nigeria campaign has received generous support from a range of development partners, including Oxfam UK, Pact/USAID, USAID Advance, USAID Prospect, Save the Children UK, the Heinrich Boell Foundation, and the Open Society Initiative in West Africa (OSIWA).[11]

STRATEGIES, METHODOLOGIES, AND TOOLS

As previously mentioned, NEITI and PWYP Nigeria work in tandem for transparency and accountability in the financial management of the extractive industries. Their strategies and methodologies were designed to complement each other's activities and to work synergistically to optimize their results.

NEITI is a government initiative (with support from the extractive companies, civil society, and professional bodies) to bring about transparency in extractive industries that will help change public perceptions of the industry. PWYP Nigeria represents the civil-society driver of that process. PWYP Nigeria has taken key strategic steps to engage the NEITI process. These steps include organizing special sessions to review the NEITI audit reports of the oil and gas industries; participation in quarterly civil society–NSWG meetings and a series of road shows organized by NEITI across the six geopolitical zones; and involvement in legislative advocacy. Both organizations' strategies, methods, and tools of engagements are further detailed below.

Nigeria Extractive Industries Transparency Initiative

The NSWG's five-team structure enables NEITI to approach its strategies and methodologies in a coordinated way, each team focusing on its own area of expertise. To cite just a few examples, the Technical Team's work resulted in the selection of Goldwyn International Strategies as the NSWG's advisor. The Legislative Team made possible the drafting of the NEITI Bill, which has institutionalized NEITI as a statutory body with the necessary powers. The Focal Team handles training programs and technical support for government agencies, while the Civil Society Team acts through its quarterly interactive forum where questions are asked and views exchanged about the day-to-day implementation of NEITI to deepen debates and strengthen constructive engagement (Asobie and others 2006).

For its part, the Media Team ensures that NEITI's work is accessible to the public—supporting the initiative's outreach both on the grassroots level and to high-level opinion leaders while also pressing for improved media coverage of relevant issues. Beyond ensuring that NEITI's work percolates to the grassroots, NEITI has always interacted with the media as a way of ensuring that its work is in the public domain, and this has led to further analysis of media reports.

Before the NEITI Act was enacted in 2007, the Media Team (anchored by Olusegun Adeniyi of *This Day* newspapers and Orji Ogbonnaya Orji, formerly of Radio Nigeria) led the process that developed NEITI's two-track (direct communication and opinion leader) communication strategy

(Goldwyn 2006; NEITI n.d.). Designed to meet Nigeria's needs and circumstances, NEITI's communication and media strategy seeks to address

- The pervasive sense of economic disenfranchisement among most Nigerians, who have suffered several decades of neglect despite the huge amount of money that has accrued from oil and gas production
- The opaqueness of the extractive industry, especially the oil and gas sector, which has fostered negative public perceptions about its management
- The disempowerment of most Nigerians, who require access, better understanding, and meaningful participation in debates about the use of Nigeria's mineral wealth

In view of the task set by the communication and media strategy, however, local people have yet to start any serious engagement with NEITI, especially when matched against NEITI's momentum under former President Obasanjo. Much is still required to create the necessary awareness of the initiative through the two-track communication strategy, which civil society is expected to help promote.

Civil society has taken advantage of the opportunity provided by the communication and media strategy for its public education and mobilization work concerning the extractive industry. PWYP Nigeria as a coalition and the Civil Society Legislative Advocacy Centre, as a PWYP member institution, have used the communication strategy effectively in their legislative advocacy work at the National Assembly. For example, PWYP Nigeria, using the media, ensured the widespread release of the NEITI Final Report on the physical, financial, and process audits of the oil and gas sector. Since NEITI came on board, the media have reported regularly about the oil and solid-mineral blocs' licensing processes.

Challenges remain, however, in reaching out to the grassroots level and in changing the people's negative perceptions about the management of oil, gas, and mineral wealth. NEITI has tried to address this challenge through a partnership with civil society that continues to assist the process through effective use of information.

NEITI's strategic process has given special consideration to women in the mineral sector by ensuring that the NEITI Bill, which seeks to complement the Mineral and Mining Act (2007), recognizes artisanal and small-scale mining, where women are most vulnerable. While the strategic framework for the new Act's special concession to women is yet to be fully unveiled, it is nevertheless anchored on the principle that, as a marginalized social group, women are most visible at the artisanal and small-scale level. NEITI has also established a single database on oil and gas exploration, mining permits, and licensing (Ezekwesili 2006).

Overall, the NEITI Act institutionalizes NEITI through support for the Obasanjo administration's overall reform agenda, mainstreaming it into government and ensuring the sustainability of the process. Synergy is also being built with civil society through its representation, particularly in PWYP Nigeria, to drive the process forward.

PWYP Nigeria

PWYP Nigeria uses many strategies, methodologies, and tools to advance its activities in the civil society component of the NEITI process. These include legislative and policy advocacy, program participation, research, and coalition and public awareness and communication to engage NEITI and the extractive industry.

At the level of policy advocacy, PWYP Nigeria has been active in addressing the conceptual and analytical gaps in mineral sector policy; writing letters and making advocacy visits to prominent policy actors and institutions in the extractive industry sector; and engaging international financial institutions and the G-8 through the World Bank Country Assistance Strategy, IMF Policy Support Instrument, and G-8–Nigeria Compact on Transparency.

PWYP Nigeria's legislative advocacy strategy also advanced its work through advocacy of legislative support for the prompt passage of the Whistle Blower Bill, the Fiscal Responsibility Bill, the Public Procurement Bill, the Freedom of Information Bill, and the NEITI Bill. All these activities build on the Obasanjo administration's overall reform agenda, which sought transparency and accountability to enhance sustainable development in Nigeria. The bills on fiscal responsibility, public procurement, and NEITI became Acts after passage by the National Assembly and the president's assent.

PWYP Nigeria has taken several strategic steps to engage the NEITI process. These include organization of special sessions to review the audit report on the oil and gas industry; the NSWG's participation in quarterly civil society meetings and in a series of NEITI-organized road shows across the six geopolitical zones; and involvement in legislative advocacy through visits and letter writing to press for passage of the NEITI Bill. All of these actions have provided a space for PWYP Nigeria's continued collaboration and strengthening of alliances with stakeholders in the extractive industries.

After the uproar generated by the release of the Hart Group Audit Report in April 2006, PWYP Nigeria reviewed the report in light of the discrepancies revealed in the oil companies' purported payments to the Central Bank of Nigeria and the latter's receipt of such payments (PWYP Nigeria 2006a). The PWYP campaign joined President Obasanjo in calling on NEITI to get the auditors back to the field to trace the missing funds. The position paper—a follow-up to a preliminary statement on the April 2006 report (PWYP Nigeria 2006b)—highlighted a lengthy list of issues the auditors should investigate when they returned to the field, including the following:

- Metering at flow stations
- An additional $510 million not finalized
- Unresolved crude exports of 10.5 million barrels
- Petroleum Profit Tax royalties on Itochu Loans and repayment
- Clarification on Nigerian National Petroleum Corporation (NNPC) payment for domestic crude
- Oil spillage figures
- Computation of education levy investment allowances
- Management of cash call allowances
- NNPC's inability to confirm payments

As part of its legislative advocacy, the PYWP campaign has used the opportunity provided by NEITI's road shows across Nigeria's six geopolitical zones to strengthen its alliances with stakeholders and ordinary Nigerians. In particular, the campaign has collected citizens' signatures to support its claim at the National Assembly that Nigerians support the codification in law of transparency and accountability in the extractive industries to stem corruption and ensure sustainable development. This strategy complements letter writing to the leadership of the National Assembly; sending of text messages to relevant National Assembly committee members; and consultations with civil society, the NEITI Secretariat, and the consultant to the Senate Committee and the Conference Committee that reconciled the House- and Senate-passed versions of the NEITI Bill for President Obasanjo's assent.

The PWYP Nigeria campaign also builds coalitions through work with representatives of member institutions, operational support for the secretariat, steering committee meetings, annual general meetings, and an active listserv where issues relating to transparency in the extractive industry are discussed and decisions made. Member institutions sometimes represent the campaign at functions held far from its secretariat.

Media campaigns, circulation of electronic newsletters, and town hall meetings to popularize PWYP at the grassroots level have proved to be useful components of PWYP Nigeria's engagement strategy. The media campaign strategy uses regular press releases to draw attention to and solicit public support for the issues that PWYP Nigeria is working on. An electronic newsletter keeps members updated on major developments in the extractive sector. The town hall meetings create vertical and horizontal spaces across the six geopolitical zones to keep farmers, community- and faith-based organizations, students, and grassroots associations informed about the campaign's work and to seek their cooperation in pressing for transparency and accountability in the extractive industries. The feedback at some of the town hall meetings, however, reveals logistical problems that the campaign must redress.

PROBLEMS AND CHALLENGES

Although NEITI and PWYP Nigeria have made strides, major challenges persist. The initiatives faced many problems and constraints in executing the NEITI process, including those explained below.

Nigeria Extractive Industries Transparency Initiative

Some critics have argued that the NEITI cannot afford to tarnish the national and global respect it has earned by constituting the NEITI NSWG in an undemocratic way. Ghana and Azerbaijan democratically elected their EITI managements, but Nigeria did not. Instead, the Nigerian government handpicked individuals for the NSWG who represent different sectors. For example, former President Obasanjo appointed the representatives of Nigerian civil society and the Nigerian Union of Journalists without consulting them. President Yar'Adua has followed suit, albeit under the provisions of the 2007 NEITI Act. Considering NEITI's transparency and accountability objectives, the CSOs—particularly PWYP Nigeria—contend that it was fundamentally and democratically wrong for the government to decide who represents them on the NSWG (PWYP Nigeria 2005).[12] The CSOs' position is that the constituencies making up the NSWG should elect their own representatives.

Another significant challenge is NEITI's financial dependence on foreign donors while the government contributes little. A significant part of NEITI staff salaries comes from foreign donors, and most of the technical and human capacity-building programs since 2004 have been funded by the World Bank, the U.K.'s Department for International Development, and the United States Agency for International Development (USAID). Although funding from Norway, the United Kingdom, the Netherlands, Germany, and the Multi-Donor Trust Fund in support of EITI in countries like Nigeria is highly appreciated, local ownership of NEITI through financial commitment by the Nigerian government is critical to the initiative's success. If the government is committed to the ideals of the global EITI, it will commit resources to NEITI. To overcome this problem, Nigerian civil society has argued that the federal government should appropriate funds for NEITI from Nigerian consolidated revenue through the National Assembly. The government has demonstrated its commitment through establishment of the NSWG and its pledge to NEITI principles, but much more financial support is expected.

NEITI activities are overconcentrated in the oil and gas sector to the detriment of other extractive sectors. The 1999–2004 NEITI Audit focused solely on the oil sector without considering the mining sector. The 2005 audit report, published in September 2009, used the same sectoral approach. While the long neglect of other extractive minerals in Nigeria may have been responsible for this, it is important that future audits increase transparency of other extractive sectors such as gas, iron ore, gypsum, tin, and so on. Remarkable progress has been made in the mineral sector. The Mining Cadastre took 18 months to complete its revalidation circle, culminating in the passage of the Minerals and Mining Act in March 2007 and the granting of the first batch of 1,002 mineral title licences in May 2007.[13]

One development in NEITI was the appointment of the founding chairperson of the initiative, Obiageli Ezekwesili, as vice president of the World Bank for Africa, effective May 1, 2007. Dr. Siyan Malomo, who replaces her in an acting capacity, was the director-general of the Nigeria Geological Survey Agency and was instrumental in shaping the Nigerian solid mineral sector, which is set to take off after decades of stagnation. Notwithstanding his familiarity with NEITI work and his technical expertise in the extractive sector, Dr. Malomo's greatest challenge is in marshaling the political and personal influence that had been Madam Ezekwesili's greatest tool as a member of the Executive Council of the Federation, a member of the president's economic team, the head of the Budget Monitoring and Price

Intelligence Unit (BMPIU, popularly known as the Due Process Unit), and as minister of solid minerals (and, later, as education minister) in the Obasanjo administration.

Inadequate or irregular communication between NSWG members and their constituencies is another problem. Most NSWG members rarely meet with their constituencies to brief and consult them on policy issues and decisions. This was the case in a recent interaction forum between NEITI and CSOs on the ongoing EITI validation in Nigeria, during which civil society representatives feigned ignorance of certain issues put on the table for consideration ahead of the exercise. This challenge is related to the way these members were selected without the prior consultation with, and agreement of, their constituencies. While election must replace selection in the future, Nigerians and their government must hold members of the NSWG accountable for inadequate information dissemination to their constituencies. Evaluation mechanisms must also be put in place by the government and the relevant constituencies to ensure the effectiveness of NSWG members.

In addition, NEITI pays too much attention to revenue transparency and accountability and little or no attention to how revenue is spent and the value for money spent. Although the Ministry of Finance used to publish monthly allocations, mainly on the extractive revenues to state and local governments, only a few CSOs have fully used such data.[14]

Several constraints impede widespread use of the data. First, CSOs lack sufficient capacity to efficiently and effectively use Ministry of Finance statistics to conduct the informed analyses of revenue expenditure monitoring that would generate enough information to support advocacy and demands for accountability. Second, recipient state governments claim that deductions are often made from published figures to settle state debts and other obligations such as contributions to the Niger Delta Development Commission and the Education Tax Fund. Third, constitutionally approved "State Joint Local Government Account" practices have created confusion about the published figures.[15] Local governments are supposed to have access to their allocations without undue interference from state governments, but they have accused the states of denying them such access through the "Joint Account" practices. In addition to increasing confusion about access to, and reliability of, the published figures, the "Joint Account" procedure also aids corruption and violates basic principles of fiscal relations. For Nigeria to overcome poverty and underdevelopment, NEITI must be holistic and not too narrow in its mandate, which includes intensification of efforts to build civil society capacity to engage related issues as they emerge.

Finally, the apparent lull in NEITI operations since the inception of President Yar'Adua's administration has caused concern about where Nigeria now stands within the global EITI. Given the Obasanjo administration's enthusiasm in pushing NEITI and the robustness of the disaggregated first audit report covering 1999–2004, little progress was seen under the current administration until the 2005 audit was conducted and belatedly released (in September 2009). Although it took two years (2004–06) to produce the 1999–2004 Audit Report, it was worrying when, three years later, the 2005 Audit Report (covering just one year) was still not forthcoming. Meanwhile, while the country continuously waited for meaningful progress to be made on the plan for the 2006–09 Audit Report.

Adding to the concerns, Nigeria and the EITI Board had agreed to a March 9, 2010, deadline to complete the validation exercise necessary to elevate Nigeria from EITI "candidate country" to "compliant country" status. The validation exercise tests candidate countries' compliance to EITI principles and operations, and failure to pass it could erode earlier progress and expel Nigeria from the list of EITI candidate countries. Even though the validation report on Nigeria was successfully submitted on deadline, Nigeria was (surprisingly) among the 16 out of 18 candidate countries to which the EITI Board granted extensions to enable them to conclude further required steps (not detailed) to conclude their EITI-compliant status, adding that they demonstrated "exceptional and unforeseeable circumstances outside the country's control."[16] Nigeria had applied for an extension well ahead of the submission of its report, it was learned from an anonymous source, because of fears that the country might not meet the deadline.

PWYP Nigeria

PWYP Nigeria has been active and has contributed significantly to the NEITI process despite several major challenges. Like NEITI, the network depends heavily on foreign donors for survival (Ikubaje 2006). Some foreign supporters could have ulterior motives and use their funding for leverage (Lubeck, Watts, and Lipschutz 2007). In 2006, three donors—OSIWA, Pact/USAID and Oxfam UK—had a meeting on how, when, and why they would continue to support PYWP Nigeria in light of their concerns about governance. They decided not to make any grants available to PYWP Nigeria until its system of governance and internal conflicts were resolved concerning the alleged excessive influence of the former national coordinator, David Ugolor, over project financial management and decision making. While it was appropriate for these donors to withhold their financial support when necessary, their decision endangered PWYP's independence and health; the campaign subsequently suffered a cash shortage and internal crises that made it impossible for PWYP to effectively engage the issues for which it was formed.

Some PWYP members also had lost confidence in Ugolor's integrity. The PWYP Nigeria listserv reflects incessant quarrels over allegations and counter-allegations of financial impropriety.[17] Some representatives of member organizations either quietly eased themselves out of the campaign or directly accused Ugolor of corrupt practices and left the campaign to work on EITI-related issues within their individual organizations, thus depleting PWYP's strength in terms of collective action.

Recognizing this problem, the PWYP Nigeria Steering Committee established an independent committee in 2006 to review PWYP's activities since its inception, including its finances, and to make recommendations on how to move the campaign forward. The five-person committee completed its assignment but not without facing problems arising from Ugolor's refusal to release funds to facilitate the committee's work, failure to release official grant papers signed by donors, and alleged harassment of the committee chair (which had resulted in the national coordinator's resignation).

The remaining committee members went ahead with the work and submitted their report to the steering committee. The report, which the remaining four members signed, clearly stated that it had no facts that indicted the national coordinator of corrupt practices. It nevertheless acknowledged that the national coordinator had exercised excessive control of the campaign's administrative, program, and financial management. The committee recommended a review of institutional structures and practices (including governance, communication, membership, and financial management) to overcome the problems identified in its report (Akiyode-Afolabi and others 2006).

The internal squabbles and conflicts among representatives of PWYP Nigeria member organizations posed another problem. Some had fully supported Ugolor, who was also the PWYP Nigeria campaign chair, while others opposed him. After the inauguration of a new steering committee in January 2007, it became even more difficult for members to reach consensus on policy and administrative issues because of the politics that brought relatively inexperienced members and organizations onto the new steering committee. As a result, the campaign's official listserv became a forum for quarrelling rather than for constructive engagement and networking on revenue management.

Technical knowledge of extractive industries remains a critical challenge for most PWYP Nigeria members, who are unfamiliar with how the sector operates and its technical terms. Only a few members of the network understand NEITI issues. Most members are interested only in how they can benefit and not in what they can contribute to revenue transparency and accountability in the Nigerian extractive industries. The few who are committed to the campaign have no access to training on how they can engage the issues. PWYP Nigeria must make a concerted effort to ensure that only members who have demonstrated commitment to NEITI issues receive training opportunities, at the same time not neglecting others whose capacity must be built. The World Bank and other donors are to be commended for supporting the campaign's capacity building, although more such training is needed to overcome the challenges and to guarantee effective engagement of the Nigerian extractive sector.

RESULTS AND IMPACTS

An appraisal of the Nigerian government's and civil society's steps to introduce NEITI and PWYP Nigeria reveals many results and impacts, which are detailed below.

Nigeria Extractive Industries Transparency Initiative

NEITI achievements since its inception in 2004 are impressive, the exception being that much more had been expected from the current Yar'Adua administration. NEITI earned Nigeria worldwide recognition for being one of the two countries leading the initiative globally (the other being Azerbaijan). Nigeria became the first country to promulgate an enabling law for EITI when President Obasanjo signed the NEITI Act on May 28, 2007 (the eve of the transition to Umaru Musa Yar'Adua as president). Liberia followed suit in July 2009.

NEITI has significantly raised awareness of the need for transparency and accountability in the extractive industries, particularly in the oil and gas sector. For example, the first audit report indicated serious irregularities in the financial records of oil transactions by Nigerian government agencies—on the order of $230 million in 2002 and $263 million in 2004 (Ikubaje 2006; PWYP Nigeria 2006a, 2006b). Today, many of Nigeria's elite understand clearly what the initiative is about and are willing to support NEITI because it saved Nigeria about $1 billion by 2007 (Adio 2007).[18] Nonetheless, more awareness is still needed, especially on the grassroots level, where there is next to no knowledge about the initiative.

The Hart Group Audit (PWYP Nigeria 2006a) promoted the transparency and accountability of local and international oil and gas companies operating in Nigeria. However, NEITI's impact is not restricted to the oil and gas sectors alone. Government agencies that have financial dealings with the oil and gas companies operating in Nigeria—including the Central Bank of Nigeria, the NNPC, the Department for Petroleum Resources (DPR), and the Federal Inland Revenue Services—have realized that it is no longer business as usual because they are now being watched by civil society and other oversight institutions. It is in this context that PWYP Nigeria raised its voice before the DPR and the presidency about the controversies surrounding the 2007 Oil Block Licensing Bid Round, in which the first right of refusal was subjected to significant criticism.[19] The complaints were that the bid round compromised due process and the principles of openness, transparency, and a level playing field and that it raised public concerns about a rushed bidding process, given that President Obasanjo was already on the verge of handing over power to the newly elected president, Yar'Adua. Of the 45 oil blocks slated for the 2007 bid round, the first right of refusal was exercised in more than 20 blocks.

The positive impact of the Hart Group Audit signaled a warning to corrupt officials in other extractive sectors. President Obasanjo instructed the government to immediately begin implementing the report's recommendations while urging further investigation of defaulting companies and government agencies for necessary sanctions. The president's response was indicative of the new commitment to do things properly— a commitment that was carried over to the mineral and mining sector, where a better-regulated regime leading to the revocation, revalidation, and approval of new exploration licenses and reconnaissance permits was subjected to the provisions of the Mineral and Mining Act 2007. The Act itself was a by-product of the same economic reform movement that led to NEITI.

One other significant NEITI achievement is that it has become an institution with statutory status. With the NEITI Act of May 2007, the institutionalization of NEITI has the potential to enhance the drive for greater results and impacts. The initiative has opened up advocacy space for CSOs working on transparency and accountability in general and in the extractive industries in particular, thereby increasing the chances for its success. NEITI opened up the opportunity for regular engagement, knowledge sharing, and capacity building on extractives.

After the release of the 1999–2004 Audit Report, an interministerial task team was established to formulate an action plan for redressing the discrepancies the audit report had identified. The major elements of the action plan covered revenue flow among government agencies, oil and gas metering infrastructure, harmonization of cost determinations, human and physical capacity development for critical government agencies, and governance of the oil and gas sector. Among the several activities undertaken by the NEITI Secretariat under this agenda are the various road shows, roundtables, and training programs for government agencies and CSOs about the extractives sector and extractive revenue management.

PWYP Nigeria

The global role of civil society in promoting transparency and accountability in the extractive sector cannot be overemphasized. The global EITI recognizes the role of civil society in promoting transparency and accountability in the extractive industries, thereby providing for civil society to actively engage in the design, monitoring, and evaluation of the EITI process and to contribute toward public debate.[20]

CSO contributions to NEITI's work can be categorized as information dissemination, capacity building, policy formulation, and monitoring and evaluation (Ikubaje 2006). The PWYP campaign has contributed significantly to awareness about the need for NEITI through information dissemination in the media and at the community level. PWYP Nigeria actively participated in the road shows organized to popularize EITI across Nigeria's six geopolitical zones in 2006, which helped to spread awareness of the initiative; consequently, 45 percent of Nigerians became aware of NEITI (Poroznuk 2006).

Since its inception, PWYP Nigeria also has contributed significantly to NEITI's policy formulation. NEITI's success to date cannot be fully separated from the contributions of the PWYP campaign. One of the civil society representatives on the NEITI NSWG belongs to a member organization of PWYP Nigeria. Another member-organization representative, Uche Igwe, is the civil society liaison officer at the NEITI Secretariat. In that capacity, he has consistently influenced the civil society component of NEITI work, even though some civil society persons have demanded regular feedback.

PWYP Nigeria's influence on NEITI policy making is being replicated at the global level. Professor Assisi Asiobe, a former civil society representative on the NSWG, was appointed a member of the global EITI advisory body prior to his eventual appointment and inauguration as the NSWG chairman in January 2008. This joint appointment adds to the leading role that Nigeria's chapter is playing in the global EITI. PWYP Nigeria's oversight of NEITI activities has greatly increased adherence to general EITI principles and operational criteria. As Ikubaje (2006) argues, "The monitoring role of NPWYP has put NEITI on its toes, working hard to avoid criticism from civil society."

FACTORS OF SUCCESS AND KEY LESSONS LEARNED

Nigeria's extractive industries are changing. The adoption of the global EITI and PWYP by the federal government and civil society is a fundamental step in that process, given that NEITI and PWYP Nigeria have been part of new institutions—including the Independent and Corrupt Practices Commission, the Economic and Financial Crime Commission, the BMPIU, and the Debt Management Office—among other measures put in place by the Obasanjo administration to bring about needed reform in Nigeria.

NEITI's exemplary leadership role has been a crucial factor in its success. Nigerians agree that their country will achieve sustainable development if corruption can be effectively tackled in the oil sector. The people have excellent ideas on how to overcome poverty and corruption in all sectors, but insufficient political will has remained a major constraint.

The commitment to and success of NEITI is also related to the conditions that international financial institutions place on extractive industry financing in developing countries. Among the reasons for NEITI's success are the conditions the International Finance Corporation imposes on potential borrowers that seek its loans to finance their extractive projects. If the EITI principles advocated by the international community become the criteria for foreign assistance, Nigeria will be a likely beneficiary. This type of foreign influence that compels poor countries to embrace transparency, accountability, good governance, and development can be used in other sectors in Nigeria.

A final important success factor is the NEITI secretariat's engagement of the right stakeholders from the beginning (the "undemocratic" appointment of its NSWG members notwithstanding). The invitation of civil society practitioners, government staff, and employees of extractive industries to NEITI's conferences, workshops, and training has enriched debates and inputs to the initiative. Whenever opportunities arise for training and capacity building on how to engage NEITI, such individuals should receive priority over NEITI staff members' friends and relatives, who may not necessarily share the same commitment for which the initiative is known.

NOTES

1. PWYP Nigeria is the umbrella body leading civil society engagement with NEITI, although other CSOs also participate. It was launched by a coalition of 47 CSOs from Nigeria's six geopolitical zones at a workshop organized by the African Network for Environment and Economic Justice, which was held in Port Harcourt, Nigeria, on February 16–17, 2004, with the support of the Open Society Initiative in West Africa (OSIWA) and Save the Children UK. NEITI was launched on February 19, 2004.

2. Nigeria has more than 40 billion tons of mineral deposits; 1 billion tons of gypsum; 42 million tons of bitumen; 3 billion tons of proven coal reserves; 7.5 million tons of bentonite; 700 million tons of barite; 1.5 million tons of rock salt; one of the world's best deposits of gemstones; an estimated 3 billion tons of kaolin; and additional deposits of bauxite, columbite, copper, diamonds, gold, phosphates, tantalite, tin, uranium, and zinc.

3. At the time, Madam Ngozi Okonjo-Iweala was minister for finance, Madam Esther Nenandi Usman was minister of state in the Ministry of Finance, and Miss Ifeuko Omoigui was the head of Federal Inland Revenue Services.

4. The standards for EITI-implementing countries to achieve EITI candidacy and compliance are detailed on the EITI Web site at http://eitransparency.org/eiti/implementation.

5. Although the World Bank study was unpublished, its influence has been widely acknowledged and cited elsewhere, notably as "a series of [2000] sector reviews and management audits by the World Bank [that] identified a number of inconsistencies and areas of concern over Nigeria's oil industry" (Bryan and Hoffman 2007, 75).

6. The 28 members of the NSWG represent civil society (2), the media (1), the National Assembly (2), state (regional) houses of assembly (2), domestic and multinational oil companies (3), the private sector (4), and federal government agencies in the extractive sector (14) (NEITI n.d.).

7. President Obasanjo made the pledge in his address to the EITI International Advisory Group at its February 2006 meeting in Abuja, Nigeria.

8. The women-focused organizations in PWYP include the Women's Advocacy Research and Documentation Centre in Lagos, Nigeria; the Women's Rights to Education Program in Abuja, Nigeria; and Rahma Women in Bauchi, Nigeria. All three organizations had been on the steering committee of the PWYP campaign until January 2007, when Rahma Women was dropped.

9. Dauda Garuba, one of this chapter's authors, served on the steering committee, which submitted its report on August 9, 2006.

10. The authors represent the Centre for Democracy and Development within the research and documentation thematic area of the steering committee.

11. The PWYP campaign implemented a two-year work plan (2005–07), which Pact/USAID and Oxfam UK supported. OSIWA signed a formal agreement with PWYP Nigeria in 2006 to further support of the campaign.

12. The campaign's position has not changed regarding the undemocratic appointment of NSWG civil society representatives, but the campaign has not stopped civil society at large from collaborating with NEITI on its transparency work in the extractive industries.

13. News about the beneficiaries of the mineral titles licenses (exploration licenses and reconnaissance permits) was published in the *Daily Trust*, Abuja, Nigeria. May 14, 2007: 19–44.

14. Among the CSOs that have engaged state governments in the Delta are the Niger Delta Budget Monitoring and Transparency Network, the Niger Delta Budget Monitoring Group, and the Commonwealth of Niger Delta Youth.

15. The "State Joint Local Government Account" system is a constitutional practice that allows state and local governments to operate the same account. See Section 162 (7) of the Constitution of the Federal Republic of Nigeria.

16. The other 15 countries granted extensions were Cameroon, the Democratic Republic of Congo, Gabon, Ghana, Kazakhstan, the Kyrgyz Republic, Madagascar, Mali, Mauritania, Niger, Peru, the Republic of Congo, the Republic of Yemen, Sierra Leone, and Timor-Leste. The candidatures of Equatorial Guinea and São Tomé and Principe were withdrawn, with the caveat that "both countries are welcome to reapply to become EITI candidate countries once the barriers to effective implementation have been addressed." See "EITI Board agrees status of 20 countries," April 16, 2010. http://eitransparency.org/news-events/eiti-board-agrees-status-20-countries.

17. The African coordinator of PWYP Nigeria, Matteo Pellegrini, confirmed the perceptions of institutional and financial improprieties ("Matteo's Travel Report, Nigeria, February 11–12, 2006" and the "Encouragement Letter" to the Annual General Meeting of PWYP Nigeria, March 2007).

18. Waziri Adio is NEITI's director of communications.

19. "First right of refusal," in this context, means granting a preferred oil company a preemptive right to match the highest bid on an oil bloc that has been determined in an open competitive bid process in which it had earlier expressed interest.

20. The EITI Principles and Criteria, http://eitransparency.org/eiti/principles.

REFERENCES

Adio, Waziri. 2007. "Gains of Extractive Transparency." *This Day* (Lagos, Nigeria), June 6, 2007.

Akiyode-Afolabi, Abiola, Akpan Tijah Bolton, Dauda Garuba, and Mohammed Salisu. 2006. "Report on Review of PWYP Nigeria Activities Since Inception in 2004." Independent committee report prepared for PWYP Nigeria. n.p.

Asobie, Humphrey Assisi. 2006. *Demystifying the Extractive Sector: Civil Society Report on EITI Implementation in Nigeria.* n.p.

Bassey, Don. 2007. "2007 Oil, Gas Bid Round of Controversy." *Sunday Independent*, May 20, 2007.

Bryan, Shari, and Barrie Hoffman, eds. 2007. *Transparency and Accountability in Africa's Extractive Industries: The Role of the Legislature.* Washington, DC: National Democratic Institute for International Affairs.

CAFOD (Catholic Agency for Overseas Development). n.d. *The Rough Guide to Transparency and Natural Resource Revenues: A CAFOD Briefing.* London: Rough Guides Ltd.

Christian Aid. 2003. *Fueling Poverty: Oil, War and Corruption.* London: Christian Aid.

Ezekwesili, Obiageli. 2006. "Solid Minerals: A Strategic Sector for National Development." Paper presented at the NEITI North Central Road Show at the Transcorp Hilton Hotel, Abuja, Nigeria, April 11, 2006.

Fayemi, Kayode. 2005. "Introduction: Towards Integrated Development in the Niger Delta." In *Towards an Integrated Development of the Niger Delta*, ed. Kayode Fayemi, Stella Amadi, and Ololade Bamidele. Lagos: Centre for Democracy and Development.

Fubara, B. A. 2002. "The Politics of the Niger Delta." In *The Niger Delta Development Commission: Towards a Development Blueprint*, ed. Peter OzoEson and Ukoha Ukiwo. Proceedings of the Fourth Memorial Program in Honor of Prof. Claude Ake. Port Harcourt, Nigeria: Centre for Advanced Social Science.

Garuba, Dauda S. 2006. "Oil and the Natural Resources Curse in Nigeria." *AfricaFiles* 3 (2): 5. http://www.africafiles.org/atissueezine.asp#art4.

———. 2007. "Contractual Breakdown: Small Arms, Intolerance and Tragedy in Nigeria's Delta Region." *AfricaFiles* 5 (4): 2–3. http://www.africafiles.org/atissueezine.asp#art1.

Goldwyn, David L. 2006. "Communication Strategy Implementation." Paper presented at the NEITI North Central Road Show at the Transcorp Hilton Hotel, Abuja, Nigeria, April 11, 2006.

Ibrahim, Jibrin, and Amina Salihu. 2004. *Women, Marginalization and Politics in Nigeria*. Abuja, Nigeria: Open Society Initiative in West Africa, Global Rights, and the Centre for Democracy and Development.

Ikubaje, John. 2006. *Corruption and Anti-Corruption in Nigeria: A Case Study of the Nigerian Extractive Industries Transparency Initiative (NEITI)*. Lagos: Joe-Tolalu & Associates.

International Crisis Group. 2006. "Nigeria: Want in the Midst of Plenty." *Africa Report* 113: 19–20.

Kar, Dev, and Devon Cartwright-Smith. 2010. "Illicit Financial Flows from Africa: Hidden Resource for Development." Paper for the Global Financial Integrity Program of the Center for International Policy, Washington, DC. http://www.gfip.org/storage/gfip/documents/reports/gfi_africareport_web.pdf.

Lewis, Peter M. 2004. "Getting the Politics Right: Governance and Economic Failure in Nigeria." In *Crafting the New Nigeria: Confronting the Challenges*, ed. R. I. Rotberg. Boulder, CO: Lynne Rienner.

Lubeck, Paul M., Michael J. Watts, and Ronnie Lipschutz. 2007. "Convergent Interests: U.S. Energy Security and the 'Securing' of Nigerian Democracy." International Policy Report, Center for International Policy, Washington, DC. http://ciponline.org/NIGERIA_FINAL.pdf.

McPherson, Charles. 2005. "Extractive Industries Governance and Transparency." Presentation at the Forum of the Corporate Council on Africa in Washington, DC, November 30, 2005.

Momoh, Abubakar, and Said Adejumobi. 2002. *The National Question in Nigeria: Comparative Perspectives*. Aldershot, England: Ashgate.

NEITI (Nigeria Extractive Industries Transparency Initiative). n.d. *Extracting Transparency: A Handbook on Transparency and Reform in the Oil, Gas and Solid Mineral Sectors*. Abuja, Nigeria: NEITI.

Obasanjo, Olusegun. 2006. "Our Commitment to NEITI Remains Strong." Address to the International Advisory Group of the Extractive Industries Transparency Initiative (EITI), in Abuja, Nigeria, February, 2006.

Poroznuk, Amber. 2006. "Nigerian Minister Obiageli Ezekwesili on NEITI." *Transparency Watch*, July, 2006. http://www.transparency.org/publications/newsletter/2006/july_2006/interview.

PWYP (Publish What You Pay) Nigeria. 2004. *Moving from Secrecy to Transparency in the Extractive Sector*. Benin City, Nigeria: PWYP Nigeria.

———. 2005. PWYP Nigeria Submission at the Nigeria EITI Capacity Building Conference for Government Agencies Relevant to Oil and Gas Revenue Management in Abuja, Nigeria, February 14–17, 2005.

———. 2006a. "Hart Group Report: Need to Return to the Field." Position paper on the Hart Group Report, PWYP Nigeria.

———. 2006b. "Preliminary Statement on the NEITI Audit Report." Abuja, Nigeria: PWYP Nigeria.

UNDP (United Nations Development Program) Nigeria. 2006. *Summary: Niger Delta Human Development Report*. Abuja, Nigeria: UNDP.

CHAPTER 8

CITIZEN CONTROL OF PUBLIC ACTION: THE SOCIAL WATCH NETWORK IN BENIN

Cyrille Chabi Eteka and Anne Floquet

I n the 1990s, the democratization of Benin's public institutions, together with government withdrawal from the production of many social goods, promoted the emergence of nongovernmental organizations (NGOs) and community-based organizations (CBOs). Initially, NGOs and CBOs were meant to take over the provision of public services. Gradually, they would also defend the interests of their members or intended beneficiaries. At the same time, civil society organizations (CSOs) from other countries intervened at the international level through multilateral summits to make other voices heard besides those of government.

Social Watch International emerged within this context by federating national networks willing to monitor the adherence to commitments made during international summits by their governments and by the international community. The Social Watch Benin network of NGOs was initially created to monitor the United Nations (UN) Millennium Development Goals (MDGs). However, because of the national issues at stake and the involvement of some of the network's members in the Benin Social Watch's Citizen Control of Public Action (CCPA) initiative at a local or sectoral level, the network broadened the scope of its activities to the national level.

The CCPA experience has allowed CSOs and grassroots participants to increase their contributions to the establishment of good governance practices to achieve the MDGs. Social Watch has also developed dialogue and advocacy capabilities with different Beninese institutions such as the Economic and Social Council and the National Assembly. In addition, Social

Watch has achieved significant results in the formulation of development policies, in the management of public affairs, and in changing authorities' perception of the competence of civil society.

This chapter presents the experience of Social Watch Benin, including a discussion of two alternative reports prepared by CSOs about the MDGs in Benin, CSOs' involvement in preparing the second Poverty Reduction Strategy Paper (PRSP 2007–09), and a critical analysis of the government's 2007 national budget.

The chapter emphasizes the original aspects of Social Watch Benin's initiative, which combines capacity building, critical analysis, research, dialogue with the state, advocacy, and demands. In addition, it describes and examines the following:

- The strong alliances built among CSOs, the media, and resource persons
- The limitations of voluntary mobilization of CSO members whose organizations have not included CCPA initiatives in their action plans or budgets
- How these processes can be institutionalized without making the mistake of delegating them to experts
- The key lessons learned

POLITICAL AND ECONOMIC CONTEXT

After its independence in 1960, Benin experienced a period of intense instability with frequent military coups and popular demonstrations. The October 26, 1972, coup opened the way to a military regime claiming to adhere to revolutionary socialist ideas. In 1975, with the transition to a single-party regime—the People's Revolutionary Party of Benin— political militancy prevailed. The people gradually lost confidence in the government and their leaders, demobilized, and lost motivation for productive activity.

The economic crisis of the late 1980s, the implementation of structural adjustment policies and their social impacts, and political tensions collectively led to the February 1990 *Conference des Forces Vives de la Nation* (Conference of the Forces of the Nation). This major national forum, the first of its kind in Africa, ushered in a political and social détente that enabled the people of Benin to adopt a new constitution by referendum on December 2, 1990. Since then, the country has made undisputed political progress. Gradually, the institutional framework and mechanisms of a formal democracy have been created. A liberal democracy was established with separation of powers and a broad multi-party system.

In principle, Benin is in a relatively enviable position regarding the right of association, the freedom of expression and the media, and the electoral process. It is one of the few countries in Africa that has held several elections since 1990 (five legislative elections and four presidential elections) in a peaceful environment of political pluralism and changes in political power. Boni Yayi won the 2006 presidential elections, bringing in an administration that swept away the team led (from 1972 to 1991 and again from 1996 to 2006) by former President Mathieu Kérékou. In December 2002, Benin organized its first local elections in accordance with the February 1990 recommendations to decentralize territorial administration to promote grassroots democracy and boost local development.

The NGOs' Service-Providing Role

Structural adjustment policies have imposed a reduction in public employees, and many public functions have been transferred to the private sector. However, private actors are less interested in unprofitable social goods, and professional organizations and NGOs have gradually taken up the training of service producers, the fight against illiteracy, providing help for undernourished children and advisory services for the agricultural sector, and so on. For example, professional farmers' organizations created a strong federation by channeling resources from the cotton market to organize a coalition of farmers' groups.

Nongovernmental service providers generally depend on external resources to carry out their mission. Some organizations are created by government agents who mobilize public resources, while others are created for patronage and election purposes and have short lives. After more than 10 years, respectable and rather solid NGOs with diversified portfolios and recognized expertise have emerged. Because they do not depend on government funding, they have gradually begun to conduct critical analysis of public action.

Benin has one level of decentralization: the commune. Decentralization laws confer upon communes great autonomy and broad jurisdiction over primary education, primary health care, social protection, water supply, sewage disposal, housing and land use, market management, road maintenance, and so on. To date, however, although basic service provision has been transferred, the government has not transferred equivalent budget resources to the communes. Therefore, people are dissatisfied with the services provided by their local governments, and pressure groups have been created to defend their interests or to demand their mayors' resignations. They voice their disappointment through local radio stations during programs with suggestive names such as "Morning Discontent." Four out of 77 mayors have been removed from office. Management of local affairs is a major issue between local authorities and citizens.

Tolls on Economic and Human Development

Agriculture is the leading sector of Benin's economy. Food production, well below its potential, barely increases at the same pace as population growth. Cotton, Benin's major export, suffers from declining global prices and poor governance. As a result, poverty tends to be higher in rural areas.

In the absence of an industrial sector, mostly commercial activities and services are being developed. Commerce is based largely on cross-border exchanges and transit. Investors benefit from variations in currency exchange rates without investing in productive infrastructure. Increasing urbanization during the past 15 years has developed focal points of growth, but most of the urban workforce is in the informal sector whose health depends on the growth of the formal sector. If at first income seemed to be rising in the cities, recent surveys show that poverty has increased there as well.

Benin's ranking in the United Nations Development Program (UNDP) Human Development Index is continuously falling; in 2004, it ranked 162nd among 174 countries. Life expectancy at birth in 2002 was 59 years. In spite of efforts to improve education and access to water and primary health care, the gap with other countries is widening. More than two-thirds of Benin's population is illiterate; the literacy rate is 48 percent for men and 28 percent for women, for a gender parity index of 0.58. Therefore, the progress in terms of democracy and governance was not accompanied by significant economic and social development.

After the UN Millennium Declaration that set the eight MDGs in 2000, Benin formulated a development policy, adopted its first poverty reduction strategy (for 2003–05), and monitored its progress. This allowed Benin to qualify in 2003 for the Heavily Indebted Poor Countries completion point, and its multilateral debt was canceled in September 2005. However, economic growth decreased from 5 percent in 2003 to 4.5 percent in

2006 against a target of 7 percent (the level needed to reduce poverty given the population growth rate).

The Growing Consensus against Corruption

Despite external debt relief, Benin faces huge shortages of funds because of a large public deficit and substantial arrears in state treasury payments. These difficulties arose partly from an unfavorable macroeconomic context (higher energy prices, lower cotton prices), but public spending was also inefficient, and a sense of impunity generated an insecure fiscal climate that was detrimental to private investment. For example, the program budgets to implement the PRSP in priority ministries have a low execution rate. In certain regions, cotton producers had to wait years to be paid for their crops although the cotton had been ginned and sold. Political and institutional reforms have not facilitated economic growth and more equitable income distribution. Corruption, injustice, and political investments are widespread.

The importance of introducing ethical standards in government had already been highlighted during the February 1990 Conference of the Forces of the Nation. In 1996, the government established an ethics committee for public management, which would report directly to the president's office. In 1998, after discussions with NGOs, the government organized a Forum for the Mobilization of Civil Society in the fight against corruption. As a result, a consensus has formed in Benin on the need to fight corruption. Newspaper articles frequently denounce corruption, and numerous radio and television programs also address the subject. However, civil society, citizens, and politicians cite different reasons for corruption, and scandals are rarely sanctioned. In such a context, an apparatus for evaluating public governance through citizen control appears to be critical.

In fact, several CSOs have undertaken initiatives to encourage citizen participation, advocacy, and control over public action. Some NGOs specialize in fighting against corruption or for human rights or consumer protection. NGOs often support user associations (for example, parents' associations, management committees for health centers and water supply points) and workers unions or professional organizations, mainly of farmers. Even though user associations encounter difficulties at the national level (professional organizations and unions have overcome similar obstacles by expanding from the local to the subregional level), they all intervene in communes as soon as the opportunities arise. Some NGOs have decided to work on capacity building of these local actors so they can become key figures in commune planning, municipality monitoring, and service quality assessment.

THE CITIZEN CONTROL OF PUBLIC ACTION (CCPA) INITIATIVE

The CCPA initiative was launched by Social Watch Benin, a network of CSOs. Its strategic actions relate to the contribution of civil society to the elaboration of the PRSP, the evaluation of the achievement of the MDGs, the analysis of the government's national budget, and specific advocacy activities. Social Watch Benin is part of Social Watch International, created in 1995 to monitor the implementation of international commitments of governments and international organizations, particularly those made during the summits held in Copenhagen (March 1995) and Beijing (September 1995).

During the UN Millennium Development Summit of September 2000, world leaders adopted a new vision of development in the form of eight MDGs. As a signatory to the Millennium Declaration, Benin took a new direction in the fight against poverty in collaboration with its development partners. Within this framework, the first government report on MDGs was prepared in 2003.

In spite of significant potential due to the national political climate, the mobilization of civil society actors as an effective pressure group within the framework of the MDGs and the PRSP was limited. Few CSOs focused on control over public action, locally or nationally. Most NGOs lack resources and instead provide services for partners. Moreover, the state undermines the determination of many CSO leaders to engage in CCPA because their organizations are sometimes funded by government-created networks. Nevertheless, some of these organizations, such as the Observatory for the Fight against Corruption and the National Front of Organizations for the Fight against Corruption have spoken out about embezzlement and corruption in public management. Their intervention was sometimes discredited by people who have limited knowledge of public management, do not trust the stated idealism of NGO leaders, claim they have more practical objectives, or believe NGOs have certain political leanings.

Proper financial management is necessary to achieve the MDGs and the PRS. Therefore, Sœurs Unies à l'Oeuvre (United Sisters at Work, or SUO) developed the idea of mobilizing Beninese CSOs in a network that would monitor government policies, the implementation of the PRS, and the achievement of the MDGs. The CCPA initiative, which built on this, was formed to promote good management in the public sector and to fight the corruption and bad governance that are poisoning public institutions in Benin. The network was created in March 2005 following a national workshop on civil society involvement during the review of the Millennium Summit, which SUO organized in collaboration with UNDP and the Netherlands Development Organisation.

SUO was in charge of the network's coordination for a three-year period. The network also has a technical committee composed of representatives of SUO, Women in Law and Development in Africa (WILDAF-Benin); Centre Afrika Obota; Réseau d'Intégration des Femmes des ONG et Associations Africaines (Network for the Integration of Women of Non-Governmental Organizations and African Associations, or RIFONGA-Benin); Groupe de Recherche et d'Action Pour le Développement (Group Research and Action for the Promotion of Agriculture and Development, or GRAPAD); and GLEGBENU.[1] More than 150 CSOs and development organizations make up the CCPA network, which operates in all Beninese communes.

The Strong Role of Women

Women have strong representation in the Social Watch network. Three of the six CSOs on the technical committee are women's organizations and are represented by women. In the national coordinating committee, composed of representatives of 17 CSOs, at least four have gender-related issues as their main objective (WILDAF, RIFONGA-Benin, ROBS,[2] and SUO), and many others work for increased social and economic integration of women (for example, the Benin Centre for Environment and Economic and Social Development [CEBEDES] and GRAPAD). Six of the national coordinating committee's members, including the coordinator and the vice coordinator, are women.

Women also take part in or are in charge of the work groups that carry out budget analyses and contributed to the preparation of the PRSP. To date, however, there has been no gender-sensitive analysis of the budget.

Social Watch Objectives and Pilot Activities

The main objectives of Social Watch are the following:

- Reinforce CSO advocacy to influence government and development partner decisions and actions to promote political changes in favor of the poor
- Participate effectively with government institutions and financial partners in the preparation, implementation, monitoring, and evaluation of the PRS
- Monitor the preparation, implementation, and evaluation of the national budget and the budgets of Benin's communes, paying particular attention to aspects that affect the poor and the use of public development aid to contribute to good public resource management
- Prepare an annual civil society report on implementation of the MDGs and PRS in Benin
- Create awareness and mobilize citizens using the press, radio, and television
- Organize civil society in communes and thematic areas for effective community participation in social development processes
- Develop monitoring activities by local Social Watch committees on the implementation of local community development plans

Activities related to the last two objectives have not been fully developed in most communes. Social Watch Benin is in its early stages, and its activities will gradually expand to include grassroots participation. Moreover, decentralization began only in 2003. Local authorities completed their first term at the end of 2007. During these first years of decentralization, communes have prepared local development plans, some of which involved different social groups, but they lacked the resources needed for implementation.

Considering that both Social Watch Benin and local authorities are still so recent, the network launched its activities in four pilot communes: one in the north (Parakou), one in the southeast (Ifangni), and two in the southwest (Athiémé and Lokossa). The network based its choices mainly on the dynamism of NGOs working in those communes.

Network activities receive technical support from the government. UNDP, Dutch and German organizations, and the Embassy of the Netherlands provide mainly financial support. Member organizations contribute member fees and their members to different activities.

STRATEGIES, METHODS, AND TECHNIQUES

As previously mentioned, Social Watch Benin launched the CCPA initiative as a mechanism for building and mobilizing citizen control to evaluate public governance. Many of its activities, therefore, bring together organizations, citizens, the media, and resource persons to monitor government policies, PRS implementation, progress toward achieving the MDGs, and national budgetary allocations. This section further describes CCPA's strategic decisions, actions, and tools—including capacity-building activities, critical analysis, research, dialogue with the state, advocacy, popular mobilization, media relations, and alliance building.

Structure and Human Resources

Social Watch Benin's permanent organization and operational structure is a compact unit. The executive secretariat is in charge of implementing the network's action plan, managing everyday tasks, compiling information, and providing members with information. The secretariat coordinates with the international Social Watch network and coordinates programs for national, regional, or international activities. It has three permanent members and temporary members for specific activities.

Depending on the activity, the network's human resources include its members, voluntary resource persons, and consultants. Ad hoc work and analysis groups are created at the national level and, increasingly, at the local level. Local presence is introduced gradually because many local authorities discredit actors or actions whose objective is to monitor or control the management of local affairs. Such resistance is why the network chose four pilot communes to test the approach and gather experience before expanding to other communes. In addition, some NGO members of the network carry out citizen control actions in other communes. For example, CEBEDES works in nine communes of the Zou Department.

Training and Other Tools

Social Watch's activities are promoted through training workshops, awareness building, advocacy, and other tools. Workshops have focused particularly on learning how to read and analyze the national budget to help trainees determine whether the budget contributes to poverty reduction, is favorable to rural areas, and takes into account the priorities of social sectors. Workshop participants include leaders of CSOs affiliated with the network and journalists of the press, radio, and television (mostly television newscasters and presenters at local and community radio stations). Particular attention is given to CSOs affiliated with the network.

Approximately 100 participants attended the first workshop, which took place in Cotonou, Benin's largest city. Two other training workshops on local budget analysis were organized by zone (south and north) and attended by 50 presenters and journalists in each zone. Even if actions undertaken by CSOs and journalists are still barely perceptible at the commune level, the network is taking measures to better prepare and reinforce their intervention capacity.

Alternative Reports on Achieving the MDGs

Social Watch used resource persons within and outside the network to prepare the first annual government-independent report on the achievement of MDGs (Social Watch Benin 2005). Six resource persons, chosen through bid invitations, completed a draft report. A review panel modified it, and the resource persons presented the findings to the network's technical committee, the review panel, and the resource persons to harmonize viewpoints. Four resource persons, members of the technical committee, then revised the report. The review panel made more changes, and a validation workshop was organized to collect comments and observations from development partners, private and public stakeholders, and CSO members. A technical committee was established to incorporate the changes gathered from the workshop and to finalize the report.

The second annual alternative report in 2006 took a different approach (Social Watch Benin 2006b). Social Watch created a thematic group for each of the 12 priority targets of the MDGs, clustered into three main themes:

1. Promoting sustainable economic growth and development of the agricultural sector
2. Improving the provision of basic social services
3. Advocating fulfillment of commitments on aid, commerce, and the promotion of Benin's cultural potential

Resource persons from these thematic groups, often members of network CSOs, were asked to work on the report. Because the resource persons were members of civil society (not involved in government actions), their views appeared representative of Benin's citizens. These resource persons studied the first report to determine their line of research. Limited resources did not allow for an exhaustive analysis, so the groups prepared a partial study of the progress achieved on the MDGs and identified the remaining challenges.

The resource persons contacted government officials in charge of MDG implementation and collected data from line ministries, state institutions, CSOs, diplomatic missions, and international organizations. Government agencies facilitated access to information, but it is not known whether the information was accurate because the resource persons had neither the time nor the financial and material resources to verify the government-provided data. Moreover, the organization of data collection did not allow for periodic monitoring of activities in the field. Objective assessment of progress left much to be desired. However, the thematic groups began by assessing the implementation of recommendations made in the first report and then submitted concrete suggestions according to each specific theme. At the end of the analysis, each group presented a draft report.

These reports were submitted to a panel of writers who merged the contributions of the thematic groups into a single draft report. After a prevalidation workshop with reviewers and editors, the writers incorporated those comments and recommendations into the draft during the validation workshop and finalized the alternative report for 2006. The report was launched with significant media coverage and in the presence of government authorities. This report had been prepared with a much larger public participation even if citizen feedback was not yet available to verify and complete the analyses. The report, however, did allow some public officials to express their thoughts on the MDG implementation process.

The 2006 report's major conclusions and recommendations included the following:

- The cotton sector suffers from governance problems, with disastrous effects on the welfare of the rural population.
- The intention of the new government to boost the economy by promoting agricultural diversification is welcome, but it must also support small producers.
- Regarding the gender issue, there has been limited implementation of important legal and institutional reforms (several laws have been passed for the protection of human rights).

- Health plans have been drawn up and are pending implementation. They must be monitored and evaluated with the participation of NGOs working in this field.
- Opaque management impedes assessment of government projects, particularly those concerning HIV patients.
- Living conditions are an important measure of poverty.
- Development aid to Benin has not yielded the expected results because of inadequate allocation of resources and poor management of funds.
- The open economy and trade liberalization have not benefited the Beninese. Social Watch recommends public dialogue before signing partnership or cooperation agreements.

The 2006 report openly denounced the government's failure to act upon most recommendations of the 2005 report. Launched during discussions for the preparation of the second PRS, the 2006 report sought to influence decision makers to consider poverty reduction objectives. It contained precise and detailed criticisms of government shortcomings (for example, the excessively centralized management of assistance to AIDS victims or the shortage of antiretroviral drugs) and proposed concrete recommendations for parliament (for example, passing laws on illicit enrichment); government (among others, a policy for protecting the interests of local producers and establishment of an effective regulatory body for the cotton sector); and civil society itself.

In the end, however, there may have been too many good ideas. The main thread of criticism was lost among too many recommendations, and the role and priorities of the civil society were not clearly defined.

Monitoring the National Budget

In September 2006, Social Watch created a Budget Analysis Unit to carry out critical analysis of the national budget. The unit is composed of three heads of the thematic groups that monitor progress on MDGs and approximately 15 "tutors" (sociologists, economists, and political and legal experts) experienced in reading and analyzing budgets.

The 2007 budget was the first to be analyzed. After several training sessions on how to read a national budget, the heads of the 12 thematic groups and representatives of civil society resource organizations met in October 2006 for an analysis workshop at the West African News-media and Development Centre in Cotonou. Workshop results were compiled in a critical report and sent to the National Assembly, the Economic and Social Council, and the government the day before the budget was to be presented at the National Assembly. Workshop participants analyzed, sector by sector and line by line, all budget allocations to make sure they were consistent with national strategies aimed at the reduction of social inequalities.

The Budget Analysis Unit noticed a reduction of budget allocations for water, urban and rural roads, housing, and so on. Taking into consideration that these cutbacks could be justified by decentralization measures that devolved powers to local authorities, the unit asked the government to indicate precisely where the budget allocated the corresponding resources to those local authorities. Concerning primary education, for example, the budget for schools did not reflect the increase in the number of students. The already meager budget of the Ministry of the Family, Women, and Children was significantly smaller, particularly in the budget provisions concerning child trafficking, social mobility, and the advancement of women.

Experience also had shown that aid to the indigent population was inefficiently managed. The report showed that management is centralized and excludes communes as well as health and social centers from the decision-making process.

The analysis unit also expressed great concern about limited allocations for housing and the imprecision of some allocations. For example, resources had not been clearly earmarked for agricultural development, and it was feared that public funds would support certain businesses to the detriment of small farmers. Moreover, the increase in the budget of the Benin President's Office was not clearly justified.

Advising and Monitoring the PRS

In Benin, civil society had played only an advisory role in the preparation of the first-generation PRSP. PRS implementation was supposed to have been monitored by committees representing different social groups, including communes, but the committees' creation was delayed and, given neither the support nor the necessary means, they failed to perform their intended role. Therefore, Social Watch collaborated with financial and technical partners and received government supports to implement a project involving civil society in effective monitoring of the second-generation PRSP.

The first action undertaken by the Social Watch project was to incorporate network representatives into the nine thematic groups organized by the former National Committee for Development and the Fight against Poverty (CNDLP),[3] which was the official body in charge of formulating the PRSP. Each thematic group conducted a diagnostic analysis and developed strategic actions to be implemented within the framework of the second PRSP. These representatives enabled Social Watch to play an active role in advocating that the PRSP take into account its effects on living conditions at the grassroots level.

The second action was the creation of a grassroots consultation mechanism that would identify people's concerns and priorities and incorporate them into the PRS. A questionnaire was prepared and validated. The collection of data covered the entire nation. Data validation at departmental and national levels was made possible by regional coordination units, Social Watch local committees, and partners of the project. While the data were being collected in the field, regular meetings were organized with Social Watch representatives from the different thematic groups to discuss ongoing debates in the thematic groups and to give network representatives the tools that would enable them to intervene effectively in the debates. The grassroots consultation process allowed Social Watch to prepare a solid contribution based on grassroots concerns and to identify the issues to be addressed to achieve the MDGs (for example, precise and decentralized actions targeting the poor, quick intervention in crisis situations, and so forth).

Social Watch data collection efforts were constrained, however, because the network did not prepare an adequate budget at the start, and it lacked the necessary resources to organize feedback workshops at the grassroots level. Workshops were organized in each department, but they could have started on a smaller scale with districts and communes.

The network's contribution to the second PRS was compiled in a single document and submitted to the CNDLP (Social Watch Benin 2006a). An evaluation of the first PRS had shown significant delays in the implementation of the reforms, explainable by poor ownership of the PRS by institutions charged with its implementation. Social Watch suggested making the MDGs operational so the PRSP can take them into consideration. For instance, the PRSP should take into account the powers devolved to communes, which are now responsible or share responsibility for the implementation of social sector infrastructure and for performance deficits. The governance issue was discussed, emphasizing the need to continue the decentralization process and CSOs' participation in monitoring local government. Finally, suggestions were aimed at developing a more operational classification of the different types of poverty. Specific actions targeting these groups were recommended, along with mechanisms for decentralized prevention and intervention.

Monitoring Local Government

Citizen control is well on its way in nine communes through a project conducted by CEBEDES and financially supported by the Danish International Development Agency. CEBEDES has worked for many years in support of decentralization, was involved in preparing local development plans in the nine communes, and continues to participate in programs that help these communes establish better dialogue with their citizens. It is also involved in other programs that build local CSOs' capacity in monitoring and control of public affairs.

In the commune-level project, after assessment and validation during feedback workshops, monitoring and control procedures were discussed in detail with NGOs, committees that manage social and community property, professional organizations, elected officials, and technical services. All actors had the opportunity to discuss what they were expected to do in monitoring the commune budget, contract awards, civil registry services, and management of infrastructure such as markets.

Building on the consensus achieved, a manual of local government monitoring procedures was prepared. These procedures are based on current legislation and may help mayors to exercise prerogatives that vested interests had questioned. (For example, the management of road transport stations where taxes on taxis and trucks can be collected was challenged by professional driver associations.) Indeed, government does not have a monopoly on bad governance!

Disseminating Information

Social Watch's work is presented and made public through community and local radio stations, newspapers, and television channels. Social Watch invited journalists to participate in budget analysis workshops in Cotonou and training sessions that were specifically organized for journalists in all Beninese departments. The research carried out by thematic groups is published and presented in conferences. Contracts are signed on a weekly, monthly, and quarterly basis with private and public media representatives to disseminate network activities. Information dissemination through these media created public awareness, explained the mission of Social Watch, and encouraged citizen support of network actions.

KEY ISSUES AND CHALLENGES

CCPA also faced several problems and constraints in executing its programs, including those in the four major areas explained below: limited leadership capacity, lack of financial resources, people's distrust or lack of knowledge about CSOs, and struggles with the government to make public information more accessible.

Leadership

The leadership of thematic groups is not as dynamic as it should be because their leaders are often not available—possibly because they must find time for network activities in addition to their responsibilities in their respective organizations and because the financial compensation they receive is far less than the services they provide. Because network activities have not been included in their organizations' planning, leaders of thematic groups are under a lot of pressure and find it extremely difficult to keep their commitments to the network. This explains the relatively little progress made by most groups.

The Budget Analysis Unit encountered fewer constraints because the Coordinating Committee hired an assistant to help the executive secretary prepare methodology notes, contact tutors who were difficult to reach because of their multiple roles, and contribute to the activities of the unit.

Lack of Resources

Internal operations are also limited by the lack of financial resources. The CCPA initiative is supported by development partners. To become a member of the network, CSOs must pay a membership fee of CFAF 50,000 and an annual fee of CFAF 25,000. However, only about 50 CSOs have paid all their fees; it is difficult for CSOs to pay their fees on time because they do not receive government support even if they are actively involved in achieving the MDGs. Only large NGOs or those with a wide range of activities (providers of services to the government or development partners) can pay their membership fees. NGOs with limited resources are willing to pay but cannot because of extremely limited means or even none at all.

Legislation could correct this situation, but unfortunately, the law does not provide for budget allocations for CSOs that fall within the framework of "humanitarian public actions." Moreover, any kind of government support to such CSOs could divert them from their ideals if the donor were to pressure them.

In addition, the young network lacks experience and has difficulty planning and preparing a budget for its activities. Many activities were assigned insufficient funds and could not be carried out. As a result, network leaders must develop activities with modest financial support, which may undermine motivation.

The network's organization—based on a General Assembly, a Coordinating Committee, and an Executive Secretariat—makes it possible to avoid conflicts over the network's actions and mission. However, in spite of the many CSOs that belong to the network, it is still difficult to have network presence in all 77 communes. In each of the former six departments, an area leader has been identified to represent the Coordinating Committee. Likewise, each commune should have a network unit to organize monitoring activities of local development policies.

Still in its early stages, Social Watch Benin has operational local units in only four pilot communes. In these four communes, the local authorities consider CSOs to be "enemies" with whom they are not quite prepared to collaborate. In addition, departmental delegations cannot function adequately because they lack the resources needed to follow up local units. Local citizen control is inadequate and does not even exist in most communes. The network does not have local representatives. In general, grassroots organizations do not try to monitor local government.

Confusion about Social Watch and CSOs

Another problem limiting the impact of Social Watch activities involves the people's perceptions of civil society. That many individuals use CSOs as a stepping stone for their political, social, or professional advancement confuses many people who cannot easily separate legitimate CSOs from fakes. Most people are convinced that CSO leaders, like political leaders, are simply trying to protect their own material interests. It is hard for them to believe that some might seek to achieve better governance and citizen advancement.

Because distrust is rampant, many CSOs with good intentions are discouraged. Constant vigilance is necessary because some CSOs do hide, behind a façade of social commitment, their true intentions of malicious criticism and personal political advantage. The confidence of elected officials that was so hard to win could quickly be lost.

Struggles to Increase Government Cooperation

Local monitoring is possible only if both sides are willing to make it work. Communes where monitoring mechanisms are implemented have mayors and local officials with an open attitude and willingness to communicate. The officials in those communes believe that monitoring will protect them from malicious gossip and will act as a deterrent to internal disorder.

Likewise, sectoral monitoring and monitoring of the national budget is possible only if the government is willing to make information public and in such a way that it can be read and understood by ordinary citizens. The national budget now appears to be available for public discussion before it is voted on by parliament, but it is not yet available in the form of program budgets with verifiable indicators. Not all ministries have undergone planning reform, and it is not possible to have an overall view of the budgetary situation. Therefore, monitoring economic governance is a difficult task. The network has criticized the lack of a clear and easy-to-read budget.

RESULTS AND IMPACTS

The CCPA experience has allowed the mobilization of CSOs and grass-roots participation to increase their contribution to establishing good governance practices for the achievement of the MDGs. Social Watch has also developed dialogue and advocacy capabilities with different Beninese institutions such as the Economic and Social Council and the National Assembly, introducing new dynamics in the process. Significant results have also been achieved in the formulation of development policies and in the management of public affairs. The CCPA initiative has also affected the authorities' perception of the competence of civil society and the positive impacts of engaging in dialogue.

Enhanced CSO Capacity

In less than two years, many CSOs have built their capacities in fundamental areas of citizen control of public action. The Social Watch network organized several capacity-building workshops that have helped its members develop a common vision on CCPA and how to put it into practice. More than 200 people from CSOs, the media, and the Budget Analysis Unit have studied Benin's public finances, budgetary procedures and mechanisms, mobilization strategies, and use of resources. These individuals have significantly increased their capacity to analyze a budget in order to suggest alternatives that will protect citizens' social and economic rights, particularly those of the poor and vulnerable. The Budget Analysis Unit prepared a guide on how to read national and sectoral budgets and how to analyze them according to each MDG. The unit's members have a good knowledge of the MDGs and of the constraints that must be overcome to achieve them. Collective skills are being developed to formulate development and poverty reduction strategies that convey the concerns of different social groups.

Increased Support for Community Action

For the first time, dozens of Beninese CSOs devoted to development mobilized and participated actively and effectively in CCPA activities. Their performance was less conditioned than usual by remuneration or similar considerations. Most members understood that citizen control requires dedication that will be rewarded by better public governance.

Improved Relations with the Media

The network has also greatly improved its relationships with the media, an area where CSO members are often lacking, thereby limiting their visibility and dissemination capacity. This visibility could be one of the benefits for CSOs that invest effort in the network. Journalists have shown through their actions that they understand and share the vision of Social Watch Benin. Communication plans were adopted to disseminate network actions, and contracts have been signed with the media to effectively support citizen awareness-building actions and develop effective and efficient citizen monitoring.

Scant Impact on Formulation and Monitoring of Development Policies

The 2006 alternative report analyzed public action in relation to the recommendations of the first report and made many suggestions. The analysis showed that few recommendations from the first report had been taken into account. Social Watch condemns this loss of a year as a result of inactivity and the misappropriation of public funds by individuals reaching the end of their careers. However, the network confirmed citizen expectations in terms of good governance and public accountability. The lack of impact may be explained by the end-of-term atmosphere before the 2006 elections, which left the newly elected team without public funds and with higher poverty indicators than in 2000.

Limited Impact on the Public Budget

Even if the contribution of the Budget Analysis Unit is limited because it cannot propose any budget allocations without matching them with additional financing, it has given its opinion on existing allocations. According to the network's executive secretary, many recommendations have been taken into consideration by the government, and the network received a copy of the revised budget, allowing Social Watch to verify that its concerns had been taken into account.

Improved Civil Society Credibility

All of Social Watch's actions have had a major impact in establishing the credibility of civil society and its capacity to carry out critical analysis and to formulate proposals. It is too early to suggest that Social Watch has had a direct impact on public policies, even though it has most likely contributed to the debate on economic development and on the types of businesses that should be promoted. Social Watch has also called attention to the existence of extreme poverty in certain areas and social groups and has proven its capacity to ensure citizen control of government action.

FACTORS FOR SUCCESS AND LESSONS LEARNED

Social Watch's CCPA initiative and its results are closely related to Benin's political process, which has been a model of democracy in Africa since

1990. The creation of opposition parties, freedom of association, freedom of expression, and freedom of the press are fertile ground for the CCPA experience that is unfolding in Benin. The nature and quality of the political environment make it possible.

In addition, Social Watch can benefit from the new Beninese political scene. The new government team does not feel threatened in any way by the criticism directed toward its predecessors. Even better, it has defined, as its political principles, the engagement of dialogue with citizens and establishment of a code of conduct for government management. Information on government activities is no longer treated as confidential. On the contrary, it is available to all. Authorities have adopted a favorable attitude toward Social Watch. Government officials who are conscious of the government's opaque and deficient management and of its inability to reform itself now welcome proposals that could help improve its performance and develop citizen control actions.

Voluntary civil participation is a sign of citizen maturity. However, CSOs must have adequate financial and human resources and be capable of supporting each other if they are to preserve their political credibility. Only then can the CSOs in Benin (a) guarantee the continuity of CCPA initiatives and widen their scope for long-term monitoring of local and sectoral actions, (b) carry out periodic evaluations of user satisfaction, (c) expand media coverage of advocacy actions, and (d) engage in concerted civil society activities at a subregional level.

NOTES

1. A part of Alliance 21 ("glegbenu" means resolute and vivacious in Fon, a national language).
2. The Beninese Health NGO Network.
3. This committee became the Monitoring Unit for Economic and Structural Reform Programs (CSPRES).

REFERENCES

Social Watch Benin. 2005. *Objectifs du Millénaire pour le Développement: Participation de la Société Civile a la revue du sommet du millenaire au Bénin.* First alternative CSO report. Cotonou: Social Watch Benin. http://www.socialwatch-benin.org/documents/ Rapport%20alternatif/Rapport%20Alternatif%202005%20des%20OSC%20sur% 20les%20OMD.pdf.

————. 2006a. "Contribution des Organisations de la Société Civile au PRSP II final, rapport d'activité." Social Watch Benin, Cotonou.

————. 2006b. *Objectifs du Millénaire pour le Développement: Deuxième Rapport alternatif des Organisations de la Société Civile sur les OMD.* Second alternative CSO report. Cotonou: Social Watch Benin. http://www.socialwatch-benin.org/documents/Rapport%20 alternatif/Rapport%20Alternatif%202006%20des%20OSC%20sur%20les%20OM D%20au%20Benin.pdf.

CHAPTER 9

SOCIAL ACCOUNTABILITY IN AFRICA: AN ANALYSIS

Mary McNeil and Carmen Malena

The case studies presented here reflect the work of early pioneers involved in enhancing citizen involvement in government decision making and implementation. In the few years since these experiences were initiated, the social accountability agenda in Africa has grown considerably, with much more emphasis on evidence-based data collection (including third-party monitoring of investment projects) and the monitoring, development, and tracking of public resources. However, without this early push toward civil society participation, these advances would not have been possible.

Chapters 2 through 8 present a rich and diverse set of these early social accountability practices in the African context. Each case is unique and is shaped and influenced by a wide range of context-specific factors. Because social accountability is about relationships and because these relationships—among individuals, institutions, and societal spheres—are determined by a complex mix of political, social, institutional, cultural, and other factors, no two social accountability initiatives are the same. Therefore, it is difficult to compare social accountability experiences and problematic to propose standardized approaches or blanket recommendations. That said, a comparative analysis of the cases presented in the previous chapters does reveal some common challenges and hints at some shared factors for success and lessons learned.

Based on an analysis of both the particularities and commonalities of the seven case studies, this final chapter aims to draw out some key findings and lessons that can inform future work. It begins by identifying crucial aspects of an enabling environment for social accountability and goes on to analyze some of the main obstacles and challenges faced by civil society and the state in seeking to promote social accountability in Africa. The chapter then discusses several factors of success and lessons learned before proposing some conclusions. It ends with an update on the current status of such work in Africa and some brief suggestions for how to best advance this agenda across the continent in future years.

ENVIRONMENT FOR SOCIAL ACCOUNTABILITY

Social accountability is strongly influenced by a range of underlying political, legal, social, cultural, and economic factors. These factors play important roles in determining the feasibility and success of social accountability initiatives:

- *Political context, culture, and will.* Opportunities for social accountability initiatives are clearly greater where the political regime is democratic, the rule of law is respected, power is decentralized, and basic political and civil rights (such as access to information and freedom of expression, association, and assembly) are guaranteed. The initiatives' success often depends on the "political will" of leaders, defined as their willingness to commit to certain actions over time.
- *Legal and policy frameworks.* Promoting or requiring public access to information, consultation, and citizen participation and oversight can also be essential to enabling and sustaining social accountability.
- *Sociocultural and economic factors.* A country's underlying sociocultural and economic characteristics have an important collective influence on factors such as citizens' expectations of, and relations with, the state; their willingness to question authority or speak out; and the capacity and means of citizens and civil society leaders to organize and act.

The extent to which the external environment is enabling or disabling for social accountability varies greatly from country to country and even from community to community. Environmental factors also change over time. This change can be gradual, as in the case of evolving social norms, or sudden, such as during a change of administration. Concerted citizen action can change the external environment by, for example, mobilizing and advocating for legal or policy reforms.

This section identifies and analyzes a range of environmental factors identified as enabling or disabling to the social accountability initiatives discussed in this book. As summarized in table 9.1, the case studies illustrate a range of environments, varying from positive and enabling (in Tanzania, for example) to highly disabling (particularly in Zimbabwe).

The environment for social accountability can always be improved, and an unfavorable environment does not mean that social accountability activities cannot be pursued. In fact, an Organisation for Economic Co-operation and Development (OECD) study of social accountability initiatives in 26 OECD countries found that most initiatives were launched in the absence of an enabling legal or policy norm, particularly at the local government level (Caddy, Peixoto, and McNeil 2007).[1]

The Zimbabwe case study presented here also illustrates that it *is* possible to successfully undertake social accountability initiatives even in a very difficult country context. However, experience shows that a disabling context can constrain opportunities for social accountability, restrict the

Table 9.1 Aspects of Enabling and Disabling Environments for Social Accountability in Africa: Case Study Evidence

Enabling environment factor	Enabling	Disabling
Political context and culture		
Democratic space		Zimbabwe
Respect for citizen rights		Zimbabwe
Decentralization	Malawi (mixed), Senegal (mixed), Tanzania	Malawi (mixed), Senegal (mixed)
Legal and policy framework		
Access to information		Benin, Ghana, Malawi, Zimbabwe
Citizen participation	Tanzania	Zimbabwe
Sociocultural and economic factors		
Social norms, power relations, and deference to authority		Several case studies
Lack of citizen empowerment and participation		Benin, Malawi, Zimbabwe
Gender inequities		All case studies
Widespread poverty and illiteracy		Zimbabwe

Source: Authors' analysis.

type or depth of social accountability initiative that is feasible, and limit outcomes and impacts. In some country contexts, actions aimed at creating a more enabling environment—for example, legal reforms that enhance access to information or guarantee press freedoms—can be critical to achieving effective social accountability outcomes.

POLITICAL CONTEXT AND CULTURE

There is little doubt that the political context and culture play fundamental roles in determining whether social accountability initiatives are launched, and, even more so, whether they bring about sustained institutional change. The countries presented here represent a range of political contexts and cultures. For example, Ghana has a longer history of decentralization—delegating budgetary authority to district assemblies that operate at the community level. Interestingly, of the countries here, only Zimbabwe has a Freedom of Information Act, yet it remains the most challenging environment in which to operate. Only Tanzania had a strong tradition of popular mobilization and a policy framework for citizen participation at the outset of the initiative. Yet the case studies demonstrate that the absence of any or all of the factors below played a role in the undertaking of social accountability initiatives.

Democratic Space

Most of the countries in the case studies could be classified as "emerging democracies," having recently (mostly in the past 15 years) undergone transitions from one-party authoritarian rule to multiparty democracy. In most cases, democratic structures and systems are still being consolidated. Nevertheless, most of the case study authors recognize that the types of activities they describe would have been impossible, or at least extremely risky, under previous authoritarian regimes. Several authors identify the new political space and freedoms created by democratization as an essential enabling factor for social accountability.

The case of Zimbabwe stands out as one example of a disabling political environment marked by government control, distrust, and violation of basic rights. This case study is instructive and exemplary in that through a high level of commitment and determination—combined with the rigorous, principled, and judicious use of social accountability approaches—the case study authors and their colleagues have managed to achieve important results, bringing concrete benefits to the women and children of Zimbabwe despite the difficult political environment. In numerous so-called hybrid states, which only partly respect democratic principles and systems, courageous social accountability practitioners have shown that it is possible, and crucial, to actively inhabit new political spaces (however limited they may be) and, through civic engagement, to enhance government accountability and expand democratic space over time.

Respect for Citizen Rights

None of the case study countries can claim to enjoy complete rule of law or guarantee of basic freedoms, but most enjoy at least a basic level of freedom and justice that allows them to undertake social accountability activities without excessive risk. Again, Zimbabwe stands out as an exceptional case where social accountability activists and practitioners have managed to establish productive working relations and carry out meaningful budget work in a context marked by state control and frequent violations of human rights.

For the purposes of this analysis, the most germane rights and freedoms include access to information, freedom of expression, press freedoms, freedom of association and assembly, and political participation. Ideally, these rights must be both guaranteed by *law* and respected in *practice*. Where basic rights and freedoms of information, association, and expression are not guaranteed, preliminary efforts may need to focus on developing these.

Decentralization

The extent to which political power and authority are decentralized and deconcentrated is an important element of an enabling environment. Local-level public authorities and services are crucially important from a social accountability perspective because they often represent the front line of citizen-state relations. Their proximity to local populations creates important opportunities for meaningful citizen-state engagement.

In practice, however, there are many significant obstacles. In many of the countries studied, decentralization processes are only partial, maintain top-down dynamics, or decentralize responsibility without matching resources. Local government authorities usually lack the resources, autonomy, capacity, skills, and incentives for effectively serving, engaging with, and accounting to citizens. Their lack of autonomy and capacity also undermines citizen interest in engaging with them. Yet there is also evidence that without the empowerment of local communities and citizen participation in project selection, decentralization does not often yield positive results (McNeil and Mumvuma 2006).

The case studies here illustrate different levels and stages of decentralization and deconcentration. In Tanzania, for example, decentralization is quite advanced, and the case study cites the Local Government Reform Program as an important and supportive factor. Senegal presents a mixed context. Although several reforms since 1972 have aimed to strengthen the power of local governments, and responsibility in nine areas was devolved to local governments, the financial resources to implement these responsibilities effectively have not been transferred. The Malawi case study illustrates how decentralization offers important opportunities but also poses major challenges to the ability of civil society organizations (CSOs) to function at the national level, even as they must also seek to decentralize their approaches and activities, which requires substantial investment in local-level networking and capacity building.

LEGAL AND POLICY FRAMEWORK

A legal framework includes a country's constitution, legislation, and public rules and regulations, all of which have the potential to enable or constrain social accountability—for example, by protecting basic rights, providing access to information, requiring public reporting, and promoting citizen participation. A country's policy environment can also influence the feasibility and success of social accountability initiatives. Of particular relevance are policies on citizen participation and civil society-state relations.

It is important, however, not to overstate the influence of legal and policy factors. Enabling laws and policies are useful but not sufficient to support social accountability, especially in contexts where the rule of law is lacking. For example, citizens' rights are often protected by law but not respected in practice. Although an enabling law or policy is always helpful, the lack of an enabling framework does not preclude social accountability activities. Examples such as Zimbabwe show that it is possible to pursue social accountability initiatives even in the context of a disabling legal and policy framework.

Access to Information

A fundamental element of social accountability is for citizens and CSOs to have access to accurate and relevant information regarding public policies, programs, services, budgets, and expenditures. The transparency of government and its capacity to produce and provide data and accounts are important.

Lack of adequate access to information is identified as an obstacle in several cases (Ghana, Malawi, and Zimbabwe). Gaining access to information about public finances (for example, budget commitments and accounts; records of inputs, outputs, and expenditures; and audit findings) is often particularly difficult. Problems in accessing data on financial transfers and expenditures have been a significant impediment to most budget monitoring and expenditure tracking initiatives.

The complicated and non-user-friendly format of financial information is also a problem. The Benin case study, for example, identified low readability of the budget as an important constraint.[2] In many countries, the initial focus of social accountability interventions has been to lobby for enhanced information rights and public transparency. Without adequate information, social accountability is virtually impossible.

Citizen Participation

International and domestic legislation are important mechanisms for ensuring that citizen participation and inclusion are not dependent on whims of politicians and changing circumstance. However, laws alone are not enough. Systems and structures for making citizen participation rights operational and mechanisms for dealing with complaints and sanctioning the state when it fails to respect these rights are also critical.

Tanzania stands out from the other case studies with regard to its strong tradition of popular mobilization and strong policy framework for citizen participation. The country's Participation Policy was considered a particularly important enabling factor by the case study authors. Social accountability practitioners in Zimbabwe point out that the nation's legal framework provides for consultation but not participation.

SOCIOCULTURAL AND ECONOMIC FACTORS

African countries are constantly changing with regard to societal and economic factors that may influence social accountability work. The case studies analyzed in this book yielded several interesting conclusions with respect to the roles played by sociocultural and economic factors in promoting or challenging the success of social accountability initiatives in the African context.

Social Norms, Power Relations, and Deference to Authority

Many traditional African cultures have strongly ingrained respect for and deference to authority, leadership, and elders. As a result, ordinary citizens (especially poor people, women, and youth) often are not accustomed to questioning authority figures, and the very act of seeking accountability from public officials can be perceived as an act of disrespect by public officials as well as by citizens.[3]

This cultural characteristic is not necessarily incompatible with social accountability, but it does pose certain challenges. As a result, many cases of successful social accountability efforts in Africa aim both (a) to seek accountability from authorities in a respectful and productive way, thus rendering the efforts more culturally acceptable, and (b) to empower citizens to actively advocate for less hierarchical and more democratic relations between citizens (of all social and economic levels) and public authorities. Successful social accountability activities also frequently involve specific efforts to educate groups such as women and youth about their right to be heard and to empower them to speak up.

Lack of Citizen Empowerment and Participation

In many counties, ordinary people have had little opportunity to learn about and socialize citizenship rights and habits. As a result, citizenship remains a hollow concept. Social accountability efforts must promote public reflection and discussion about the meaning of citizenship, educate both citizens and governments about citizens' rights and responsibilities, and create opportunities and mechanisms for genuine citizen participation. Especially in countries that are emerging from an authoritarian past during which questioning of government actions or policies was not tolerated (such as in Benin and Malawi), citizens need information about their rights and opportunities to develop and exercise their civic competencies.

Gender Inequities

Many societies in Africa and around the world are marked by systemic discrimination against women. Lack of respect for women's rights deprives women of access to productive resources, basic services, and decision-making processes. Women's incomes, literacy, and school enrollment rates are less than those of men. Women are largely excluded from government institutions at all levels, have less access to information about government and public affairs, and have less contact with traditional and political authorities. In sum, women suffer the most from political and social injustices and are least able to seek accountability from public authorities.

Virtually every case study presented in this book acknowledges gender inequity as a glaring social injustice, a constraint to development, and an obstacle to social accountability. Therefore, social accountability initiatives must go hand in hand with efforts to affirm women's rights and empower women to seek accountability and justice.

Widespread Poverty and Illiteracy

Poverty and illiteracy are widespread in many African countries and frequently cited as a barrier to citizen participation. People living in poverty, especially extreme poverty, clearly face numerous barriers to making their voices heard and holding government accountable. Poor people, for example, are frequently less aware of their rights and enjoy less access to information and education than people who are better-off. They also suffer from social and political exclusion and may lack the time, confidence, and resources to participate in citizen organizations or public events.

Several of the case studies demonstrate that poverty and illiteracy are not insurmountable barriers to social accountability. Many social accountability practitioners, including those who have contributed to this book, have successfully developed and used methods and tools specifically adapted for effective use by illiterate groups. The view held by some that poor or uneducated people cannot understand budgets or evaluate public services has been repeatedly refuted. In some cases, economic adversity is even cited as a factor facilitating greater civic participation. In Zimbabwe, for example, participatory budgeting practitioners found that adverse economic environments led communities to push for more involvement in local budgeting and planning.

Social accountability initiatives simultaneously benefit from and contribute to the development of a more enabling political culture, legal and regulatory framework, policy environment, sociocultural setting, and economic climate. The lesson is not for potential social accountability initiators and promoters to wait for a more enabling environment to emerge before taking action, but rather to work proactively toward the creation of a more enabling environment while taking advantage of existing opportunities to initiate actions that are possible and productive under the current circumstances, however challenging.

KEY CHALLENGES

Social accountability involves a relationship between two essential groups of actors: (a) state actors and (b) citizens and citizens' organizations. These actors work within an enabling environment (made up of political, legal, social, and other factors as discussed above) that both influences their capacities and relationships and can be affected by them. This general model is not intended to imply that state actors and citizens or CSOs are homogeneous or clear-cut groups. To the contrary, in real life, each category contains a spectrum of highly diverse actors, and the relationships both within and between the two groups are inevitably dynamic and complex.

In addition to officials in the executive branch of government, state actors include mayors and local councilors, members of parliament, executive branch officials, bureaucrats, and public service providers as well as those who work within "independent" government institutions such as the judiciary, ombudsmen, and anticorruption agencies.

Important civil society actors include ordinary citizens, community-based membership organizations, community leaders and activists, independent media, advocacy organizations, social movements, professional associations, trade unions, academics, think tanks, and nongovernmental organizations (NGOs).

As the case studies show, any of these actors can initiate social accountability efforts, which, more often than not, involve a wide variety of state and nonstate participants. Many other actors—from the private sector or international donor community, for example—also influence and participate in social accountability processes.

In some cases, the boundaries between spheres of societal actors break down, and the roles the actors play can become interchangeable. For example, CSOs sometimes become service providers, local government authorities or parliamentarians join forces with civil society leaders to lobby for legal reforms, and private companies sometimes engage the state as corporate citizens. Other groups of great potential importance to social accountability, such as traditional authorities and political parties, also do not fall clearly into either the state or civil society sphere and are sometimes perceived as inhabiting the fuzzy border area between them.

Despite this model's limitations as an oversimplified description of reality, it nevertheless provides a useful framework for analyzing some of the crucial issues and challenges that social accountability practitioners encounter in the initiatives described in this book. Some issues regarding the enabling environment have already been discussed above. The principal challenges regarding the attitudes, capacities, and roles of state actors, citizens and CSOs—and the relationships between these two broad groups—are summarized in table 9.2 and discussed in detail below. Potential strategies for addressing these challenges also are identified and explored.

Citizens and Civil Society

Civil society plays a critical role in social accountability. It offers a space for citizens to engage with one another and to organize and amplify their demands on government. In almost all the case studies, CSOs play important initiating, organizing, and mobilizing roles. They also contribute financial support and technical knowledge and expertise. Citizens and communities rarely mobilize and organize spontaneously on their own without support or assistance from an intermediary CSO.

The major challenges that CSOs face in seeking to promote and support social accountability fall within these four broad categories: building capacities and skills, raising resources, mobilizing citizens on the grassroots level, and ensuring civil society's own credibility and accountability.

Building capacities and skills for social accountability. In Africa, CSOs have a general problem of institutional weaknesses—more specifically, a lack of capacities and skills to implement social accountability measures. Over the past two decades, development-oriented CSOs in Africa have grown and expanded considerably. Traditionally, many of these organizations have taken a welfare or service delivery approach. A more recent

Table 9.2 Challenges for Social Accountability in Africa: Case Study Evidence

	Challenges for citizens and civil society				Challenges for state actors[a]		Challenges for relations between state, citizens, and CSOs		
	Capacity	Resources	Grassroots mobilization	Assurance of credibility and accountability within civil society	Patronage and partisanship	Political will	Building trust	Interface mechanisms	Inclusiveness
Benin		X	X	X					X
Ghana		X	X	X					
Malawi	X	X	X	X			X	X	X
Nigeria	X		X			X		X	
Senegal		X	X		X	X		X	X
Tanzania			X				X	X	
Zimbabwe	X			X	X		X	X	X

Source: Authors' analysis.

Note: This table summarizes some of the key problems encountered by actors in the various case studies. Although some of these obstacles ultimately proved to be major challenges, many were successfully overcome through innovative strategies and determination on the part of the involved organizations.

a. Two other challenges for state actors—"capacity" and "building a culture of genuine democracy"—were indirectly mentioned or implied in several case studies.

phenomenon is the development of CSOs focused on governance, citizen empowerment, and social accountability. Across Sub-Saharan Africa, the number of organizations engaging in such issues is still quite small and, generally speaking, capacities and skills are limited.

As the case studies have shown, seeking social accountability can be quite a difficult and demanding task requiring considerable skill and rigor. For some efforts, such as applied policy and budget work, considerable knowledge and technical expertise are required. Successful social accountability initiatives often require a mix of research, analysis, and advocacy skills that civil society sorely lacks. Even in those countries with a relatively strong and dynamic civil society, social accountability may be relatively new territory and institutional knowledge, capacities, and skills limited. Major issues include CSOs' capacities to research, analyze, demystify, and disseminate relevant information; to build public support; and to interact and negotiate with government. Many CSOs themselves lack knowledge about laws, policies, and budgets. They are not necessarily familiar with public planning, budgeting, and decision-making processes.

The Malawi Economic Justice Network (MEJN) had significant capacity for undertaking social accountability activities but still was pressed to keep up with rapidly growing demand for its training, document simplification, budget demystification, and related services. In Zimbabwe, the lack of qualified personnel was identified as a problem. In Nigeria, many Publish What You Pay (PWYP) members lacked technical knowledge of extractive industries, were unfamiliar with how the sector operated and its technical terms, did not understand Nigeria Extractive Industries Transparency Initiative (NEITI) issues, or were interested only in how they could benefit, not in what they could contribute to revenue transparency and accountability in Nigerian extractive industries. There remains a strong need for training, capacity building, and institutional development support for African CSOs that are active or interested in social accountability approaches.

Raising resources for social accountability. In many parts of Africa, CSOs have a weak financial resource base and are highly dependent on donor funding. As a result, agendas are driven largely by foreign donors, and a large proportion of available funding is linked to short-term project outputs rather than longer-term programmatic goals. Donor dependence raises important issues about local ownership, vision, and sustainability (of both CSOs and their activities).

Beyond general resource constraints, obtaining resources for social accountability activities can be particularly difficult. Social accountability is a relatively new agenda within the donor community, and only a few donors are willing and able to support such work. Some donors are reluctant to fund work that appears too political or cannot promise quick or concrete results. Funding for research, analysis, and advocacy activities remains limited.

Lack of resources is considered problematic in almost all the case studies and is identified as a crucial constraint in the cases of Benin, Ghana, Malawi, and Senegal. The Benin and Senegal case studies highlight the challenges and limitations of relying on volunteerism, especially over the longer term. In these cases, leaders and facilitators had to find time for network activities in addition to responsibilities in their own respective organizations and families, leading to some eventually dropping out or asking to be replaced.

Given the challenges of relying on volunteers and the problems associated with donor funding, an alternative solution is to work toward institutionalizing systems and funding related to social accountability. For example, the Senegalese case study recommends institutionalizing resources to allow local governments to work in a more participatory manner. This recommendation is supported by the Tanzania case study, in which the costs associated with participatory budgeting were assumed largely by the local government, which found that the direct costs of the exercise were low (less than 20,000) and highly cost-effective in the long term.

While institutionalization is an important recommendation and a potential long-term solution, it may not be feasible, or desirable, in all cases. Some social accountability practices—for example, those aimed at monitoring government budgets or denouncing malfeasance—must remain independent and would be jeopardized by government funding. The question of who pays for social accountability, especially in the long term, remains a problematic one.

Mobilizing grassroots groups. Public mobilization is an essential function of civil society and a fundamental element of successful social accountability initiatives. The ability to organize and mobilize at the grassroots level and to make effective links between the local- and national-level actors and processes proved a primary challenge in almost all the case studies.

It is exceptional to find organizations whose presence stretches from the local to the national level. In Nigeria, for example, the national CSOs' constituency links proved inadequate. In Malawi, MEJN worked hard to consolidate local-level links among district-level CSOs and networks to MEJN district chapters (committees of 10 volunteers). In Ghana, participation of the poor was facilitated when researchers involved community institutions in administering the questionnaire and the focus group discussions.

In many countries, due to weak notions of citizenship and little tradition of civic engagement, substantial effort is required to educate the public about citizen rights and responsibilities and to mobilize for action on public issues. The Ghana case study, for example, identified lack of public interest as a significant constraint.

Lack of effective local associations is another common constraint, as the Senegal case study reported. In Benin, social accountability practitioners found that most local-level groups were not accustomed to such activities and not accustomed to directly engaging the government. In Tanzania, to support local-level organizations, the municipal government devoted extensive effort to training and supporting a network of community development workers and 22 community-level planning and budgeting support teams.

Ensuring credibility and accountability within civil society. To be effective in demanding government accountability, CSOs must themselves be credible, representative, and accountable actors. Many CSOs have limited ability or willingness to seek government accountability, however, because of their own potential weaknesses in this regard. Poor internal governance, lack of transparency, and weak accountability are important problems that can limit CSOs' effectiveness and undermine their legitimacy and credibility.

In Benin, the great majority of people are convinced that CSO leaders, like political leaders, are trying only to protect their own material interests. It is hard for them to believe that some civil society leaders might truly seek to achieve better governance and citizen advancement. Constant vigilance is also necessary because some CSOs do hide agendas of personal gain behind a guise of social commitment.

In several case studies, strong CSO integrity and credibility were important to the initiatives' success. In both Zimbabwe and Malawi, for example, lead CSOs have worked hard to prove their integrity and meet rigorous ethical and operational standards. The Zimbabwe case study also identifies the strategy of capitalizing on the credibility of respected organizations. Unfortunately, in Nigeria, the PWYP campaign suffered from an internal leadership scandal, conflict among member organizations, and a lack of CSO integrity and credibility. CSO internal governance and credibility were also issues in Ghana.

There is a need for institution building within civil society to help CSOs build their representational legitimacy (for example, by strengthening links to their membership and constituency) and enhance their credibility (by improving internal management and governance practices and introducing mechanisms for transparency, participation, and downward accountability).

For building of credibility of the sector as a whole, it is also important to work toward the establishment of commonly agreed-upon CSO codes of ethics and effective self-regulation mechanisms. Donors can contribute to these goals by linking funding to compliance with basic standards of transparency and accountability, providing much-needed core institution-building support to help CSOs meet these standards, and supporting efforts to develop sectorwide coordination and self-regulation.

State Actors

The willingness and ability of state actors to disclose information and to listen to, engage with, and account to citizens is also crucial for social accountability. The principal challenges here include building a culture of genuine democracy and downward accountability, overcoming problems of patronage and partisanship, nurturing political will and leadership, and building state capacities for social accountability.

Building a culture of genuine democracy and downward accountability. Despite democratic gains, political cultures and structures in many African countries remain strongly top-down. Dominance by the executive is frequently accompanied by a strong sense of upward accountability (accountability of civil servants and public officials to governmental authorities) and a weak sense of downward accountability (government's accountability to citizens).

One of the most fundamental challenges in promoting social accountability is to nurture, in both government and citizens, this basic notion of downward accountability—and, through social accountability mechanisms, to put into practice the democratic obligation of government to account to the people and the fundamental political right of citizens to demand public accountability.

Overcoming patronage and partisanship. Political systems in Africa are frequently marked by patronage and partisanship. The logic of patronage is contrary to principles of public probity, equity, and accountability. Transforming clients into citizens (charged with expectations, rights, and responsibilities) and patrons into public duty bearers (obliged to account to the people and equitably serve the common public interest) is a profound challenge but also an evolution that is fundamental to the realization of democracy and social accountability. This evolution—resulting from progressive political leadership as well as ongoing awareness raising, public education, and advocacy—is at the heart of several of the case studies described in this book.

Excessive partisanship is a major political challenge in Africa. When loyalty to party superiors takes precedence over service to citizens and when partisan interests reign over the common public interest, democracy and social accountability suffer. The Senegal rural councilors are selected more by political parties than by the choice of local people, so the councilors often feel more accountable to their political parties than to their constituents. The Zimbabwe case study laments the limited effectiveness of members of parliament as representatives and advocates of the people due to party politics.

In many countries, any CSO that dares to question or criticize is vulnerable to charges of partisanship. Several case studies reported that state actors commonly label CSOs that promote social accountability as opposition forces. The Malawi and Zimbabwe studies emphasize the crucial importance of rigorous research and evidence-based advocacy in promoting objectivity and protecting against charges of partisanship.

Building political will and leadership. Although some government actors play prominent roles in introducing and supporting social accountability initiatives, others may be initially hesitant or feel threatened by such initiatives. Many social accountability initiatives are undertaken independently by civil society and are not reliant on government approval or support, but these initiatives have a greater chance of long-term success if state actors understand and support social accountability approaches.

Strategies for building political will for social accountability may vary based on whether an individual in the public sector is already supportive or, instead, needs more knowledge or sensitization. In the former case, CSOs can actively seek out and nurture social accountability champions within the public sector who genuinely believe in and are willing to support the approach. In the latter case, CSOs might invest time and energy in sensitizing government actors about the benefits of social accountability (for example, through in-country demonstration pilots and cross-country exchanges or study tours). Experience shows that the absence of political will is not an external factor that must be passively accepted; rather, political will can be actively created and nurtured (Malena 2009).

Experience also shows that enhanced social accountability offers important potential benefits for governments, including enhanced effectiveness, legitimacy, popularity, resources, and stability. Sharing such experiences with reticent public sector actors or, better yet, facilitating exchanges with peers who can share their own firsthand experiences with social accountability experiences can go a long way toward achieving political will.

Several of the case studies demonstrate the importance of political leadership. The Senegal initiative, for example, succeeded partially because of open and proactive rural council leadership. In Nigeria, NEITI became possible because of President Obasanjo's direct support and influence. Both cases demonstrate the vital role that a political leader can play in making social accountability possible, but they also highlight the fragility of initiatives that are highly dependent on a particular individual. The Nigeria study, for example, indicates some of the difficulties associated with the departure of a government champion and the subsequent leadership vacuum.

Building state capacities for social accountability. Beyond political will, the capacity of governments to engage in and respond to social accountability initiatives is also a challenge. The primary capacities relevant to social accountability include the capacity to manage and share information, to consult and seek feedback from citizens and CSOs, and to provide grievance mechanisms.

In recent years, numerous African governments (encouraged by civil society and donors) have taken important steps toward enhancing their capacity to share information and account to citizens. Such actions, as witnessed in some of the case study countries, include improved information management and disclosure systems as well as enhanced resources for communication and outreach. A strong need remains, however, to further strengthen the capacities of state actors to effectively communicate and engage with and account to citizens.

Citizens' and CSOs' Relationships with the State

The nature of relations between civil society and government actors lies at the heart of social accountability. Social accountability involves strengthening information sharing and dialogue between citizens and the state. The primary challenges identified by the case studies include building trust between citizens and CSOs and the state, establishing effective mechanisms of citizen-state interface, and striving for inclusiveness.

Building trust. In many country settings, interactions between citizens and civil society and the state are marked by suspicion or distrust. Building trust between citizens and the state is both a major challenge and an important potential benefit of social accountability.

In Ilala, Tanzania, local government authorities won increased citizen trust and support by openly sharing information (for example, about revenues and expenditures) and by introducing clear and defined mechanisms for dialogue and negotiation. In Malawi and Zimbabwe, social accountability practitioners built trust and positive relations by ensuring a high level of rigor, objectivity, and professionalism. The case studies also show that focusing on solutions rather than problems and ensuring that engagement remains constructive (even when it includes criticism) are good strategies for building trust.

Establishing effective interface mechanisms. In Africa, as elsewhere, often there is no established framework for ongoing dialogue or collaboration and weak mechanisms for formal and systematic exchange between civil society and the state. When interactions do take place, they tend to be ad hoc and do not necessarily influence decision making. This lack of effective dialogue breeds continued misunderstanding and distrust. Citizens and CSOs feel distant from government decision-making processes and distrustful of state institutions and officials.

Therefore, a fundamental challenge for social accountability initiatives is to introduce and strengthen mechanisms for improved information exchange, dialogue, and negotiation between citizens and the state. Each of the case studies describes various ways to do so. Some examples include consultations between civil society actors and parliamentarians in Zimbabwe, interface meetings between citizens and public service providers in Malawi, mechanisms for participatory budgeting in Senegal, and joint community-level management committees in Tanzania.

The core challenge of social accountability is not just to bring citizens and state actors together, but also to enhance the quality, effectiveness, and impact of their interactions. Because of their positions of power, state actors often tend to dominate such interactions. State actors decide who will participate, what will be discussed, and whether expressed ideas and inputs will be taken on board. Where this is the case, social accountability involves creating or claiming new spaces of interaction and redefining the terms of engagement to be more equitable and accountable. Government domination of exchange forums also enhances the risk of (real or perceived) co-optation of civil society participants. Civil society actors who become too closely associated with government processes can suffer weakened links with their constituencies or a loss of legitimacy. To mitigate this risk, forums for state-civil society dialogue and negotiation must be made as open and transparent as possible.

The Nigeria case illustrates the challenges of dealing with government domination of the NEITI working group. Although the group was established as a joint working group allowing for quarterly exchanges between civil society and the state, that the government dominates the group and selects the civil society participants has reduced the group's effectiveness as a forum for genuine and meaningful dialogue.

Striving for inclusiveness. Linked to the dialogue issue is the frequent exclusion of marginal voices. In particular, the voices of women, youth, and other traditionally marginalized or critical groups remain unheard and unheeded. As with almost any development intervention, social accountability initiatives risk being captured by more powerful or influential stakeholders. Even if unintentional, processes of dialogue and negotiation with government frequently end up involving a group of "usual suspects" or "well-behaved" NGOs. The maximum benefits of social accountability processes are gained, however, when a full spectrum of societal viewpoints are represented. Constant and explicit efforts are therefore required to ensure the meaningful inclusion and participation of less organized or less powerful groups.

Several of the cases described in this book focus on serving and promoting the equitable participation of marginalized groups. The initiatives in Benin, Malawi, Senegal, and Zimbabwe, for example, all collaborate directly with women's groups to promote women's participation. The Zimbabwe case study involves the direct involvement of children, and the Tanzania case study describes specific attempts to target and involve poor and disadvantaged groups at the local level. In each case, however, inclusiveness is an uphill struggle, and equitable representation and influence remain elusive.

FACTORS OF SUCCESS AND LESSONS LEARNED

There are no standard formulas or recommendations for enhancing social accountability. As the various case studies have shown, a wide range of diverse approaches, strategies, and tools can be used to hold government accountable. Which approaches are used, and how, will inevitably vary according to the particular political and cultural context, the specific objectives of the social accountability initiative, the priority needs of target populations, and the available resources and expertise.

As the field of social accountability develops, and a variety of initiatives and experiences are documented and shared, common factors of success and lessons learned are emerging. As table 9.3 summarizes, the success factors include use of the media, the combination of technical skills and popular mobilization, experience with social accountability practices, sustained commitment, a solution-based approach, coalition building, and international support.

Factors of Success

Each case study in this book identifies several important factors of success and operational lessons, many of which echo the experience of social accountability practitioners elsewhere (McNeil and Mumvuma 2006).[4] Some of the most common, and important, factors of operational success cited by the implementers of social accountability initiatives highlighted in this book are described below. These factors are presented not as prescriptions for success but rather as potentially important elements for those implementing or supporting social accountability initiatives to keep in mind and use as appropriate.

Use of media. The media constitute an important and powerful tool for achieving social accountability. By keeping citizens informed about government activities, investigating and exposing wrongdoing, and providing a shared space for citizens to voice ideas on public matters, the media play a critical role in promoting social accountability. Almost all successful

Table 9.3 Success Factors for Social Accountability in Africa: Case Study Evidence

	Use of media	Combination of technical skills and popular mobilization	Previous experiences with social accountability practices	Sustained commitment	Solution-based approach	Coalition building	International support
Benin	X					X	X
Ghana	X						X
Malawi	X				X	X	X
Nigeria						X	X
Senegal	X		X		X		X
Tanzania			X	X	X	X	X
Zimbabwe	X	X			X	X	X

Source: Authors' analysis.

206

social accountability initiatives have used traditional and modern media strategically to raise awareness around public matters, disseminate social accountability findings, express popular opinion, and create public pressure.

Many of the case study authors identify the use of media as instrumental to the success of their initiatives, citing the following activities:

- Press conferences in Ghana
- Press statements, news bulletins, television programs, and workshops with the media in Zimbabwe
- Media campaigns, electronic newsletters, and town hall meetings in Nigeria
- Use of community radio and a local-language newsletter in Senegal
- Workshops on budget analysis and training sessions organized for invited print, radio, and television journalists by Social Watch Benin— which also signed weekly, monthly, and quarterly contracts with private and public media representatives to disseminate network activities through community and local radio stations, newspapers, and television channels
- Media advocacy campaigns, live radio debates and phone-in programs, television programs, produced videos and music CDs, and leaflets disseminated to the main newspapers by the Malawi Economic Justice Network

Combination of technical skills and popular mobilization. Successful social accountability requires a combination of technical expertise and popular mobilization. Social accountability is, by definition, an open and public endeavor. It cannot take place behind closed doors or among a small group of experts. The principal strength of social accountability approaches is that they bring information, issues, and actions into the public sphere. They directly involve the general public and aim to create and strengthen relationships between ordinary citizens and a wide range of public authorities and power holders.

The Zimbabwe case study, for example, emphasizes grassroots involvement and seeks to create opportunities for children to articulate their own needs and to interact directly with decision makers. Community involvement is at the heart of the Tanzania case study. The Benin case study stresses the importance of judicious use of experts in combination with popular mobilization.

Previous experiences with social accountability practices. Authors of the two case studies involving participatory local budget and policy formulation attributed the success to previous experience with participatory approaches that also helped develop good government-civil society relations.

The Fissel rural commune in Senegal benefited from many years of experience in community development, dynamic local organizations that have been engaged in awareness and capacity building for decades, many local officials more inclined to be open to a participatory approach to decentralization, and a long tradition of collaboration between the rural council and grassroots community organizations.

In the Ilala, Tanzania, case, many citizens had some previous experience with participatory processes, including the citywide consultative process to develop the city environmental profile, service-delivery user satisfaction surveys, two stakeholder consultations for the Medium Term Expenditure Frameworks, and Poverty Reduction Strategy Paper consultations.

Sustained commitment. Several case studies identify sustained government and CSO commitment as a critical success factor. Social accountability is not a short-term project but a long-term agenda requiring time and persistence.

The Tanzania central government provided enduring political will and steadfast support to civic involvement at the central and local levels of government. The Tanzanian institutional and regulatory environment allows for the autonomy of local government authorities and for the direct participation of citizens in grassroots levels of administration. In fact, numerous laws require citizen participation in policy and budgeting processes in addition to service delivery satisfaction surveys.

It can be difficult and demanding to sustain such efforts, especially if political will, public interest, or financial support are lacking. In Nigeria, for example, some CSO participants in the PWYP campaign began to demand per diems or other economic incentives to justify their continued involvement. According to the Malawi Economic Justice Network, successful social accountability work requires a spirit of selfless service, not self-interest.

Even when one round of an initiative is relatively successful, it may not be sustained. Many of the case study initiatives have not been repeated because of a lack of political will and financial support even though public interest remains high.

A solution-based approach. In Senegal and Tanzania, close collaboration between government and civil society was considered crucial to success. Indeed, the initiatives that include collaboration and joint action on the part of the state and civil society tend to achieve more concrete results. In situations where civil society–state relations are more difficult or where social accountability activities are of a more independent nature (for example, where civil society is playing an independent monitoring role), it is nevertheless desirable to maintain a productive and solution-focused (rather than problem-focused) approach.

The Malawi case study underlines the importance of adopting a realistic and balanced approach to advocacy and ensuring that criticism is constructive. In Senegal, an important guiding principle was for citizens and CSOs to help strengthen local government rather than just criticizing it. The Zimbabwe case emphasizes the importance of ensuring objectivity in research and advocacy and adopting a constructive (even if critical) stance.

Coalition building. In the context of citizen-state dialogue and negotiation, public officials are often in a position of strength because of their political power and greater access to financial and human resources. For civil society actors, networking and alliance building are important strategies to compensate for their lack of power and resources. Coalitions can frequently advocate from a stronger vantage point than individual organizations and are less vulnerable to charges of partisanship or representing special interests.

Coalition building not only brings a variety of skills and capacities to the cause but also helps to make crucial links between different issues, actors, and levels of intervention. The most effective coalitions are often those that span sectors or include state, private sector, and civil society actors. However, these are also often the most challenging coalitions to establish and maintain. Linking local and national-level actors and issues is a particularly important challenge in Benin, Ghana, Malawi, and Nigeria.

CSO coalitions are critical to several of the initiatives described:

- In Benin, the social accountability initiative involves a network of more than 150 organizations.
- In Zimbabwe, the Child-Friendly Budget Initiative was established by a coalition of nine NGOs, and it formed coalitions with other networks and private sector groups.

- In Malawi, the Malawi Economic Justice Network is made up of 27 CSOs and it formed strategic alliances with several sector-based NGO networks, thus creating a network of networks.
- In Ilala, Tanzania, participatory planning and budgeting efforts include thematic, sector-based, territory-based, labor, faith-based, women's, and other CSOs as well as government, political parties, private sector organizations, and donor agencies.
- In Nigeria, the case study illustrates not only the importance of CSO coalitions—such as the various members of the PWYP campaign—but also the challenges and potential problems of collective action, including issues of leadership, trust, and effective communication and power sharing among members.

International support. Almost all of the case studies mention some form of external support—in the form of either international funding, networking, or learning—as an important factor of success. All the initiatives benefit directly or indirectly from the financial support of international donors, including support for operational programming and for learning, capacity development, and institution building.

In Nigeria, both NEITI and the PWYP campaign are linked to global coalitions that provide opportunities for international networking, support, and learning. One of the reasons why NEITI is successful is that the International Finance Corporation imposes conditions on potential borrowers who seek its loans to finance extractive projects. In Benin, Social Watch is supported by the global Social Watch network.

Similarly, numerous CSOs have seized on poverty reduction strategies, or PRSs—prepared and implemented by national governments with the support of international development partners—as an opportunity for dialogue, advocacy, and civic engagement. Practitioners from Malawi, for example, describe how participation in the Africa-wide Social Forum was an important opportunity for learning and networking.

Lessons Learned

The previous section discussed the factors that contributed to the success of the social accountability initiatives included in this book. Each of the initiatives has also encountered a range of obstacles and constraints, which have required and inspired ongoing innovation, problem solving, and learning. Again, in a spirit of sharing operational learning, this section describes some of the practical lessons that have emerged from the social accountability experiences described in this book, which table 9.4 summarizes.

Invest in awareness raising and capacity building. In many countries and communities, social accountability practices are new territory. Ordinary citizens—even civil society actors and community leaders—are often unaware of their civil and political rights, unfamiliar with social accountability practices and tools, and lack the required skills to engage effectively with the state and seek accountability. Especially in contexts where there is little experience of active citizenship or civic engagement, social accountability practitioners must often initially invest considerable time and energy in raising awareness of rights, building consensus around fundamental principles of social accountability, and laying the groundwork for future social accountability activities. In most cases, these efforts are not only necessary to get initiatives off the ground but also must be sustained over the long term to achieve impact.

Virtually all of the cases discussed in this book have required significant investments in building awareness, capacities, and skills (from the local to national levels) and in targeting ordinary citizens as well as civil society actors, leaders, and professionals. The authors from Ghana, Senegal, and Tanzania all flag the importance of training and capacity building, and the Nigerian case study emphasizes the necessity of investing in public education.

In Malawi, MEJN's experience particularly demonstrates the importance of investing not just in short-term goals but also in longer-term capacity development. MEJN has devoted, and continues to devote, enormous effort to building the knowledge, capacities, and skills of its own staff; the staff of its member organizations; its partners; and target populations through sustained public education, skills training, capacity-building activities, and other learning events.

Seek broad-based, multistakeholder involvement. A lesson that emerges from almost all the case studies concerns the importance and related challenges of engaging with multiple stakeholder groups. Because accountability is essentially about relationships and, in the case of social accountability, about relationships between a large and diverse range of citizens and public power holders, initiatives to enhance accountability inevitably involve identifying and interacting with a wide spectrum of

Table 9.4 Lessons Learned about Social Accountability in Africa: Case Study Evidence

	Invest in awareness raising and capacity building	Seek broad-based, multistakeholder involvement	Inclusiveness is essential, albeit elusive	Political analysis and timing are important	Impact is greatest when strategies are multidimensional and systemwide	Flexibility and innovation are crucial	Pay attention to incentives and sanctions
Benin		X					X
Ghana	X	X					
Malawi	X	X		X			X
Nigeria	X	X		X			X
Senegal	X	X		X		X	X
Tanzania	X	X			X	X	X
Zimbabwe		X	X	X			

Source: Authors' analysis.

different societal stakeholders. Social accountability practitioners must identify who these stakeholders are, carefully analyze existing and desired power relations and accountability relationships among them, and develop strategies for engaging multiple stakeholder groups in a way that will enhance social accountability.

Assessing and building relationships is a highly challenging but essential aspect of social accountability, especially if different stakeholder groups have no history of interaction or if relations are contentious. Often, one of the greatest contributions that social accountability initiatives can make is to create or strengthen links among different stakeholder groups, especially between state and nonstate actors.

The case studies highlighted in this book illustrate a wide variety of stakeholder roles and relationships. Each of the initiatives involves the participation of a range of government actors and citizen and community groups. Other stakeholder groups that are identified as playing significant roles in social accountability initiatives include parliamentarians (in Malawi and Zimbabwe) and private sector actors (for example, oil companies in Nigeria and local investors in Tanzania).

In the African context, traditional authorities represent another potentially important group of stakeholders in social accountability. Relationships between traditional chiefs and local government authorities are frequently unclear or contentious, and the accountability of traditional chiefs themselves is often considered problematic. Experience shows, however, that traditional authorities often wield considerable social influence and convening power at the local level. Hence, they can potentially become important allies—for example, in rallying community support or in acting as a check on local government authorities.

Inclusiveness is essential, albeit elusive. One of the most significant features of social accountability approaches is their potential to serve the interests of those groups of citizens that traditionally lack political voice and power. However, reaching out to the marginalized, giving voice to the unheard, and empowering the weak all involve swimming against the strong tides of the mainstream. There is a constant and real danger that the voices of the poorest and weakest will be drowned out, whether purposefully or inadvertently, by more powerful, more organized, or better-connected groups. Even within civil society, marginalized groups tend to be underrepresented, both as leaders and members. Groups who claim to speak for the poor, for example, are too often dominated by the non-poor.

Therefore, it is crucial to design explicit strategies and dedicate specific resources toward ensuring the direct, equitable, and effective participation of women, youth, poor people, and other marginalized groups in social accountability initiatives. Despite best intentions, experience shows that the only initiatives that seem to make serious headway are those that explicitly emphasize and prioritize the interests of specific disadvantaged groups while also directly involving and empowering members of those groups.

For example, many social accountability initiatives pay lip service to gender issues (perhaps by attempting to ensure a minimum percentage of female representation on committees or working groups), but only when gender issues are identified as core priorities and women's groups are directly involved in designing and implementing initiatives do real benefits become discernible in terms of respect for women's rights and improvements in women's livelihoods. The women-friendly and child-friendly budget work in Zimbabwe provides examples of social accountability initiatives that not only prioritize but also focus exclusively on the rights and specific needs of women and children.

Political analysis and timing are important. Although much of the literature on social accountability focuses on methods and tools, one experienced practitioner described social accountability as "20 percent technical and 80 percent political." This comment does not refer to partisan politics but to the broad political processes whereby decisions are made in a society. Experience shows that successful social accountability initiatives seek to understand political structures and processes, nurture political will, and seize political opportunity. For many CSOs, especially those new to civic engagement or social accountability, developing political analytical skills and political savvy is a significant challenge.

Although we talk about broad categories of state and nonstate actors, it is important to unpack these terms to get a sense of the political landscape within both spheres and to identify potential allies within government and civil society. Techniques such as social forces analysis and power mapping can help social accountability practitioners to chart political and power relations among various societal actors and identify potential supporters, partners, and opponents, as the following examples illustrate:

- In Malawi, members of parliament proved to be important allies, joining forces with CSOs to oppose government attempts at privatization.
- In Senegal, social accountability practitioners capitalized on the political space created by progressive political leaders. For instance, participatory

budgeting innovations were made possible by a dynamic and open-minded rural commune leader.

• In Nigeria as well, a proactive president created space for NEITI and the PWYP campaign.

• In Malawi, social accountability practitioners highlight the importance of political timing, describing how election periods provide an important opportunity for public education, mobilization, and citizen-state dialogue.

• In Zimbabwe, activists take advantage of midterm fiscal and monetary reviews as strategic opportunities to engage on budget issues.

• In Benin, Social Watch practitioners were able to seize on political opportunities offered by regime change.

Impact is greatest when strategies are multidimensional and systemwide. Social accountability activities are often, at least initially, small-scale experiences targeting one particular public service or one particular stage of the governance cycle (such as budget formulation or service delivery). However, the successful social accountability initiative in the Zimbabwe case study reveals the need for additional work at other stages or levels of governance. For example, if budget advocacy succeeds in ensuring that more resources are allocated to meet the specific needs of Zimbabwean women or children, then, to ensure ultimate impact, it becomes necessary to monitor expenditures to ensure that funds are spent according to the budgetary provisions.

Similarly, social accountability tools (such as community scorecards) frequently detect service delivery problems at the local level that are linked to problems (such as bottlenecks and leakages) higher up in the system and thus can require further investigation into resource flows at the national and district levels.

One-off forms of citizen participation have their place and can have useful effects. Over time, however, experience shows that the impact is greatest when the strategies are multidimensional and systemwide. The case of Ilala, Tanzania, for example, is a good illustration of the importance and impact of promoting popular participation throughout the local public management cycle, from planning and implementation to monitoring and evaluation of public service delivery.

Flexibility and innovation are critical. Social accountability initiatives and approaches must be demand-driven by local situations rather than by prescribed formulas or tools that have developed elsewhere. Management staff and the elected decision makers have to be flexible, innovative, and persistent in responding to citizen demands and must have the will to change procedures to ensure the effectiveness and sustainability of the process.

In Tanzania, citizens' priorities were not clear at first, and their proposed budgets were unrealistic, but with additional rounds of the participatory budgeting process and more training, the budgets became more realistic and the priorities much clearer. In Senegal, the budget planning process was subject to a fixed and rigid schedule that was sometimes incompatible with the flexible and repetitive nature of the participatory process, but in time the participants began to accept the schedule and planned their activities to meet the legal deadlines for budget presentation.

Pay attention to incentives and sanctions. The case studies show that both incentives and sanctions are important for achieving enhanced social accountability. Ideally, a mix of rewards for accountable behavior and the prospect of sanctions for unaccountable behavior appear to be most effective. The case studies illustrate that CSOs use a range of mostly informal incentives and sanctions.

In the cases of local-level initiatives in Senegal and Tanzania, the incentives for undertaking participatory budgeting were quite clear and direct. Citizens could easily see the direct benefits of participating in budgeting processes (and influencing the use of municipal resources), and local government actors quickly realized the benefits of increased popularity and the greater willingness of citizens to contribute to projects and pay local taxes.

In the national-level initiatives, incentives for state actors to respond to calls for accountability are less evident. Practitioners in Malawi took advantage of upcoming elections to create an incentive for political candidates on the campaign trail to engage with and respond to citizens. In Nigeria, the government saw the opportunity to improve its international reputation as a strong incentive to agree to NEITI.

Regarding sanctions, the experiences in the case studies are largely limited to informal strategies and mechanisms—for example, creating public pressure and the potential for public shaming through media coverage, public forums, and public interface meetings between citizens and state officials. Initiatives in Benin, Malawi, and Nigeria also seek to take advantage of international pressures and the potential sanctions (again, mostly informal) of failing to live up to commitments made in the Poverty Reduction Strategy, Extractive Industries Transparency Initiative, or Millennium Development Goal guidelines and goals.

A common characteristic and potential limitation of most of the case studies in this book is a lack of formal means of sanction or enforcement. Such potential mechanisms include public litigation, legal action, or appeals to formal accountability institutions such as anticorruption agencies or public ombudsmen.

CONCLUSIONS

While social accountability is emerging as a priority in the international development community, much still needs to be done to ensure international organizations' adaptation to the African context and their timely responsiveness to African culture and concerns. Chief among the issues affecting social accountability in Africa is the use of new technologies—cell phones, digital maps, and SMS (short message service) text messaging, among others—that enable citizens to more readily provide feedback and data that can be collected and organized through open-access software. This information can then be broadly displayed to country populations.

The case studies presented here demonstrate other crucial factors. An increasing number of initiatives are being captured and codified to glean lessons for moving ahead.[5]

Social Accountability Is Crucially Important in the African Context

Achieving social accountability is highly challenging, but it is possible. At its core, social accountability is about power relations and how power is perceived and exercised; the nature of relationships between public power holders and citizens; and the various ways in which power is monitored, checked, and shared. Social accountability is about establishing effective and just relationships between citizens and civil society and the state, enhancing demand for good governance, and achieving the government's responsiveness to that demand. Social accountability initiatives must take into account strengths, weaknesses, opportunities, and challenges on both the supply and demand sides and focus on improving the interface between the two.

Social Accountability Does Deliver

Many of the case studies demonstrate important process-oriented results such as enhanced civil society confidence, capacity, and skills; increased citizen interest and rights awareness; and improved civil society-government relations and trust.

The Zimbabwe initiatives have achieved policy changes, including the introduction of a public financial management system to call for fiscal discipline through effective monitoring of government budgets and the decentralization of some government services. NEITI's achievements in the past five years are impressive and have earned Nigeria worldwide recognition as one of the two countries leading the initiative globally; NEITI also had saved Nigeria about $1 billion by 2007 through reduced corruption and leakages.

Evidence of the direct impact of social accountability initiatives on human well-being is less frequent, given the early stages of most interventions, and it is also more difficult to measure. However, several cases reported such effects—for example, in enhanced budget allocations for women and children (in Zimbabwe) and in employment creation and the increased number and sustainability of development projects (in Tanzania).

Recent anecdotal evidence outside of the case studies presented here also points to the results of social accountability initiatives, but the evidence of their impact on development outcomes remains limited. Research is underway to address this gap—in particular, to identify attitudinal and behavioral indicators that are direct outcomes of these approaches.[6]

Social Accountability Is Spreading

Even modest beginnings have led to replication and learning. In Senegal, the Fissel rural commune organized a forum on budget transparency for 30 rural communities, presented a workshop for members of the National Assembly, and hosted councilors from almost 70 municipalities to learn about its experience. Even two mayors from Burkina Faso visited Fissel. In addition, Fissel and four other communes were selected to host the field visits organized during an international conference organized by the World Bank. Other Senegalese municipalities and rural communes have adopted participatory budgeting processes. In Malawi, at least 10 notable CSOs have adopted economic literacy among their core programs.

These examples represent only a small part of the growing social accountability experience in Africa. Facilities supporting the social accountability agenda are emerging across the continent and include— but are not limited to—the Center for Social Accountability at Rhodes University and the Affiliated Network for Social Accountability (ANSA) based at the Institute for Democracy in South Africa (IDASA), both in South Africa;[7] Forum Syd[8] and Twawezi! East Africa, both in Tanzania; and the International Budget Partnership,[9] among others.

Accountability Starts at Home

Social accountability requires accountable behavior from all actors. Government, CSOs, and development partners must all practice what they preach and abide by the same principles and standards that they demand of others. Donors should set an example by ensuring that their own programs emphasize and require transparency, information sharing, citizen participation, and downward accountability. Several initiatives greatly improved their relationships with the media. Their achievements have had a major impact in establishing the credibility of civil society and its capacity to carry out critical analysis and to formulate proposals.

Social Accountability Must Be Nurtured with Care

External support is important but must avoid social engineering. Some appropriate roles for development partners include supporting capacity building and the development and implementation of demand-driven initiatives; promoting an enabling environment; and facilitating the sharing of knowledge, lessons, methods, and tools.

A recommendation for donors is to enhance support for social accountability and democracy building but in a manner that respects and promotes locally driven approaches and initiatives rather than the imposition of predefined strategies or methods. International partners can help by sharing information about methods, tools, and lessons learned globally.

Moreover, because social accountability approaches are highly dependent upon the context in which they are applied, decisions about what methods to use, whom to involve, whether to take a more political or pragmatic approach, and the extent to which social accountability mechanisms should be independent or institutionalized must be made in-country and not imposed by external actors.

Donors can also make an important contribution by working with government counterparts to adopt principles of transparency and accountability, thus creating a more enabling environment for social accountability. In some contexts, donors can play an important role as brokers between civil society and the state, especially where relations are antagonistic. In certain country settings, this type of facilitation and intermediation can be more important than financial support.

NOTES

1. Study conducted by the Innovation and Integrity Division, OECD Public Governance and Territorial Directorate.
2. The 2008 Open Budget Index developed by the International Budget Partnership found that out of the seven countries presented here, only Ghana fell into the category of "providing some information," with Malawi evaluated as providing "minimal information." The remaining countries fell at the bottom of the index, earning "scant" or "no" information ratings. The Open Budget Project evaluates whether governments provide public access to budget information and opportunities to participate in the budgeting process at the national level.
3. This factor is implied though not directly discussed in several of the case studies.
4. For example, those identified in the context of the broader social accountability stocktaking in McNeil and Mumvuma 2006.
5. For other case studies and examples, see the *Social Accountability in Africa Sourcebook* (Pretoria: ANSA-Africa, 2010).
6. For more about this research, see two recent publications from the Department for International Development (DFID): Menocal and Sharma (2008); and Holland and Thirkell (2009).
7. See http://www.icount.org.za and www.ansa-africa.net.
8. See http://www.africa.forumsyd.org.
9. See http://www.internationalbudget.org.

REFERENCES

Caddy, Joanne, Tiago Peixoto, and Mary McNeil. 2007. "Beyond Public Scrutiny: Stocktaking of Social Accountability in OECD Countries." World Bank Institute Working Paper. Washington, DC: World Bank; Paris: Organisation for Economic Co-operation and Development.

Holland, Jeremy, and Allyson Thirkell. 2009. "Measuring Change and Results in Voice and Accountability Work: Social Development Direct." DFID Working Paper 34, U.K. Department for International Development, London.

Malena, Carmen, ed. 2009. *From Political Won't to Political Will: Building Support for Participatory Governance.* Sterling, VA: Kumarian Press.

McNeil, Mary, and Takawira Mumvuma. 2006. *Demanding Good Governance: A Stocktaking of Social Accountability Initiatives by Civil Society in Anglophone Africa.* Washington, DC: World Bank.

Menocal, A. Rocha, and Bhavna Sharma. 2008. "Joint Evaluation of Citizens' Voice and Accountability." Synthesis report. U.K. Department for International Development, London.

INDEX

Boxes, figures, maps, notes, and tables are indicated by *b*, *f*, *m*, *n*, and *t*, respectively.

A

Abbey, Charles, xvii, 4, 71
accountability
  of CSOs and NGOs, 182, 199–200
  defined, 4–6
  downward versus upward, 200
  elections and, 5–6
  good governance and, 1–2, 5
  social accountability providing overall
    improvement in, 13–14, 64–65, 126.
    See also social accountability in Africa
Action Aid International, 105
action-oriented research, 117–18
Active Youth Initiative for Social
  Enhancement, 105
Adeniyi, Olusegun, 146
Adio, Waziri, 156, 161*n*18
ADP (African Development Programme),
  78, 86
Affiliated Network for Social Accountability
  (ANSA), 219
Africa. *See* social accountability in Africa
African Development Programme (ADP),
  78, 86
African Network for Environment and
  Economic Justice, 159*n*1
African Network on Debt and Development
  (AFRODAD), 134*n*2
African Union, 137
AFRODAD (African Network on Debt and
  Development), 134*n*2

agency, social accountability enhancing, 20–22
aid. *See* overseas development assistance
  (ODA) in Africa
AIDS. *See* HIV/AIDS
Angola, access to information in, 27*n*3
ANSA (Affiliated Network for Social
  Accountability), 219
Asiobe, Assisi, 158
Association for Progressive Women, 105
authority, cultural deference to, 192
awareness raising
  investment in, 211
  MEJN public awareness campaigns,
    105–6, 211
  rights, citizen and human, 19, 189
Azeem, Vitus A., xvii, 4, 71
Azerbaijan, EITI management in, 150, 155

B

Benin. *See also* Social Watch Benin, CCPA
    initiative
  CBOs in, 163
  corruption in, 167–68
  CSOs and NGOs in
    adequate resources, need for, 183, 198
    enhanced capacity, 163–64, 181
    increased credibility of, 182, 199
    initial limited impact, 168
    public perception of CSOs in,
      179–80, 199
    service-providing role, 165–66
  decentralization in, 165–66
  HIV/AIDS in, 174
  media in. *See under* media